# Police Leadership

## M. R. Haberfeld, Ph.D.
*John Jay College of Criminal Justice*

PEARSON

Prentice
Hall

Upper Saddle River, New Jersey, 07458

Library of Congress Cataloging-in-Publication Data

Haberfeld, M. R. (Maria R.),
    Police leadership / M.R. Haberfeld.
        p. cm.
    Includes bibliograhical references and index.
    ISBN 0-13-114971-7
    1. Police—Supervision of. 2. Leadership. 3. Interpersonal relations. I. Title.

HV7936.S8H36 2006
363.2'068'4—'dc22

                                                                        2004060085

**Executive Editor:** Frank Mortimer, Jr.
**Associate Editor:** Sarah Holle
**Executive Marketing Manager:**
  Tim Peyton
**Editorial Assistant:** Kelly Krug
**Managing Editor:** Mary Carnis
**Production Liaison:** Brian Hyland
**Production Editor:** Janet Bolton
**Director of Manufacturing
  and Production:** Bruce Johnson

**Manufacturing Manager:** Ilene Sanford
**Manufacturing Buyer:** Cathleen Petersen
**Design Director:** Cheryl Asherman
**Senior Design Coordinator:** Miguel Ortiz
**Cover Design:** Miguel Ortiz
**Cover Image:** AP Wide World Photos
**Composition:** Integra
**Electronic Art Creation:** Integra
**Printing and Binding:** R. R. Donnelley
**Copy Editor/Proofreader:** Maine
  Proofreading Services

---

Pearson Education LTD.
Pearson Education Australia PTY, Limited
Pearson Education Singapore, Pte. Ltd.
Pearson Education North Asia Ltd.
Pearson Education Canada, Ltd.
Pearson Educacion de Mexico, S.A. de C.V.
Pearson Education—Japan
Pearson Education Malaysia, Pte. Ltd.
Pearson Education, Upper Saddle River, New Jersey

10 9 8 7 6 5 4 3 2 1

ISBN 0-13-114971-7

To the memory of my beloved grandfather,
Jakub Rudenski—you were the best proof that water
can be as thick as blood.

# Contents

Preface                                                                        xiii
Acknowledgments                                                                 xvii

**1  Introduction: The Pentagon of Police Leadership                              1**

The Case for Early Career Leadership Training   1
The Training Gap   3
The Pentagon of Police Leadership   7

**2  Integrity, Ethics, and Police Leadership                                     15**

Ethics and Transformational Leadership   16
Integration of Behavior and Values   18
Stewardship Model   19
Ethical Leaders' Characteristics   20
The Triangle of Police Integrity   21
The Pentagon of Police Leadership   26

**3  Partnership in a Small Force: Team Theory                                    31**

Overview of the Theory   31
Functional Team Leadership   32

The Leader-Management Model   35

Self-Managed Teams   36

Team Policing   36


**4    In-Groups and Community-Oriented Policing:
      Leader-Member Exchange Theory                           46**

Overview of the Theory   46

Measurement of the Quality of the Dyadic
      Relationship   48

The Dyadic Relationship and Effectiveness   49

Antecedents to High-Quality Dyadic
      Relationships   51

Leader-Member Exchange Theory and Bias   52

LMX Theory and the Cases of Commissioner
      Lee P. Brown and Chief Darrel Stephens   53


**5    When the Chief Becomes the Force:
      Transformational Theory                                 71**

Overview of the Theory   71

Importance of Charisma in Leaders   73

Meta-Analytic Studies on Transformational
      Leadership   76

Transformational Leadership in Military Contexts   77

Transformational and Transactional Leadership
      Styles and the Cases of Chief Reuben Greenberg
      and Chief Daryl Gates   79


**6    Parameters for Empowerment and Trust: Style Theory   94**

Overview of the Theory   94

Ohio State University Leadership Studies   94

Michigan University Leadership Studies   95

Harvard University Studies   97

The Managerial Grid   97

Style as a Universal Theory    99

Style Theory and Military Leadership    99

Style Theory and Police Leadership    101

Style Theory and the Cases of Chief Earl Sanders
and Chief Dennis Nowicki    101


**7**    **When the Event Is Just Too Much to Handle:
Situational LeadershipTheory                        114**

Overview of the Theory    114

Situational Leadership Theory and Employee
Burnout    117

Simplified Situational Leadership Theory    118

Politics and Situational Leadership Theory    118

Policing and Situational Leadership Theory    119

Situational Leadership Theory and the Cases of Chief
Charles A. Moose and Chief Bernard Parks    122


**8**    **Doing Things Right or Doing the Right Thing:
Contingency Theory                                  138**

Overview of the Theory    138

Military Leaders and Contingency Theory    142

Cognitive Resources Theory    142

Leader Substitutes Theory    143

Vroom-Yetton Contingency Model    143

Dyadic Approach to Contingency Theory    144

Criticisms of Contingency Theory    144

Contingency Theory of Leadership and
the Cases of Chief William O'Brien and
Chief Tom Koby    145


**9**    **Winning Minds and Hearts: Path-Goal Theory        160**

Overview of the Theory    160

Path-Goal Theory and Military Leadership    163

Path-Goal Theory and the Cases of Commissioner
William Bratton and Chief Richard Pennington   164

**10   Leadership and Command of the Critical Incident:
Psychodynamic Approach                                    180**

Overview of the Approach   180

Birth Order   183

Transactional Analysis   184

Psychohistory   185

Personality and Leadership   185

Psychodynamic Approach to Leadership and
the Case of Commissioner Bernard Kerik   187

**11   Soliciting and Entertaining 100 Ideas: Skills Approach   197**

Overview of the Approach   197

Learned Leadership Skills   198

Leadership in Context   198

Social Judgment as Social Intelligence   200

Emotional Intelligence   201

U.S. Army Studies   202

Skills Approach to Leadership and the Case
of Commissioner Paul F. Evans   202

**12   Career of Leadership: Trait Theory                       211**

Overview of the Theory   211

Modern Applications of Trait Theory   212

Social Scientific Evaluation of Leadership Traits   216

Trait Theory and the Case of Chief George
Edwards   219

**13**    **Into the Future: The Big Hairy Audacious Goal
          and Catalytic Mechanisms**                              **228**

          Anticharismatic Leadership   229

          Level 5 Leadership   231

          Choice of the Right People   234

          Hedgehog Rule of Management   235

          Big Hairy Audacious Goals (BHAGs) and
              the Formal and Informal Goals of Policing   236

          **Index**                                               **241**

# Preface

This book is a product of years of research, teaching, and thinking about the importance of developing police leaders. No other profession has a more dire need for these skills. Leadership is, after all, a set of skills and traits that could and must be absorbed and learned by each police officer. The word "leadership" connotes many associations, and over the years and through many cultures, it has gained various definitions and interpretations.

Most of us think of leadership as something ultimately positive and very much desirable. However, leadership in general, and (in the context of this book) in police environments, can be also negative in nature. A Pakistani high-ranking police officer whom I met a few years ago, and whom I invited to give a guest lecture in my graduate class titled Police Leadership, started his comparative lecture about leadership in the Pakistani police force by referring to an example of his supervisor who, according to him, was a *good but corrupt leader*. The students and I looked at him in disbelief, trying to figure out if it was an improper use of the English language or if he really meant something that we had previously not discussed in class (nor something I had ever come across in a vast overview of literature on leadership). We asked for an explanation and received a very profound and telling one, especially with regard to the idea of effective policing. The good and corrupt police leader happened to be somebody who did things right— a true cold-blooded bureaucrat who did what was right for the police organization but did not do the right thing for the police officers.

I inquired during the guest lecture whether the word "corrupt" was too strong when used in reference to his actions. After all, to do things right for an organization sometimes entails putting the goal of the organization ahead of some personal needs of its employees. However, this was not the case. There is a tension between police organizations' formal goal of protecting the public and the informal goal of protecting politicians in power and maintaining the political status quo. This police supervisor was willing to engage in the most unethical behaviors in order to sustain the informal goal of police organizations.

The tensions between the formal and informal goals are an eternal conflict for police leaders. The Pakistani police leader took it a step further by identifying completely with the task and totally sacrificing the relationship aspect of the leader-follower exchange. This sacrifice earned him the label of good but corrupt leader. It was definitely a lesson I learned about police leadership.

A few years later, I taught the same class for New York Police Department officers. When one of the students complained bitterly about his supervisor, I asked him if he would consider his supervisor to be a good but corrupt leader. After some initial consternation on the part of the students and my in-depth explanation of the concept, he agreed—his supervisor was indeed a good leader but also a corrupt one.

A word of caution is mandatory here: In the same way that we accept many definitions for the word "leadership," there are also many definitions for the word "corruption." Corruption has many facets and angles, and not all of them have to do with being on the take or shaking the drug dealers or accepting a bribe from a speeding motorist. A corrupt leader can be very effective from the perspective of the informal goals of a police organization but at the same time remain corrupt from the perspective of human relations, whether within or outside the police organization.

This book highlights various leadership theories that were compiled by many authors who published in this area. Chief among them was a book by Peter Northouse, *Leadership: Theory and Practice* (2004). His book offers the most comprehensive overview of leadership theories applicable for police environments (although it was not written for that specific audience). Borrowing from his medley of leadership theories, I have customized the concepts for the police environment, matching these theories with police chiefs and commissioners to highlight the application of a given approach to the reality of everyday police life. Each chief and commissioner has a unique history, as do the events that make up each biography; so do the daily struggles of police supervisors and police officers, from the first day on the job. While the magnitude of events such as 9/11 is certainly not replicated in other environments, the potential for terrorist action is a definite problem for police leaders. The same can be said about events of police misconduct, problems with high crime rates, high-profile murder cases, racial tensions, and major innovations. Each police chief or commissioner has a unique story, but the leadership approach exhibited, whether conscious or subconscious, could be applicable in similar situations that are evolving and will continue to evolve on a daily basis in police work around the country.

In one of my previous works, a book on police training, I defined police leadership as the ability of each police officer, starting with the first day on the job, to take control of a situation on the street. Any type of situation that requires assertion of control would fall under this definition. As police officers progress in their careers, the level and degree of control change. Due to the fact that police work is based on the mandate to use coercive force to achieve compliance, police leadership is about the ability to take control. This book attempts to provide a template for police leaders, from street-level officers to the highest-ranking police chiefs, on how to look at a given situation, adopt an informed perspective—even when all that is available is the proverbial split second—and make the right leadership decision.

The book starts with an overview of police integrity and ethics and how they relate to the issue of leadership. Usually books on leadership end with the ethics chapter. For me, this is a fundamental mistake with regard to the entire concept of leadership. Leadership is about integrity and ethics, and this is where one should start the discussion of leadership concepts, not where it should end. Police leadership will frequently be immersed in a clash between the concepts of doing things right and doing the right thing, and the final judgment about what is the right approach is not something that this book aims to emphasize. Instead it does focus on the issue of situational integrity that is a product of a specific leadership approach of an individual chief—one that can be either emulated or modified by the readers, as customized for the relevant environment and situation.

The final chapter is an optimistic approach. It identifies the concept of the Big Hairy Audacious Goal, encouraging leaders to take hold of what seems like an impossible goal and to make it a reality. An approach that can manage the seemingly impossible is needed and appropriate in the police context, where effective policing is constantly challenged by the competing formal and informal goals of policing. If there ever was a Big Hairy Audacious Goal, bridging the gap between these two seemingly opposing goals would be it. Nevertheless, it is a goal worth achieving, and we owe it to the idea of democracy for which we all ultimately strive.

# Acknowledgments

People rarely read the Acknowledgment pages, but the truth is that these pages are sometimes as important as the text itself, particularly for authors. It is especially true with regard to a book that deals with concepts of leadership. Leadership, as a behavior, is always a product of some sort of human interaction and support. Writing a book is also definitely an outcome of some sort of human interaction and support.

To this end I would like to introduce those who helped make this process come to fruition, through various degrees of interaction and support. I define each such support mechanism as a unique form of leadership interaction worth modeling and replicating. Leadership, as a concept, should be viewed as a source of modeling and inspiration. Behaviors of the individuals listed below not only inspired my work but also enabled it to see the light of day and made it so much better than what I envisioned at its inception.

For this I would like to thank, from the bottom of my heart, the following leaders, each one with a unique capacity for influencing and shaping this book.

**Thank you all for your . . .**

> **Ethical Leadership:** Evan Mandery, Lydia Segal, Brian MacNamara, Heath Grant, Karen Terry, Vincent del Castillo, Delores Jones-Brown, and Adina Schwartz
> **Courageous Leadership:** The NYPD students

**Knowledge Leadership:** The NYPD Police Certificate creators and faculty: Pat O'Hara, Jannette Domingo, Michael Walker, William Fraher, David Humen, Peter Casamento III, William MacDonald, Brian Onieal, Agostino von Hassell and Robert Louden

**Supportive Leadership:** Malgorzata Niepokoj-Laszczka and Anat Tal-Shir

**Faith Leadership:** The Prentice Hall team, Frank Mortimer Jr. and Sarah Holle

**Family Leadership:** My parents, Colonel (retired) Michael Sadykiewicz and Dr. Lucja Sadykiewicz; my husband, Gabriel; and my daughters, Nellie and Mia

And last and certainly not least, my two most wonderful research assistants, without whose talent and incredible devotion to this project this book would have never been completed:

**Implementation Leadership:** Johanna Bjorken and Staci Strobl

# Police Leadership

# 1

# Introduction

*The Pentagon of Police Leadership*

Many law enforcement agencies face real problems in identifying good leaders when a position becomes available. One reason for poor pools of candidates is because the development and training of leadership skills start too late. Another reason is because the potential leaders think more about management than leadership. Developing a leader is a long-term process in which encouragement, modeling, and support are combined with natural skills, and "the training should begin on the first day of an officer's career" (Bergner, 1998, p. 16).

This author firmly believes that leaders are both born and made. Since we have no control over the limited number of "born" leaders, our duty in establishing effective community-oriented law enforcement is to "make" more leaders. Baker (2000) suggests that the quality of police leadership directly affects the quality of life of police officers and the way they deliver their services. Police leaders have the potential to inspire officers but also to sabotage their efforts.

## THE CASE FOR EARLY CAREER LEADERSHIP TRAINING

A common assumption is that police leaders are by definition the upper ranks. According to Swanson et al. (1998), police departments can be divided into three supervisory planes, each associated with a mix of leadership skills. These planes are based on ranks and consist of three basic skills: human relations, conceptual, and technical skills. Top management, composed of chiefs, deputy chiefs, and majors, predominantly use the conceptual skills, with marginal use of human relations and technical skills. Middle management, composed of captains and lieutenants, use many conceptual skills but also use human relations and technical skills. Finally, first-line supervisors, that is, sergeants, make relatively little use of conceptual skills, instead concentrating on the equal mix of human relations and technical skills (Swanson et al., 1998).

Criticisms of this depiction are numerous. For one, the degree to which each of the mix of skills is distributed among the three may vary, based on factors such as the size of an agency, its political environment, crime problems, and economic conditions. However, a much more important missing link relates directly to what Bergner (1998) mentions in his writings: Developing police leadership cannot ignore the leadership skills that line officers use on a daily basis. Line officers are the true leaders on the streets, using their leadership skills in daily encounters with the community, and police executives and policy makers need to realize it.

While human relations and technical skills play a very important role in line officers' work, conceptual skills, which are fundamental for problem solving, have particular applicability in the era of community-oriented policing. Many decision-making and other responsibilities previously left to middle and top management now have been placed on the shoulders of line officers; of course, not all such responsibilities were channeled "down." However, some common features of community-oriented policing—for example, decentralizing the chain of command, empowering employees, problem solving, and downsizing and flattening the organization—clearly require leadership skills.

Swanson et al. (1998) define conceptual skills as the ability to understand and interrelate various parcels of information, which are often fuzzy and appear to be unrelated. According to the authors, the standards for handling the information become less certain and the level of abstraction necessary to handle the parcels becomes greater as one moves upward through the chain of command. This author begs to differ with their interpretation. Line officers in the 21st century are expected to create innovative solutions, involve themselves in conflict resolution, solve problems of the most intricate nature—all of which require well-developed conceptual skills.

Furthermore, the reactive nature of police work is much more pronounced on the street than behind a desk. Top and middle management have the luxury of having to make the right or wrong decision in the comfort of their offices; line officers are frequently forced to make split-second decisions in front of a particularly watchful audience—the community they serve. Sometimes such decisions are literally a matter of life or death. More commonly, police work is frequently composed of split-second decisions when a police officer must take control of a situation where a wrong approach may escalate a potentially benign circumstance to irreversible damage. The definition of police leadership must include *the ability to make a split-second decision and take control of a potentially high-voltage situation that evolves on the street.* It is time to recognize this reality and equip officers with the necessary tools.

Vinzant and Crothers (1998) examine the leadership skills of public service workers—police and social workers—"who serve at the relative *bottoms* of their organizations and physically deliver services to the public" (p. 5). They also examine some of the prevailing leadership theories—trait, skill, situational, and transformational—as practiced in the scenarios that such employees meet in day-to-day work. Public servants' leadership can be divided into categories based on what kind of discretion the individuals have. They exercise leadership when they can exercise discretion in the *process* of responding to the incident (for example, how to execute a search warrant), discretion over the *outcome* (for example, whether to give someone a breathalyzer test when making a traffic stop), or both (for example, how to respond to a domestic violence call) (Vinzant & Crothers, 1998). In exercising process-oriented discretion, situational leadership skills are most relevant; in exercising outcome-oriented discretion, street-level leaders should use transformational models while considering the higher goal of society's greater interest when making their decisions on how to act.

If, indeed, leadership skills have become so profoundly important for line officers, one would expect to find an extensive leadership training module included in basic training at police academies. Unfortunately, this is not the case. Most basic training programs at police academies not only do not offer an extensive leadership module but also do not include even the most basic introduction to the leadership skills during basic training.

## THE TRAINING GAP

The literature on leadership, in various contexts and forms, can fill the shelves of many bookcases; however, there is an absolute dearth in the area of leadership training and leadership theories that are applicable for and within police environments. Trainers and educators often integrate various ideas into their leadership training module, but the abundance of literature in this field can be overwhelming. The numerous leadership theories can be classified, in general, into four categories (Northouse, 2004):

1. "Great Man" and genetic theories
2. Traits approach
3. Behavioral explanations
4. Situational theories

Without clear examples from the world of policing, even overviews of the theories that appear to be most relevant for police environments will be of minimal utility for improving leadership in day-to-day policing. The traditional approach to what can be defined as "leadership-related issues" in police organizations is replete with terms relating more to management than to the pure issue of leadership.

An earlier book by this author, *Critical Issues in Police Training* (2002), discusses the need for leadership training to be introduced from the very first day of police basic training. This critical aspect of police basic training has been completely ignored by police organizations in the United States, as well as by those of many other countries that claim to have fully functional, democratic police forces. *Critical Issues* identifies some theoretical concepts of leadership and describes, in an overview, some of the rare existing training modules in the hope of inspiring much-needed programs that would be incorporated into basic academy training. However, *Critical Issues* only describes the contours of the problem. This book takes the issue a few steps further by identifying, in a much broader way, a number of leadership theories that are and should be applicable to various situations faced by law enforcement personnel on a daily basis.

Many police departments around the country experiment with a variety of leadership training modules, some developed and customized by the West Point Military Academy, others by the F.B.I. National Academy, and still others endorsed or developed by the International Association of Chiefs of Police. Some departments opt to expose their supervisors to leadership training developed and offered by private consultants or academic institutions, such as colleges and universities with leadership institutes. Others attempt to customize the available programs and ideas to the needs of the specific environment. The NYPD, LAPD, Santa Barbara PD, Boston PD, a number of police departments in Washington, D.C., and Virginia (Arlington and Alexandria), and other predominantly large organizations lead these efforts.

Despite being clearly dedicated to the development of leadership skills, all such efforts continue to ignore the most needy target population—line officers. In their approach to leadership training, many organizations continue to utilize the traditional skills approach, based on a reactive instead of proactive training paradigm. (Reactive training focuses on delivering training, in various degrees of intensity, to the supervisory-level employees. A proactive training paradigm, advocated by this author, is leadership or any other new skills training delivered, in the most extensive manner, to line officers during their basic academy training.)

This proactive training paradigm is particularly applicable given potential flaws in the civil service system, which is usually used to select police supervisors. Proactive training can serve as a natural screening device and can identify early in their careers those individuals who have greater leadership potential. Every agency struggles with political interference and pressure from both inside and outside the organization when making appointments. While proactive training offers no solution to the problems that arise from the political nature of policing and the influence of politics on police leadership, providing leadership training to each and every member of the organization at the very outset of their careers will produce a pool of potential candidates that will be hard to ignore, even by the savviest of politicians.

In the classroom, this author has frequently come across the best and the brightest students who, due to the bureaucratic nature of their police organizations, remained line officers for years before being given the opportunity for advancement. If leadership skills, like any other type of skill, are better absorbed by some than by others, police organizations will benefit by identifying those people early and taking advantage of their talents.

The focus of this book is as much on the theories as it is on their practical implementation. It categorizes and describes many of the applicable relevant theories and then illustrates those theories with practical examples from U.S. police departments. The examples focus on the highest echelon of the police hierarchy—the police chiefs and commissioners. The question that begs to be answered is, Why does a book on police leadership that so strongly emphasizes the need for early police leadership training focus on events and situations in which the major players are the top executives and not the line officers?

The answer is pretty simple. It is very hard to learn from mundane examples that lack prominence, mystery, and real drama as experienced by others. Yes, this author could have included scenarios or even real-life stories from the daily routine encounters of line officers on the job: the arrival at a crime scene, an angry demonstrator, a traffic violation, a high-speed pursuit, or a domestic violence encounter. The definition of police leadership is *the ability to make a split-second decision and take control of a potentially high-voltage situation that evolves on the street.* Such situations have to be absorbed by the recruits from the standpoint of what is expected of them as a leader. A recruit, entering the police academy, will not absorb easily or quickly the notion of being a leader on the first days on the job. It will be too amorphous a concept, and the focus will be more on understanding practical operating procedures.

However, if one teaches leadership through the prism of established position, then it will be much easier for the recruit to understand the nature of the problem, grasp the relevance of abstract concepts, and apply them to the lower tiers. For example, the struggles with issues of integrity and ethics faced by the police chief of New Orleans can be easily understood and analyzed by a police recruit in the same way that they can be easily understood and analyzed by any student of police science, whether or not he/she is a police officer. On the other hand, if one were to start learning about the problems of integrity and ethics from the street-level perspective—for example, by looking at a line officer being offered a bribe by a motorist—it becomes too personal, close, scary, and even immobilizing because it requires an almost immediate split-second response with regard to what is right and wrong, without having the room not only to understand and analyze but also to be able to argue the pros and cons of doing things right versus doing the right thing. When the examples or scenarios one is supposed to learn from hit too close to home, our reactions tend to lean more toward what we know is expected of us rather than toward what we really feel and think about the issue at hand. That is why it will be much easier, for example, to look at the behavior of Chief O'Brien (who decided not to involve the mayor of Miami in his operational decision regarding Elian Gonzales) and to analyze the pros and cons of his leadership approach in this given situation than to learn the same lessons from a situation that involves a line officer having to make a decision that goes against the departmental rules but that makes moral or ethical sense to the line officer. Learning leadership concepts from top-ranking supervisors, and then adapting them to line-level situations, is a much safer approach to this complex topic.

There is one disclaimer that cannot be repeated often enough. Anyone's career is a complex three-dimensional entity, and no matter how many pages are dedicated to describing it, they will not capture every phase and nuance of it. The cases that were chosen to illustrate the theories depict only a small facet of any chief's career—isolated situations or particular characteristics. Furthermore, no one real-life situation will ever exactly model the ideal of an abstract theory. The point of applying the theories to the chiefs is to open discussion, to further explore the theories through practical examples. There is nothing written in stone, and disagreement and debate will only further deepen understanding.

## THE PENTAGON OF POLICE LEADERSHIP

There are five model components leading to effective leadership, introduced here as the *pentagon of police leadership,* that can be emulated in police training academies. The five components of the pentagon are recruitment, selection, training, supervision, and discipline (see Figure 1–1).

**FIGURE 1–1    PENTAGON OF POLICE LEADERSHIP**

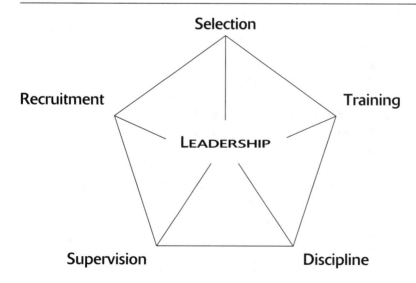

*Source:* J. Bjorken, 2004, based on model by M. H. Haberfeld.

The efforts to develop future police leaders can certainly be traced to the early stages of recruitment and selection. The process of *recruitment* and *selection* of recruits with potential to lead, on the streets as well as behind desks, is just the initial stage of the five-prong approach to be applied to the development of the police leadership cadre. By offering the leadership *training* (the third prong) at the basic academy level, it will be possible to identify the level of readiness of the officers for future supervisory positions within the department and to expose them to advanced leadership training, customized to their level of readiness and individual style, further down the road. Advanced leadership training will then concentrate *primarily on the issues pertinent to the functions of supervision and discipline*, the fourth and fifth prongs of the pentagon of police leadership.

This book is a tool for that process. By evaluating the ways in which police recruits look at the cases presented in this book, the ways they analyze behaviors and look for other and/or better leadership approaches, the academy trainers will be able to distinguish those who have the highest potential to climb the supervisory ladder and in doing so identify, at the earliest stage, those who should be given additional opportunities to hone their natural predispositions.

This book discusses some of the prominent theories of leadership that are applicable to the policing context, in the format of case studies accompanied by an in-depth overview of the theories. The basic models put forward by leading academics and other theorists are summarized. Then the biography of a police chief is used to illustrate how that particular theory can be applied to practical circumstances. The chapters end with an invitation to consider how other theories the student has learned might be applied to the chief's or commissioner's circumstance.

Police work is full of temptations to err and to experience the consequences of those errors of judgment on the most profound level, consequences that touch not only other people's lives but also the officers'. The police chiefs and commissioners who were chosen to illustrate the theories were probably not even conscious of the fact that their decision-making process was informed by one leadership approach or another. Some of them, as well as some readers, will disagree with the label attached to them by the author. The true beauty of social science is the ability to argue and dispute many notions and perceptions. Experimentation with concepts and ideas is truly a building process in this complex maze of skills, traits, and approaches that can and will make the life of police officers and those they police much more worth living.

The reader of this book, whether a police recruit, trainer, ranking officer, or student with interest in police work, is strongly encouraged to familiarize himself/herself with the following summary of the basic tenets of each leadership theory (see Table 1–1). This will serve as a foreshadowing and will also be useful when reading the case studies. It is important for the reader to be able to grasp the basic differences among the theories in order to fully appreciate all the subtleties and nuances that differentiate the approaches. This preparation will enable the reader to go back and forth and to experiment with a number of alternative approaches that could/would be beneficial in a given situation for a specific police chief or commissioner and from there to be able to deconstruct and translate the example into a street-level reality, one that each one of us can and will face on a daily basis.

**TABLE 1–1   LEADERSHIP THEORIES**

| Theory | Basic Concepts |
| --- | --- |
| Team | • Leadership involves the solving of complex organization problems.<br>• Leadership of teams involves team performance and team development.<br>• Leaders must monitor and diagnose problems that could impede organization and group performance, plan appropriate solutions, and then implement them, in an effort to adapt to changing conditions (Zaccaro et al., 2001).<br>• Four processes of leadership determine team productivity: cognitive, motivational, affective, and coordination (Zaccaro et al., 2001).<br>• Self-managed teams involve either rotated leadership and democratic decision making or emergent leadership in which an individual steps forward to assume the leadership role (Erez et al., 2002). |
| Leader-member Exchange | • This theory focuses on the interactions between leader and subordinates.<br>• Each subordinate has a dyadic relationship of vertical linkage with the leader (Liden & Graen, 1980). There are two types of relationships, with subordinates forming an in-group and out-group in relation to the leader (Graen & Uhl-Bien, 1991).<br>• Subordinates in the in-group go beyond their mere job descriptions and as a result receive more information, have better confidence, and elicit more concern from the leader (Graen & Cashman, 1975).<br>• Effective leaders should develop in-group exchanges with all subordinates if possible (Graen & Uhl-Bien, 1991). |

**TABLE 1–1    LEADERSHIP THEORIES    (*continued*)**

| Theory | Basic Concepts |
|---|---|
| **Transformational** | • Transformational leaders raise motivation and morale in subordinates (Burns, 1978), often through charisma (House, 1976).<br>• Transformational leaders cause followers to engage beyond mere job description by raising consciousness, motivating a transcendence of self-interest, and promoting the attainment of higher-level needs (Bass, 1985).<br>• As social architects, transformational leaders shape shared meanings in organizations and direct mutual values and norms (Bennis & Nanus, 1985). |
| **Transactional** | • Transactional leaders exchange things of value (e.g., contingent reward: work for a paycheck) with subordinates. Both leaders and subordinates engage in the transaction for their own self-interest (Kuhnert, 1994).<br>• Management-by-exception characterizes the leadership style. Active management-by-exception refers to daily monitoring by the leader of problems with subordinate performance. Passive management-by-exception involves intervening only when standards are in jeopardy (Northouse, 2004). |
| **Style** | • Leadership effectiveness is dependent on behavior.<br>• There are two broad categories of behavior: task and relationship (Northouse, 2004), for example, consideration and initiation of structure (Stogdill, 1974) or concern for structure and concern for people (Blake & Moulton, 1985).<br>• According to Blake and Moulton (1985), the intersection of the two behavior dimensions forms a grid of styles of management.<br>• Each leader has one style that is used in all situations. |
| **Situational** | • The type of leadership behavior that is most appropriate depends on the situation.<br>• To determine the correct behavior, the leader takes into consideration the competency and commitment of subordinates.<br>• According to Hersey and Blanchard (1977), there are four main leadership styles: delegating (low directive-low supportive), supporting (low directive-high supportive), coaching (high directive-high supportive), and directing (high directive-low supportive).<br>• A leader may have to use a variety of styles throughout a career, depending on situations faced. |

**TABLE 1–1    LEADERSHIP THEORIES** (*continued*)

| Theory | Basic Concepts |
| --- | --- |
| Contingency | • Fiedler's (1967) contingency theory attempts to match leadership styles to specific situations.<br>• There are three variables associated with a situation: leader-member relations (confidence and loyalty), task structure (clarity of task), and position power (amount of leader authority). Certain leadership styles (task versus structure) are better in certain situations.<br>• Therefore, not all leaders are good for all situations. Leadership is effective to the extent that the leader is compatible with the situation (Northouse, 2004). |
| **Vroom-Yetton Model** | • The Vroom and Yetton (1973) contingency model focuses on the autocracy-participation dimension of leadership style. The model looks at leadership as a problem to be solved. In order to handle the problem, the leaders may or may not share their decision making with subordinates.<br>• The level of participation represents a continuum of five levels of employee participation, from no participation to democratic participation. The leader decides which of the five levels to adopt based on seven rules, which are designed to either protect the quality of the decision or protect the acceptance of the decision by subordinates (Vroom & Yetton, 1973).<br>• According to the model, a single leader should be flexible enough to vary the style across the continuum as needed; therefore, a person has the capacity to be both autocratic and participative (Bryman, 1986).<br><br>**Leader Substitutes**<br><br>• This theory is based on the notion that group processes can produce effects similar to interpersonal, hierarchical leadership (Tosi & Kiker, 1997). The idea was developed by Kerr and Jermier (1978) from the observation that situational factors can actually negate a leader's ability to be effective.<br>• The model makes a distinction between two kinds of situational variables: substitutes (what makes leader behavior unnecessary or redundant) and neutralizers (what nullifies the effects of the leaders) (Yukl, 1994).<br>• Formal leadership may be unnecessary in the presence of capable subordinates (Kerr & Jermier, 1978). |

**TABLE 1–1  LEADERSHIP THEORIES  *(continued)***

| Theory | Basic Concepts |
| --- | --- |
| **Path-goal** | • Path-goal matches leadership style with the characteristics of subordinates and the work environment.<br>• Subordinates are only motivated when they believe they can perform their work, that they can achieve their goals, and that there are benefits to doing so. The leader's task, therefore, is to remove obstacles to success, to coach subordinates, and to instill motivation (House, 1971). |
| **Psychodynamic** | • This approach was derived from Freud (1921, 1939). Deep-seated emotional factors influence leaders.<br>• Childhood family experiences affect leaders who always take a paternal role with subordinates. Based on family experiences, leaders exhibit behaviors along continuums of authoritative to permissive, of supportive to critical, of dependent to counterdependent to independent (Northouse, 2004).<br>• Based on Jung (1923), leaders must understand their own shadow self, or their unconscious, including repressed needs and desires, in order to effectively lead.<br>• Berne (1961) posited that an effective leader operates out of an adult ego state, reflecting emotional maturity.<br>• Because of the different psychodynamic outcomes leaders embody, leaders will match better with some subordinates than others, depending on subordinates' psychodynamic variables. Leaders' awareness of their own personality types will help them relate to subordinates more effectively (Kroeger & Theusen, 1992). |
| **Skills** | • A leader's success is determined by skills and abilities, which are not innate but which can be learned and developed.<br>• Leaders must be able to use their skills to solve complex organizational problems.<br>• Technical, human relations, and conceptual skills are the primary skills, according to Sheriff (1968).<br>• In addition, social intelligence (Kobe et al., 2001) and emotional intelligence (Feldman, 1999) are leadership skills that produce effectiveness. |
| **Trait** | • Individuals' traits determine their success as leaders. Traits are innate, according to the "Great Man" theory, on which the trait theory is based.<br>• Traits associated with leadership are intelligence (Lord et al., 1986; Mann, 1959; Stogdill, 1948), insight, responsibility, persistence, self-confidence, initiative, sociability (Stogdill, 1948), cognitive ability, motivation, drive, task knowledge, and integrity (Kirkpatrick & Locke, 1991). |

# REFERENCES

Baker, T.E. (2000). *Effective police leadership: Beyond management*. New York: Looseleaf Law Publications, Inc.

Bass, B.M. (1985). *Leadership and performance beyond expectations*. New York: Free Press.

Bennis, W.G. & B. Nanus (1985). *Leaders: The strategies for taking charge*. New York: Harper & Row.

Bergner, L.L. (1998, November). Developing leaders begins at the beginning. *Police Chief*, 16–23.

Berne, E. (1961). *Transactional analysis in psychotherapy*. New York: Grove.

Blake, R.R. & J.S. Moulton (1985). *The managerial grid III*. Houston, TX: Gulf.

Bryman, A. (1986). *Leadership and organizations*. London: Routledge & Kegan Paul.

Burns, J.M. (1978). *Leadership*. New York: Harper & Row.

Erez, A., J.A. Lepine & H. Elms (2002). Effects of rotated leadership and peer evaluation of the functioning and effectiveness of self-managed teams: A quasi-experiment. *Personnel Psychology*, 55, 929–948.

Feldman, D.A. (1999). *The handbook of emotionally intelligent leadership: Inspiring others to achieve results*. Falls Church, VA: Leadership Performance Solutions Press.

Fiedler, F.E. (1967). *A theory of leadership effectiveness*. New York: McGraw-Hill.

Freud, S. (1921; 1959). *Group psychology and the analysis of the ego*. London: Hogarth Press.

——— (1939; 1964). *Moses and monotheism*. London: Hogarth Press.

Graen, G. & J.F. Cashman (1975). A role making model of leadership in formal organizations: A developmental approach. In J.L. Hunt & L.L. Larson (Eds.), *Leadership frontiers* (pp. 143–165). Kent, OH: Kent State University Press.

——— & M. Uhl-Bien (1991). The transformation of professionals into self-managing and partially self-designing contributions. Toward a theory of leader-making. *Journal of Management Systems*, 3 (3), 33–48.

Haberfeld, M.R. (2002). *Critical issues in police training*. Upper Saddle River, NJ: Prentice Hall.

Hersey, P. & K.H. Blanchard (1977). *Management of organizational behavior: Utilizing human resources*. Englewood Cliffs, NJ: Prentice Hall.

House, R.J. (1971). A path-goal theory of leader effectiveness: Lessons, legacy and a reformulated theory. *The Leadership Quarterly*, 7 (3), 323–352.

——— (1976). A 1976 theory of charismatic leadership. In J.G. Hunt & L.L. Larson (Eds.), *Leadership: The cutting edge* (pp. 189–207). Carbondale: Southern Illinois University Press.

Jung, C. (1923). *Psychological types*. New York: Harcourt & Brace.

Kerr S. & J. Jermier (1978). Substitutes for leadership: Their meaning and measurement. *Organizational Behavior and Human Performance*, 22, 374–403.

Kirkpatrick, S.A. & E.A. Locke (1991). Leadership: Do traits matter? *The Executive*, 5, 48–60.

Kobe, L.M., R. Reiter-Palmon & J.D. Rickers (2001). Self-reported leadership experiences in relation to inventoried social and emotional intelligence. *Current Psychology*, 20 (2), 154–163.

Kroeger, O. & J.M. Theusen (1992). *Type talk at work*. New York: Delacorte.

Kuhnert, K.W. (1994). Transforming leadership: Developing people through delegation. In B.M. Bass & B.J. Avolio (Eds.), *Improving organizational effectiveness through transformational leadership* (pp. 10–25). Thousand Oaks, CA: Sage.

Liden, R.C. & G. Graen (1980). Generalizability of the vertical dyad linkage model of leadership. *Academy of Management Journal*, 23 (3), 451–465.

Lord, R.G., C.L. Devader & G.M. Alliger (1986). A meta-analysis of the relationship between personality traits and leadership perceptions: An application of validity generalization procedures. *Journal of Applied Psychology*, 71, 402–410.

Mann, R.D. (1959). Review of the relationship between personality and performance in small groups. *Psychological Bulletin*, 56 (4), 241–270.

Northouse, P.G. (2004). *Leadership: Theory and practice* (3rd ed.). Thousand Oaks, CA: Sage.

Sheriff, D.R. (1968). Leadership skills and executive development: Leadership mythology vs. six learnable skills. *Training and Development Journal*, 22 (4), 29–34.

Stogdill, R.M. (1948). Personal factors associated with leadership: A survey of the literature. *Journal of Psychology*, 25, 35–71.

———— (1974). *Handbook of leadership: A survey of theory and research.* New York: Free Press.

Swanson, C.R., L. Territo & R.W. Taylor (1998). *Police administration: Structures, processes, and behavior* (4th ed.). Upper Saddle River, NJ: Prentice Hall.

Tosi, H.L. & S. Kiker (1997). Commentary on "substitutes for leadership." *Leadership Quarterly*, 8 (2) 109–112.

Vinzant, J.C. & L. Crothers (1998). Street-level leadership: Discretion and legitimacy in front-line public service. Washington, DC: Georgetown University Press.

Vroom, V.H. & P.W. Yetton (1973). *Leadership and decision-making.* Pittsburgh: University of Pittsburgh Press.

Yukl, G. (1994). *Leadership in organizations* (3rd ed.). Englewood Cliffs, NJ: Prentice Hall.

Zaccaro, S.J., A.L. Rittman & M.A. Marks (2001). Team leadership. *The Leadership Quarterly*, 12, 451–483.

# 2

# Integrity, Ethics, and Police Leadership

Police integrity is defined in many different ways by many different actors. For the purpose of this chapter, the author will be using the following definition, developed during a study of 30 police departments in the United States that were surveyed by the author and her colleagues between the years 1996 and 1997:

> Police integrity is the normative inclination among police to resist temptations to abuse the rights and privileges of their occupation. (Klockars et al., 1997, 2002)

Using the word "integrity" appears to be less threatening for police organizations than the word "ethics." Ethics somehow connotes that if somebody is in need of ethical training or exposure to ethical decision-making processes, there is something deficient in that area that needs to be addressed and/or corrected. Therefore, substituting "integrity" for "ethics" creates a somewhat more appealing notion—that the ethical foundation is in place and that what we are really looking for is some form of enhancement and maintenance of otherwise ethical environments. Integrity is simply a much more user-friendly word than ethics, and this is an especially poignant point with regard to police environments.

This chapter will provide a general overview of literature related to the concept of ethics within the leadership context and proceed to identify ways police leaders could and should create and maintain environments of integrity in their organizations. These practical applications are as relevant for first-line supervisors as they are for chiefs and commissioners; it is not a coincidence that this chapter opens the door to various theories of and approaches to leadership within police organizations.

Leadership scholars underemphasize leadership ethics. According to Ciulla (1995), "good leadership" implies two realms: 1) effective leadership and 2) ethical leadership. Yet a majority of leadership studies focus only on the first consideration. Ciulla argues that the focus on scientific assessments of leadership has neglected the softer analysis required of leadership ethics. "[N]o matter how much empirical information we get from the 'scientific' study of leadership, it will always be inadequate if we neglect the moral implications" (Ciulla, 1995, p. 14). Ciulla explains that each of the normative theories in leadership studies has inherent philosophical underpinnings that beg ethical questions.

Ethical considerations are important because confidence in leaders, and thus their effectiveness, falters if followers do not perceive a sense of ethical responsibility from leaders (Martinez-Carbonell, 2003). Maintaining trust in leadership is a critical component in a healthy organization. "If an atmosphere of misinformation and distrust exists, work activities may continue even though the workplace is hampered by rumors and suspicion. However, motivation and efficiency will be hindered" (Eckhart, 2003, p. 6).

## ETHICS AND TRANSFORMATIONAL LEADERSHIP

Ethics as it relates to transformational leadership has been the subject of the bulk of articles on leadership ethics in general (see the table in the Introduction and Chapter 5 for an overview of transformational theory). Burns's (1978) *Leadership* focuses on the notion that people can be lifted up to become their better selves through the transforming power of leadership. Leaders are to encourage followers to develop a set of values that emphasizes justice, liberty, and equality. This is what gives transformational leadership its moral purpose. The moral calling of transformational leadership is then contrasted with transactional leadership. Burns finds transactional leadership to lack a moral center because it is inherently uncritical of the people involved in the leadership exchange. It is enough that people operate in their own self-interest; there is no encouragement to ascend to higher-order moral functioning. Giampetro-Meyer et al. (1998) come to a similar conclusion, arguing that transactional leadership can lead to ethically questionable behavior on the part of leaders. This is because of what they term "craft ethics" (p. 1731), in which leaders do not reflect on what they personally think is right but merely follow what those on the job or in the workplace believe is ethical.

Similarly, for Kuhnert and Lewis (1987), transformational leaders transcend self-interested goals to a more mature set of values, culminating in a sense of universal ethical principles of fairness, equality, and justice. These values form ends in themselves for the mature leaders. In fact, moral reasoning has been empirically connected to leadership effectiveness, using a measure of moral reasoning (Defining Issues Test [DIT]) and subordinates' ratings of leaders in a sample of managers. Moral reasoning is considered a cognitive function that can develop over a life span. Leaders with the cognitive capacity to reason morally will use this higher degree of transformational leadership and will be more likely to behave in a way that serves the collective good. Leaders who use the transactional style of leadership, however, do not become more effective regardless of whether they have the capacity to reason morally. This is because, by definition, transactional leadership is merely a dyadic exchange to satisfy individual needs (Turner et al., 2002). Contrastingly, however, in a study of U.S. military cadets, emergence of moral reasoning abilities in the first year of military training was not predictive of emergence as a leader in later years. This suggests that in strong hierarchical organizations, moral reasoning may not be critical to performing well as a leader. Such environments may be inherently transactional, lacking the flexibility for moral reasoning and transformational leadership to come into play (Atwater et al., 1999).

One of the problems with the above conception of the moral superiority of transformational leadership is that it assumes that leaders know and operationalize the values to be instilled in followers and that they have the will to proceed as such:

> An analysis of the ethics of transformational leadership is thus closely connected to the question of why leaders behave immorally. On the standard view in applied ethics and moral theory, ethical failures are essentially volitional, not cognitive. We behave unethically because of problems of will, not because of problems of belief and knowledge. (Price, 2003, p. 69)

Aside from problems of will, Price argues that leaders can behave immorally because they are blinded by their own values. Transformational leadership may actually lead to a dangerous moral superiority in which leaders believe they are justified in doing as they wish, even exempting themselves from ethical behavior. This is similar to Bass and Steidlmeier's (1999) notion of the pseudo-transformational leader who purports to be moral but in fact is manipulative and victimizing. Price explains that leadership is not so black and white and that the real test of authentic transformational leadership is whether leaders can apply moral requirements to themselves.

However, Kanungo (2001) argues that transformational and transactional leadership can both be ethically based. They reflect two different value systems and motives. Unlike most other theorists, Kanungo does not believe that transformational leadership is morally superior. For him, transformational leaders possess an organic worldview characteristic of a deontological perspective. Such a perspective asserts that leaders' actions have a morally intrinsic value. An act is moral when, as a means to an end, it is executed with a sense of duty to others and guided by Kantian pure reason; this is referred to as genuine or moral altruism:

> While acting out of a sense of duty, the leader is prepared to suffer the harmful consequences for him/her self. Sometimes, the leader knowingly causes harm to him/her self, a strategic move that convinces others of the leader's unbending commitment to the organizational objectives. (Kanungo, 2001, p. 261)

In contrast, transactional leaders reflect teleological ethics in which ends or outcomes are emphasized. The leader has an atomistic worldview, meaning that he/she feels separate from others, with an emphasis on independence rather than interdependence. Under this paradigm, actions that provide the most benefit to subordinates in the end are considered moral; this is referred to as mutual altruism. In this mode of influence, transactional leaders are only unethical if they follow their own self-interest without providing a beneficial end result for subordinates.

## INTEGRATION OF BEHAVIOR AND VALUES

Other theorists have written about the problem of integrating behavior and values in the context of leadership in general rather than merely in transformational leadership. Weber (1989) believes that organizations can potentially stifle the moral maturity of leaders in favor of other organizational values such as competitiveness and efficiency. Although a leader may be able to reason in a morally mature fashion, research has not established a connection between this and the capacity or opportunity to behave morally.

Heifetz (1994) writes about leadership as the capacity to behave in a manner that is commensurate with moral reasoning and values. Leaders assist subordinates in resolving fundamental value conflicts that occur in organizations in which people have different job functions, social roles, and personal interests. In essence, leadership is adaptive work that "consists of the learning required to address conflicts in the values people stand for and the reality they face" (Heifetz, 1994, p. 22). Further, effective leadership involves fostering situations in which followers can learn to reconcile values with reality and thus develop their moral compasses.

## STEWARDSHIP MODEL

Under the stewardship model, leaders serve their followers and put their needs above their own self-interest. In other words, the leader becomes a steward whose job is to protect the interests of subordinates:

> [T]he steward is motivated by deep intrinsic values based upon a moral theory that a prima facie priority of interests is owed to those who have a stake in the organization's success. The underlying mechanism is that the steward is driven by an underlying social contract. (Caldwell et al., 2002, p. 161)

This is similar to Greenleaf's (1977) servant leadership, which centers around the need for leaders to be attentive to the interests of their followers. Under this model, leaders are charged with nurturing subordinates, helping them to develop their intellect, independence, and personal leadership abilities. In essence, the leader is a servant to followers. Giampetro-Meyer et al. (1998) point out that Greenleaf's conception is particularly moral: "Servant leaders are concerned with the least privileged in society and strive to help others grow as persons. . . . Servant leaders show awareness of how the decisions they inspire affect others" (p. 1734).

Caldwell et al. (2002) explain that an effective steward is a "facilitating idealist" (p. 156). Stewards recognize that reality is complex and ultimately unpredictable. They also accept that individual perception is imperfect and limited even in the best of circumstances and with the most conscientious of stewards. However, leaders as stewards proceed to make decisions that serve the best interest of all stakeholders. This requires adaptability, flexibility, and commitment to continual learning.

Stewardship also requires a self-exploration of beliefs, values, and assumptions that inform stewards' decision-making process. Schein (1977) provides a framework for assessing these assumptions. One should reflect on these areas:

- Beliefs about the self and about ways stewards view their own talents, goals, and worth
- Beliefs about others, including beliefs about the nature of people and organizations, and about stewards' social responsibility
- Beliefs about the past and how it has influenced current events
- Beliefs about the current reality as a process of filtering data and interpreting information
- Beliefs about the future, including goals and spiritual tenets

## ETHICAL LEADERS' CHARACTERISTICS

Ethical leaders have been characterized in a variety of ways. The main characteristics fall into three broad categories: being nurturing and service-oriented, being just and honest, and being committed to common goals.

### Nurturing and Service-Oriented

Burns (1978) indicates that leaders must instill in subordinates an awareness of their needs and values; they must be nurturing. Similarly, Greenleaf (1977) emphasizes the service of followers, encouraging them to develop their values and moral visions. Caldwell et al. (2002) emphasizes that effective leaders are committed to all stakeholders in a given issue and pursue integrative solutions. Further, leadership should not force followers to a certain end, nor should it ignore the interests of subordinates (Bass & Steidlmeier, 1999).

### Just and Honest

Effective transformational leaders have a sense of social responsibility and fairness (Kanungo, 2001; Kuhnert & Lewis, 1987), follow established rules, and are objective evaluators of the facts underlying any decision (Caldwell et al., 2002 ). Lying is often cited as one of the most destructive behaviors that a leader can exhibit because it leads to a breakdown in trust, the foundation of any relationship. "One of the critical 'cures' for . . . an organization is truthfulness. . . . Being truthful involves taking active steps to promote understanding, especially when misperceptions persist" (Eckhart, 2003, p. 6).

## Committed to Common Goals

Burns (1978) and Bass and Steidlmeier (1999) describe transformational leadership as the development of common goals that are beneficial to both leaders and followers. Moreover, a sense of the common good should be broadly interpreted by leaders and includes the public interest as well as the interests of leaders and their subordinates.

## THE TRIANGLE OF POLICE INTEGRITY

In the policing environment, three general topics—recruitment, selection, and training—are viewed in the context of integrity and corruption. The very essence of this chapter has to do with and is predicated on the assumption that whatever does not lead to integrity will, by default, actually or potentially lead to corruption. The word "corruption" connotes numerous interpretations, some of which include noble cause corruption, abuse of power, excessive use of force, and corruption for gain (Crank and Caldero, 2000; Klockars et al., 2002; Punch, 1999). For the purpose of this chapter, however, corruption will be viewed as any misconduct or inaction exhibited by a police officer that can be directly tied to poor and/or inadequate mechanisms of recruitment, selection, and training.

There are three crucial topics in which the theoretical models of ethics in leadership apply to policing. These are recruitment, selection, and training—three of the five prongs of the pentagon of police leadership (discipline and supervision are the other two). Each has a relationship to integrity.

## Recruitment

The relationship between recruitment and integrity can be approached from a number of theoretical angles. First, the overall endeavor

## Framing the Problem

1. NOBLE CAUSE CORRUPTION (Crank and Caldero, 2000)
   a. *Noble cause:* Not directly making choices for personal gain
   b. *Victim:* Acting on behalf of victims and doing "the right thing"
   c. *"Tower":* Choosing to run toward the sniper on the tower instead of away from him and belief that this gives one the right to act in a certain way—not necessarily by the book
2. ADAPTATION (Crank, 2004)
   a. *The Asshole:* Viewing everybody, including self, as such
   b. *Cynicism:* Resulting from viewing the worst that humans are capable of
   c. *Means-end conflict:* Doing the right thing or doing things right
3. ECONOMIC CORRUPTION (Kleinig, 1996)
   a. *Stages—the slippery slope:* Starting with something small that leads to more
   b. *Typology:* Using different types of corruption for gain
   c. *Corruption of Authority:* Being involved in the following:
      Kickbacks
      Opportunistic thefts
      Shakedowns
      Protection of illegal activities
      Traffic fixes
      Misdemeanor fixes
      Felony fixes
      Direct criminal activities
      Internal payoffs

---

devoted to the recruitment process indicates whether a given agency views the outreach effort as an important component of its internal infrastructure. An agency that invests significant resources, from qualified manpower to adequate facilities, in its recruitment process sends a powerful message about its professional standards to potential applicants.

The intensity and variety of outreach efforts are closely related to integrity. An agency that attempts to recruit in narrowly defined environments, such as military facilities or community colleges, or that narrows its recruitment effort to a recruitment office within that agency can be considered to have a much skewed interest in the quality of potential applicants. On the other hand, an agency that is highly engaged in proactive recruitment, attempting to reach out to applicants of diverse socioeconomic, educational, ethnic, racial, and other backgrounds, sends a signal about its ethical orientation and motivation (orientation and motivation which might originate from political pressures but which, nevertheless, are omnipresent). A recruitment staff composed of selectively chosen career-oriented officers, as opposed to a small number of unmotivated employees, projects an image of professionalism and high standards. Recruitment offices located in temporary or poorly maintained facilities, equipped with old or broken furniture, cast an image of neglect on the force they represent. On the other hand, well-equipped, modern, and permanently located offices project a sense of importance and seriousness about the activities taking place inside.

In sum, a combination of resource allocation, marketing techniques, and careful planning, exemplified by the intensity, diversity, and quality of effort devoted to recruitment, bears an important correlation to the integrity of a department.

## Selection

The actual and potential relationship between the selection process and integrity is the second theme. A number of theoretical questions need to be addressed in order to clarify the importance of the selection process. To begin with, if it is a fundamental premise that there are certain characteristics that applicants must possess to be attractive to a police agency, this premise invites two questions:

1. If such characteristics indeed exist, which of them, individually and in combination, are indicative of future ethical behavior?
2. If individuals do exhibit such characteristics, is it because of their moral character, prior life and work experience, education, physical agility, medical history, or age?

Reviewing the selection efforts of police departments in the United States, one might ask these questions:

1. Are there any generalizable evidence-based characteristics that could be looked on as profiling the "ideal" prototype of an ethical police professional?
2. Is the entire selection enterprise highly influenced by a number of themes unrelated to integrity?

Some of these themes stem from political pressure, some from budget constraints, and yet others from a complete ignorance of the posited desired skills and qualities. Profiling is important to consider because frequently individuals who engage in corrupt behavior are associated with various characteristics or lifestyles.

The second theoretical theme is based on the premise that a direct but complex and dynamic relationship between the selection process and integrity can be observed by looking at the planned efforts dedicated by the agency to the selection process. This begins with the allocation of resources and manpower (devoted to the verification of those "minimum standards"), followed by a closer look at the rationale behind the minimum standards required of the potential applicant. These allocations of resources and manpower relate directly both to the role the police play in a given society and/or community and to the culture of policing within the organization on a micro level and within the governmental and societal structures on a macro level. Various types of transformations—economic, societal, political, and cultural—contribute to observable changes in the distribution of resources to the organizations that serve the government and the community.

## Training

The component of police training is somewhat more problematic. Police training is defined as a process of socializing a less than homogeneous group of people into police work, during which necessary rules and values of a given organization, system, and culture are communicated to the recruits. Police training, on a basic academy level, is delivered through an in-house police academy, a regional academy, or a state academy. Only departments with their own in-house programs have the ability to invest and maintain real input into the curriculum, number of hours allocated to a given topic, selection of instructors, and instructional materials, facilities, etc. Any police academy, regardless of its size, length of existence, or location, serves a certain role in creating and maintaining police integrity. Training, in general, can be defined as a three-step process in which necessary rules and values of police organization are explained, demonstrated, and practiced. In the course of this process, certain situations and behaviors are addressed, and the instructors are responsible for showing the police recruits how to behave and/or respond under a range of challenging and oftentimes complex circumstances and how to do this without sacrificing personal and/or police organizational integrity. This happens almost irrespectively of the quality of the instruction and the instructors. Police recruits are socialized and acculturated to the life of a policeman—getting to work on time, listening to and following instructions, and learning other discipline-related issues as well as being subject to "vulnerability" reinforcing or promoting pressures. These explanations, demonstrations, and practices establish a certain type of an "integrity character."

It is reasonable to assume that there is a general relationship between the number of hours allocated to a given training topic and the issue of police integrity. The longer the period dedicated to the topic, the better is the socialization to the discussed values. Having noted this, the reality is that for any educational and/or training process, it is rare that generalizable evidence-based data exist that form the basis for making staffing and materials choices and decisions as well as making possible the necessary conditions for achieving the selected goals or targets. It is no different for police training.

When looking at the three components of the training process—explanation, demonstration, and practice—we can assess the quality of experience for a given applicant. In the case of integrity/ethics training, the following four steps help to identify the importance of such topics to a given police academy:[1]

1. Examining whether a particular topic is part of the curriculum makes it possible to deduce something about the overall importance of that topic to the given organization at a given point in time or with regard to its future planning. Given the fact that each state mandates the number of hours and the mandatory topics each academy must include in its training, the choice of additional topics is basically an arbitrary decision made by the training director and/or police chief.

2. By reviewing and analyzing how this topic is demonstrated (or not demonstrated) to police recruits, we can begin to see what the academy (or the organization during the on-the-job training) actually trains its "screened-in" recruits to do.

3. We may further engage in investigating the police training process to find out and to better understand what is necessary

---

[1] This chapter does not look at supervision and built-in feedback and their relationship to the three components of training discussed in this segment. Future researchers would be well advised to look at these components as well.

for a person to know about ethical policing in a democratic society and how to do it before (or after) recruits become police officers.

4. By following the process involved in practicing the policing "gospel," we might arrive at a final conclusion as to whether or not a given topic is actually treated with the ultimate necessary seriousness by the police organization. Looking at the materials used to instruct a given topic, further conclusions might be reached.

No matter how positive the overall conclusion about the triangle of integrity of recruitment, selection, and training, an environment of integrity relies on the two additional prongs of the pentagon: supervision and discipline. Without proper supervision and discipline, it will be impossible to maintain environments of integrity in a world filled with opportunities and temptations to abuse the rights of the position of police officer.

## THE PENTAGON OF POLICE LEADERSHIP

As previously discussed, police officers operate in a world full of temptations. Nothing describes it better than a statement made by a representative of the British police force during a meeting sponsored by the Council of Europe in 1999 in Strasbourg, France: Given the nature of police work, it is no shame to find corruption within the service; the shame is not doing anything about it.

> *Given the nature of police work, it is no shame to find corruption within the service; the shame is not doing anything about it.*
>
> Anti-Corruption Task Force, 1999.
> Association of Chief Police Officers, U.K.

Environments of temptation can consist of many prongs and angles. It might be the classic economic gain corruption, it might be the noble cause corruption, or it might be ambiguity of a law that leaves officers with an impression that discretion is about manipulation and situational integrity, exempt from objective evaluation. No matter what the cause, reason, or motivation, the fact remains that police misconduct is rarely tolerated by the public and is certainly not something that should be tolerated by a police leader, no matter how high or low he/she is on the leadership ladder.

It is very hard for this author to make a value judgment about the various situations that require or at least appear to require some manipulation. Nevertheless, the pentagon of police leadership can provide a useful tool for understanding the nature of the problem and how it can be controlled.

It needs to be reiterated that policing is about using ethics and integrity and about differentiating between right and wrong. Police accomplish these ends through their ability and mandate to use coercive force. Force does not have to be just ultimate brute physical force; sometimes just the implied notion of the ability to use this force can be as detrimental. Therefore, no effort should be spared to ensure that the ends are accomplished in the most effective and straightforward manner. Every police officer needs the ability to lead, to take control, and to use force, force that can be lethal if not handled by the right people.

The idea of effective policing will always be a balance between the two prevalent leadership concepts:

1. Doing things right
2. Doing the right thing

A third concept, related to number two, that is of critical importance in police work takes the concept a step further by making it as explicit as it can be and in a provocative way:

3. Sometimes it's right to do the wrong thing

This third concept underscores why developing ethical police leaders cannot be emphasized enough: Individuals who have the mandate to use coercive force against others, and who have the discretion to choose one of these three concepts, need to be very carefully chosen, trained, supervised, and, if needed, disciplined.

This is where one of the leadership theories, presented in more detail later on in this book, becomes more applicable than others where ethical leadership is concerned: the path-goal directive approach (see table in Introduction and Chapter 9). While conducting research in three large police departments in the United States, the author and colleagues looked at integrity management from many different angles. The conclusion reached by the team of researchers produced a five-step approach to integrity management that appears to be replicable in other police environments as well. These five steps are best implemented through the use of the path-goal directive approach to leadership.

## The Path-Goal Theory of Leadership

1. Subordinates will be motivated if:
    a. They are capable of performing their work.
    b. Their efforts will result in a certain outcome.
    c. The payoffs for doing their work are worthwhile.
2. Leaders help subordinates define their goals and clarify their work.
3. Leaders remove obstacles and provide support.
4. Leaders select a style of leadership that is best suited to their subordinates:
    a. *Directive* leadership gives subordinates instruction about the task (complex).
    b. *Supportive* leadership attends to the well-being and the human needs of subordinates (repetitive).
    c. *Achievement-oriented* leadership establishes a high standard of excellence (excel), consults with subordinates, and integrates their suggestions (control).
    d. *Achievement-oriented* leadership establishes a high standard of excellence (excel).

The directive approach of the path-goal theory posits that when faced with a complex situation, leaders should give subordinates clear and straightforward instructions about how to complete the task. There is nothing more complex in police work than the issue of police ethics and leadership. While there is room for discussion and dialogue, at the end of the day each and every police officer needs to know what to do and how to do it. Effective supervision and swift and certain discipline will ensure that this knowledge of what and how will not be diluted or otherwise distorted.

If police leaders follow Klockars et al.'s five steps of integrity management, chances are that the complex topic of police ethics will become a tiny bit less complex.

The steps are composed of five questions and answers; readers can customize those questions and answers to the reality of their police organizations and their own status within the organizational structure. Sometimes the nature of the offense or misconduct will allow for a further modification.

Ethical leaders must be developed to handle these complex issues of integrity properly. Policing is about discretion, policing is about use of force, policing is about ethics and integrity—only leaders can handle such heavy ideals and loads. We are not born with the ability to exercise discretion and authority without

## Five-Step Approach to Integrity Management

*Question 1.*   Do officers in this agency know the rules?
*Action Response.* If they do, fine. Where they don't, teach them.

*Question 2.*   How strongly do they support those rules?
*Action Response.* If they support them, fine. Where they don't, teach them why they should.

*Question 3.*   Do they know what disciplinary threat this agency makes for violation of those rules?
*Action Response.* If they do, fine. Where they don't, teach them.

*Question 4.*   Do they *think the discipline is fair?*
*Action Response.* If they do, fine. Where they don't, adjust discipline or correct their perceptions.

*Question 5.*   How willing are they to report misconduct?
*Action Response.* If they are willing, fine. Where they are not, find ways of getting them to do so.

(Klockars et al., 2002)

---

abusing it and hurting others as a result. The same can be said about the use of force; we do not know how to use it without hurting others. The ability to use force, the ability to use discretion in issues of life and death, the ability to make ethical decisions—those are leadership skills that need to be honed and developed. Hopefully this book will contribute to this process by providing an opportunity to consider the theories, the concepts, and the situational applications.

# REFERENCES

Atwater, L.E., S.D. Dionne, B. Avolio, J.F. Camobreco & A.W. Lao (1999). A longitudinal study of the leadership development process: Individual differences predicting leader effectiveness. *Human Relations*, 52, 1543–1562.

Bass, B. & P. Steidlmeier (1999). Ethics, character and authentic transformational leadership behavior. *Leadership Quarterly*, 10, 181–217.

Burns, J.M. (1978). *Leadership.* New York: Harper & Row.

Caldwell, C., S.J. Bischoff & R. Karri (2002). The four umpires: A paradigm for ethical leadership. *Journal of Business Ethics*, 36, 153–163.

Ciulla, J.B. (1995). Leadership ethics: Mapping the territory. *Business Ethics Quarterly*, 5 (1), 5–28.

Crank, J.P. (2004). *Understanding police culture.* Cincinnati, OH: Anderson Publishing, Inc.

_____ & M. Caldero (2000). *Police ethics: The corruption of noble cause.* Cincinnati, OH: Anderson Publishing.

Eckhart, D.E. (2003, March). What do ethical leaders follow? The way of truth. *PA Times,* 6.

Giampetro-Meyer, A., S.J.T. Brown, M.N. Browne & N. Kubasek (1998). Do we really want more leaders in business? *Journal of Business Ethics,* 17, 1727–1736.

Greenleaf, R. (1977). *Servant leadership: A journey into the nature of legitimate power and greatness.* New York: Paulist.

Haberfeld, M. (2003). Recruitment, selection, and training—The triangle of police integrity or corruption? In M. Amir & S. Einstein (Eds.), *The uncertainty series: Corruption, policing, security & democracy.* Huntsville, TX: Office on International Criminal Justice, Inc.

Heifetz, R.A. (1994). *Leadership without easy answers.* Cambridge, MA: Belknap Press.

Kanungo, R.N. (2001). Ethical values of transactional and transformational leaders. *Canadian Journal of Administrative Sciences,* 18 (4), 257–265.

Kleinig, J. (1996). *The ethics of policing.* New York: Cambridge University Press.

Klockars, C.B., S. Kutnjak Ivkovich, W.E. Harver & M.R. Haberfeld (1997). The measurement of police integrity. Final report submitted to the National Institute of Justice, NIJ Grant #95-IJ-CX-0058, *The cross cultural study of police corruption.* Also published as the NIJ Research in Brief Report, May 2000.

_____, W. Geller, S. Kutnjak Ivkovich, M.R. Haberfeld & A. Uydess (2002). *Enhancing police integrity: A final report to the National Institute of Justice.* Washington, D.C.: National Institute of Justice, 2–7.

Kuhnert, K.W. & P. Lewis (1987). Transactional and transformational leadership: A constructive/developmental analysis. *Academy of Management Review,* 12, 648–657.

Martinez-Carbonell, K. (2003, March). Inching toward ethical leadership. *PA Times,* 7.

Price, T. (2003). The ethics of transformational leadership. *The Leadership Quarterly,* 14 (1), 67–81.

Punch, M. (1999). Police misconduct and "system failure": European perspective. Unpublished paper presented at the International Conference of Police Integrity and Democracies, May 20–23, 1999, in Florence, Italy.

Schein, E. (1977). *Organization culture and leadership* (2nd ed.). San Francisco: Jossey-Bass.

Turner, N., J. Barling, O. Epitropaki & V. Milner (2002). Transformational leadership and moral reasoning. *Journal of Applied Psychology,* 87 (2), 304–311.

Weber, J. (1989). Managers' moral meanings: An exploratory look at managers' responses to moral dilemmas. *Academy of Management Proceedings,* Washington, D.C., 333–337.

# 3

# Partnership in a Small Force

## *Team Theory*

## OVERVIEW OF THE THEORY

Use of teams in organizations began in the United States in the 1980s when industries were being negatively affected by Japanese competition and began to form work teams in order to informally discuss ways of improving performance. In many organizational settings, management creates teams in order to solve a particular problem, and the teams are temporary in nature. In other settings, teams reflect the primary units within the organization (Dumaine, 1994). In this chapter, the relationship of two officers from the small department of Montclair, New Jersey—Chief Dave Harman and Deputy Chief Frank Viturello—illustrates how the theories of team leadership can be applied in practice in a police environment.

Teams are typically defined as sets of two or more people who cooperate toward a common goal and who have specific functions to perform. Team members are interdependent, coordinated, and synchronized. Information exchange is integral to team coordination (Salas et al., 1992). Teams are also adaptive in that they can maintain a level of performance even with challenging external pressures (Zaccaro et al., 2001). They also may be able to accomplish tasks that could not be accomplished outside the team environment:

> Team leader effects go beyond those of each individual member inter-acting with the leader. There may be an assembly bonus effect for the team so that the team does better than the sum of its members. (Bass, 1990, p. 611)

## FUNCTIONAL TEAM LEADERSHIP

One model of team leadership is functional team leadership. This perspective considers the use of teams as a form of social problem solving. Effective team leaders diagnose problems that could impede organizational and group performance, plan appropriate solutions, and implement them (Zaccaro et al., 2001). The theory holds that most teams originate from a particular environment; therefore, effective leaders are in tune with external events and demands (Ancona & Caldwell, 1988). Leaders interpret and define the outside context for the team. Factors to interpret in the outside context include cognitive, social, personal, political, tech-nological, financial, and staffing concerns. Thus, the core of func-tional team leadership is that the circumstances surrounding the team prescribe leadership activities. Effective team leaders possess the skills to respond to and organize in a given situation. These skills are not a specifically defined set of behaviors (Zaccaro et al., 2001).

---

### Effective Team Leaders

- Effective teams often display smooth processes of distributed leadership.
- Groups and teams move through stages of development. Good team leaders understand and manage them.
- Effective team leaders understand the importance of clarifying membership, purpose, and leadership processes early in the team's life cycle.
- Effective team leaders will find ways to revisit the team's vision while it is per-forming its task to keep energy and motivation high.
- Effective team leaders understand and are able to manage the team's response to changing environmental and internal conditions and events.

(Clawson, 2003)

---

Zaccaro et al. (2001) reflect that leadership influences team effectiveness through four types of means: cognitive processes, cohesion, affect, and coordination.

## Cognitive Processes

Cognitive processes involve the emergence of shared mental models. This occurs when team members are able to anticipate each other's action, usually derived from experience, and thereby decrease the amount of planning and communication needed to accomplish a goal. Cannon-Bowers et al. (1993) identify various mental models, including the equipment model (knowledge of the equipment used by the team), task model (tasks, procedures, and strategies), and team model (skills, attitudes, and preferences), and the interplay between the collective and individual needs of the team. According to Zaccaro et al. (2001), the above mental models originating in the leaders are the determinants of the mental model developed by the team, which thereby influence team coordination and performance.

As the team matures and the leader has imparted the mental modeling necessary for performance, there can be a shift toward self-management when the leader provides less guidance. With self-managed teams, leaders do not direct specific team activities as much as they work toward developing the individual and collective capacities of the team to manage itself (Kozlowski, 1998). As such, most models of team leadership emphasize a participatory rather than directive style of leadership. In general, participatory leadership has been shown to be more effective in teams rather than large groups (Bass, 1990). For example, participatory leadership has been shown to increase information sharing and performance of the team (Larson et al., 1998; Tesluk & Mathieu, 1999). Leaders who encourage meta-cognitive practices (reflection on the processes used in problem solving) have also been shown to lead to better team performance than those who do not (Tannenbaum et al., 1998). This suggests that leaders who provide for training, self-critique, and feedback are more likely to have an effective team.

However, Janis (1982) indicates that cohesive groups are susceptible to groupthink, an extreme concurrence in decision making that thwarts realistic evaluation of alternative options and courses of action. Conditions such as directive leadership, undue pressure for an end product, and insulation of the team from external sources of information are likely predicators of groupthink. In another study, the key component in the occurrence of groupthink was not the level of cohesiveness but the existence of a directive leadership style on the part of the leader (Bass, 1990).

## Cohesion

Group cohesion is another key component in team performance. Cohesion is both what attracts and keeps members in the group as well as how the group resists external disruptions. Zaccaro and McCoy (1988) find that members of teams with high coherence are more likely to be committed to the job, devote more effort to it, and set higher performance norms. Therefore, creating group cohesion is another way to effectively lead teams. Teams often must work together for a length of time and develop a stable structure of relations before cohesiveness can fully develop (Bass, 1990). In a study of 203 military cadets, cohesiveness moderated the effect of leaders' consideration and initiation of structure on subordinate teams (Bass, 1990; Dobbins & Zaccaro, 1986).

According to Zaccaro et al. (2001), a common theme in the literature on team leadership is the importance of collective efficacy as originally conceptualized by Bandura. This refers to members' beliefs that they are capable of accomplishing their objectives. When teams have high collective efficacy, they tend to work harder even when faced with challenges. Zaccaro et al. (2001) argue that the leaders' role as builders of collective efficacy is similar to the empowerment process characterized by transformational leadership.

## Affect

Although they may suggest raising the level of passion in the workplace, leaders also must control the emotional affect of the team. Collective negative moods lead to more internal conflict and less motivation to complete tasks:

> Teams performing under stressful conditions can be highly susceptible to emotional distress across members. As team environments become more aversive . . . , team members obviously need to maintain a collective calm. If the team succumbs to stress, member interactions become more and more narrowly focused among a subset of the team, information becomes increasingly less shared among team members, decision alternatives are not fully explored, and decision making accuracy declines. (Zaccaro et al., 2001, p. 471)

Studies have shown that teams suffer from less emotional reactions to stress when leaders provide clearly outlined objectives, job descriptions, and performance strategies (Isenberg, 1981; Sugiman & Misumi, 1988). Emotional affect can also be controlled by creating a climate in which conflict is handled constructively rather than in a manner that involves personal blaming. The leader in essence develops the interaction patterns necessary for team performance (Zaccaro et al., 2001).

## Coordination

Effective team leaders also help their team members coordinate actions. This can be accomplished by setting up orientation functions, distributing resource information, working on timing functions (pace and speed of task), working on detecting errors (system monitoring), and making sure operations conform to established standards (procedure maintenance) (Zaccaro et al., 2001). As Kozlowski et al. (1996) point out, when the complexity of the demands of the team grows, established interaction can become insufficient. Leaders can adapt by reorienting the team to new patterns. Team leaders can encourage flexibility among individuals on the team. As noted by Zaccaro et al. (2001), "In teams such as military units, or those in more traditional organizational forms, which are typically organized in a strong hierarchical structure, a major portion of the variance in performance may reside in factors associated with leadership" (p. 477).

## THE LEADER-MANAGEMENT MODEL

Team leadership has also been conceptualized using the MacKenzie (1969) leader-management model. Leadership is broken down into three categories: conceiving, organizing, and accomplishing. At the beginning of the life of the team, ideas are generated and plans made, representing the conceiving phase. The organizing phase refers to deciding how to implement the plans. This is followed by the accomplishing stage, which involves the events that drive the project to the desired objectives. Weinkauf and Hoegel (2002) studied 39 industrial teams through a survey designed to identify activities that fall into the above categories. Their findings support situational leadership, in that types of leadership activities were performed when needed, depending on the stage the team was in, rather than being consistently performed over the life of the team.

## SELF-MANAGED TEAMS

Another model of team leadership is that of self-managed teams. Decision-making authority on these teams, usually consisting of between 8 and 15 members, rests with the individual team members. They engage in "whole work" by being involved in planning, measuring, and executing entire operations (Jessup, 1990). Leadership is often rotated among the team members so that each member feels he/she plays a part in the team's overall performance (Erez et al., 2002). Rotated leadership has been compared to that of club officers in which everybody is a leader (Jessup, 1990). Kerr (1983) hypothesizes that rotated leadership leads to a greater likelihood that team members will pull their weight in accomplishing tasks.

Another form of leadership in self-managed teams is emergent leadership, in which the team relies on individuals to step forward to take the leadership role. Some theorists believe that a natural selection process occurs in small groups from which the most qualified leader organically emerges (Erez et al., 2002). In a quasi-experiment testing the effects of peer evaluations and rotated leadership in self-managed teams, Erez et al. (2002) report that differences in team design impact effectiveness. Specifically, the use of peer ratings on teams promotes workload sharing and cooperation, which all lead to higher team performance. Similarly, rotated leadership promotes cooperation, which enhances team performance.

## TEAM POLICING

In the 1970s, team policing was practiced in some jurisdictions in an attempt to decentralize command in the move toward community-oriented policing. In its idealized form, it is envisioned as a flexible participatory structure in the form of a self-managed team with rotated leadership. Administrative procedural guidelines do not apply to team members. Goals are set at team meetings, with direct input from citizens. For example, in Holyoke, Massachusetts, teams consisted of 15 members and a director who held the rank of captain. The team provided for peer evaluation and could set its own goals with the help of a police-community relations council. Team policing did not succeed ultimately. One reason may be that a team would be implemented in the midst of the existent hierarchical structure of policing. In team experiments in Los Angeles, middle managers who were left out of the experiment would sabotage the democratization of teams. It also set up differential treatment among officers by management based on whether or not each officer was on a team. Reports on team policing in Cincinnati indicated that flexibility and autonomy could lead to corruption among patrol officers (Toche & Grant, 1991).

Brewer et al. (1994) studied a sample of Australian police teams and show that monitoring team performance and soliciting self-reports lead to higher performance. They used the Komacki et al. (1986) notion that effective supervisors would be more likely to also provide clear expectations and appropriate consequences. Using a sample of 20 police patrol sergeants, each of whom supervised a stable team of officers, the researchers analyzed the sergeants' performance evaluations (written by their superiors) as well as directly observed the sergeants with their teams, evaluating whether each sergeant communicated expectations and consequences. The researchers found that sergeants spend 53 percent more time on average supervising subordinates than supervisors in insurance, newspaper, and bank work environments. Even though inadequate feedback characterizes most police organizations, sergeants' use of performance monitoring and consequences was strongly correlated with effective team performance. This suggests that the team model may be compatible with the quasi-military chain of command if implemented properly.

Nahavandi (2003) differentiates between two crucial concepts— teams and groups (see Table 3–1). This differentiation clearly points to the fact that in police environments it will be very hard to find a real team (as defined by Nahavandi); instead, group environments are primarily encountered. The five ingredients necessary to create a true team will occur very rarely, precluded by the organizational and cultural or subcultural structure. It is very rare to find a team whose members are fully committed to developing a mission of police organization. Accountability is usually individual, not mutual. Trust or a collaborative culture is frequently contradictory to police subculture, which more often emphasizes a suspicious and dubious view of the

**TABLE 3–1    GROUPS AND TEAMS**

| Groups | Teams |
|---|---|
| Work on common goal | Are fully committed and develop a mission |
| Accountable to manager | Mutually accountable |
| Conflict—no clear culture | Trust—collaborative culture |
| Leadership assigned to one person | Shared leadership among members |
| May accomplish their goal | Achieve synergy (2+2=5) |

(Nahavandi, 2003)

world. Leadership sharing is individual rather than delegated (in the full sense of the concept). Similarly, leadership is routinely associated with higher rank, and an officer with higher rank is the one who sets the final perimeters to any kind of empowerment. Finally, achievement of true synergy can only be accomplished when one steps out of the box, not just in symbolic terms but with the risk-taking approach, and risk taking in police environments is only encouraged within certain clearly defined and liability-oriented parameters.

On the other hand, working on common goals, being accountable to one's supervisor, being exposed to an esoteric subculture that is unique and that differs between units and teams, and experiencing the overall environment of conflict in which one may or may not accomplish a goal (formal or informal) appear to characterize many, if not all, police organizations, regardless of their size and location. These elements lend themselves to creating environments destined for group rather than team orientations.

## CAREER HIGHLIGHTS    Team Leadership Approach

**Chief David Harman and Deputy Chief Frank Viturello**
*Montclair Police Department, New Jersey*

One cannot completely exclude the possibility of finding a true team approach in police organizations, and an example of such collaboration can be found in the very real, and rare, cooperation between Chief David Harman and Deputy Chief Frank Viturello of the Montclair Police Department in New Jersey.

Most of the police chiefs depicted in this book come from large and/or notorious police departments. This choice was not coincidental. It is much easier to collect information about police chiefs and departments that are large and well known, particularly if there has been scandal or misconduct. The nature of events, a geographic location, and its prominence or lack of prominence in the daily media will dictate the level of coverage that will, in turn, be available to researchers. Small police departments also frequently undergo interesting challenges and exhibit leadership characteristics worthy of wider dissemination. It is a rare opportunity to get insight into a smaller police department where things and events are known primarily to the local community and written about only in the local newspapers.

The partnership between Chief Harman and Deputy Chief Viturello exemplifies, as closely as possible, the five ingredients of the team approach to leadership (as defined by Nahavandi, 2003). Although their police careers and personal backgrounds did not necessarily make them an obvious match, their dedication to the police profession, their basic values, and their ethical consciousness created a synergy that can and should be looked upon as a model approach to team leadership in police environments. To fully understand the uniqueness of this partnership, it is necessary to follow their careers on the force, on an individual level, and identify the traits and qualities that brought them together and that allowed them to experience the level of comfort necessary for the implementation of the team leadership approach. Of course, this summary only highlights certain aspects of their relationship and careers—the choice of these was intentional to illustrate the team leadership theory.

Montclair, New Jersey, is a township of approximately 39,000 people that prides itself on its diversity; approximately 59 percent of the population is white, 32 percent is African American, and the majority of the remainder of the minority population is Latino or Hispanic (U.S. Census, 2000). Its median family income is above the state average at $96,000, and significantly more of its inhabitants have bachelor's degrees (or higher) than the state average ("Montclair, New Jersey," n.d.).

The Montclair Police Department had 111 sworn members in 2004, of whom 28 percent were minorities or women. Harman served in the Montclair Police Department for 25 years, retiring in May 2004 after serving 3 years as chief (Zadrozny, 2004; Brubaker, 2004). An African American whose family moved to Montclair when he was in high school, Harman served as a military police officer before joining the Montclair Police Department in 1978 (Harrell, 2001a). Harman was an early rising star, ascending quickly through the ranks. He made detective 28 months after joining the force in 1979. He spent more than 7 years at detective and then was promoted after scoring second on the sergeant's promotional exam. He was first put in charge of the patrol division and later put in charge of the detectives. After 13 years on the job, he became a lieutenant and within 7 months was promoted to deputy chief. In 2001, he was promoted to chief, the first African American appointed to that position in the history of the force.

Viturello retired from the force as deputy chief in 2003. An Italian American, he joined the Montclair Police Department in 1970, after graduating from the police academy first in his class. A union leader, Viturello views one of his accomplishments as successfully advocating for the introduction of a merit-based promotional system within the force, introduced in the 1980s. It was only after this system was put in place that Viturello's career advanced; the prior system had relied on political favoritism that excluded Viturello, partially due to his ethnicity and his outsider status (he did not live in Montclair). After the introduction of the

*(continued)*

system, he gradually made his way up through the ranks. Although formally he became part of a senior management team with Harman when Harman appointed him deputy chief in 2001, they had a close working relationship from long before that time, when Viturello served as Harman's sergeant when Harman made detective.

Harman and Viturello both describe their working relationship as "being on the same page." They held similar goals for the department: to increase its diversity and equitability. Before they assumed positions of leadership, the department had been run according to a "good old boys' network" (D. Harman, personal interview, June 20, 2004). Both Harman, as an African American, and Viturello, as an Italian American, had experienced discrimination early in their careers. Viturello, as a union member, advocated and was instrumental in stating a merit- and examination-based system of promotion and career advancement. Harman increased the level of minority representation on the force through a commitment to recruitment he describes as "a continuous job. You have to be highly motivated. It will take a lot of time, and the chief of police has to be 100 percent behind that."

The recruitment policy change was one of the first major changes brought in by the department after Harman became chief. When Harman took over the force, less than 20 percent were minorities or women (Harrell, 2001b; Thorbourne, 2003). With town officials, he changed recruitment policies so that Montclair residents were given priority on the recruitment test. Given the ethnic makeup of the township and the fact that 92 percent of those who took the first test offered were minorities, the numbers of minorities increased significantly (Thorbourne, 2001).

Montclair also was the first department in the state to implement a policy designed to monitor racial profiling; video cameras were installed in patrol cars, and information on the race, ethnicity, and gender of those stopped was logged and recorded statistically (Harrell, 2001c). Eighteen months after the policy was implemented, results showed that the racial makeup of those stopped reflected the township's ethnic makeup (Thorbourne, 2002).

During the period Harman and Viturello led the department, there were several scandals. A police officer was accused of beating an epileptic man and contributing to a seizure episode (Harrell, 2001d). Another officer resigned after being accused of sexually assaulting a woman whom he had followed back to her apartment after she had no documents during a traffic stop (Harrell, 2001d).

Harman and Viturello describe the key aspects of their management and leadership in similar terms: a commitment to demonstrating integrity through example, treating all employees fairly, and motivating people to work by making them want to do the work rather than forcing them to do it. This shared vision was one that was present near the beginning of their relationship. Viturello describes their relationship as developing over a number of years but that the shared vision they had was something innate to both of them; it was the common bond they shared through these values that strengthened their partnership.

As an example of their shared vision, they had similar approaches to managing subordinates when subordinates' requests (for example, for time off) could not be fulfilled; both preferred the style of explaining the reasons and justifications for the denial rather than simply playing the authority card. Viturello gave one such example:

> For example, the chief says, "Look, we've got to cut back on vacation, so get guys to keep guys on deck." A weak guy would go the squads and say, "It's not me. The chief said we have to do it. It's not me." Me, I would say, "Guys, we have a problem; we have a crime wave. You've got to work with me. If you ask for time off, I'm not going to be able to give it to you now. If you work with me, I'll be there for you later." That's being honest. Most of the time they appreciate it. (Personal interview, June 16, 2004)

Harman gave an example illustrating the same approach:

> When I took over, there was a big problem with overtime. We had to get people to seriously look at staffing. From 1993 to 1999, the department had received over 3 million dollars in grants, and they hired more police officers. But the grants were drying up. But the [community] had expectations, expected a certain level of service. And supervisors expected to be able to provide that level of service. But there was no money for it. So people had to know why, and I'd explain it to commanders. I'd look over the schedules and say, "Look, you hired two people to work this shift. Why?" So I started on top and worked my way down through the ranks, to get everyone on the same page. (Personal interview, June 20, 2004)

Furthermore, both Harman and Viturello emphasize trust and collaboration in their approach not only to their subordinates but also to each other. There can be no doubt that the partnership of Harman and Viturello was a tight unit. Viturello describes their relationship in emotional terms: "His love and respect for me, and my admiration for him, that's what made our relationship tight" (Personal interview, June 16, 2004). Harman describes Viturello as someone who "always had my back" (Personal interview, June 20, 2004).

Although not exactly key to the team itself, motivation was a key element of the team's leadership style for the force. Harman and Viturello both emphasize that believing in their subordinates was key to motivating them. Harman used the key term "empower":

> As for my style, what I do is empower my personnel. I involve them in the decision-making process; I know I can't do it alone. We need to be on the same page, and I let them know that. It makes for a better department. You can't make someone follow you, but they will do it if they want to follow you. (Personal interview, June 20, 2004)

(continued)

Viturello used similar language, illustrating with an example of an officer to whom he gave a second chance:

> For example, one guy was on the border for abusing sick time, and I had even scolded him for a poor traffic report. He knew he was in trouble, and I found an opportunity for him. I said I need someone to review reports. Why? I knew he had ability; I knew he was intelligent. I saw some of myself in him, and I saw that the difference was because I had the urge to fight. Certain things I saw, I would fight them and go to the chief. I'm not afraid to reward those who needed to be rewarded. Not afraid to stand up for those who needed to be stood up for. . . . I felt I had to motivate. I tried not to raise my voice, but to do it through discipline. People will work when they want to, not when they have to. Somewhere I got this principle. I wanted to have people want to work for me. (Personal interview, June 16, 2004)

The two were also unique in their willingness to take risks in order to solve problems. For example, there was an explosive incident in the community when gang members wanted to erect a memorial for one of their members after a shooting (this followed in the wake of a large community memorial for a youth who had died after pushing his girlfriend out of the way of an oncoming train). Viturello described how the two found a solution to placate the competing demands of the members of the community (who did not want to be seen rewarding gangs) and the gang members (who might take action that would lead to further gang violence if the tensions were not resolved):

> The community didn't want this; there was a lot of pressure to say no. We could have said that graffiti is defacing public property. We went down and spoke to the gang leaders and said that it was defacing property, etc. They said, "If you leave us alone, after two or three days, we'll clean it up." I said that it was better to have two to three days of graffiti than months of cop overtime. (Personal interview, June 16, 2004)

Harman also described the reaction in the community and his response:

> And you have to see the whole picture. We had intelligence that said that if we stepped in and tore it down, it would be trouble. We even talked to some of our informants in town, and they said the same. I hired more cops on overtime [for the memorial service]; they kept an eye on things. In the end, there was no violence. We knew, on the other hand, that if we stepped in, it would be violent. . . . Well, you have to understand; the community, they understood. Again, the problem was something in the media. People, they understand; they have to live there. People in gangs live there too, and they have to live next door [to them]. Do you really want to provoke problems? On the other hand, if you respect them, look, they came in and cleaned it up afterwards. That's what I mean. Sometimes you have to take a stand. You have to look at the whole picture and understand what would give you the most serious repercussions. (Personal interview, June 20, 2004)

As a result of the willingness of Harman and Viturello to consider a creative approach, the memorial was peaceful, and the gang members cleaned up the area of the memorial, resulting in no further public criticism or outcry.

### Exercise

The relationship between Dave Harman and Frank Viturello (the police chief and his deputy from Montclair, New Jersey) detailed in this chapter has been examined through the prism of team leadership theory. Using what you have learned from other theories in this book or from the summaries (as indicated in the Introduction) you have read thus far, it is possible to consider their approach through the lens of different theories. What other theories can you find that are applicable to these chiefs? Are there lessons to be learned from those applications, or do those theories indicate alternative paths or approaches that might have yielded a more successful outcome?

## REFERENCES

Ancona, D.G. & D.F. Caldwell (1988). Beyond task maintenance: Defining external functions in groups. *Group and Organization Studies*, 13, 468–494.

Bass, B.M. (1990). *Bass and Stogdill's handbook of leadership: A survey of theory and research*. New York: Free Press.

Brewer, N., C. Wilson & K. Beck (1994). Supervisory behaviour and team performance amongst police patrol sergeants. *Journal of Occupational and Organizational Psychology, 67*, 69–78. *Personnel Psychology*, 55, 929–948.

Brubaker, P. (2004, May 19). May the force be with them: Sabagh named new chief of police, Terry is new deputy. *The Montclair Times*. Retrieved July 22, 2004, from http://www.montclairtimes.com/page.php?page=7616.

Cannon-Bowers, J.A., E. Salas & S. Converse (1993). Shared mental models in expert team decision making. In N.J. Castellan, Jr. (Ed.), *Current issues in individual and group decision making* (pp. 221–246). Hillsdale, NJ: Lawrence Erlbaum.

Clawson, J.G. (2003). *Level three leadership: Getting below the surface*. Upper Saddle River, NJ: Pearson Education, Inc.

Dobbins, G.H. & S.J. Zaccaro (1986). The effect of group cohesion and leader behavior on subordinate satisfaction. *Group and Organization Studies*, 11 (3), 203–229.

Dumaine, B. (1994). The trouble with teams. *Fortune*, 130 (5), 86–92.

Erez, A., J.A. Lepine & H. Elms (2002). Effects of rotated leadership and peer evaluation on the functioning and effectiveness of self-managed teams: A quasi-experiment. *Personnel Psychology*, 55, 929–948.

Harrell, J. (2001a, February 2). Russo to have respite before taking new post. *The Montclair Times*. Retrieved July 22, 2004, from http://montclairtimes.com/page.php?page=1872.

_____ (2001b, February 22). Montclair aims to diversify police force. *The Montclair Times*. Retrieved July 22, 2004, from http://www.montclairtimes.com/page.php?page=1882.

_____ (2001c, March 1). New policy announced to track police racial profiling with statistics. *The Montclair Times*. Retrieved July 22, 2004, from http://www.montclairtimes.com/page.php?page=1884.

_____ (2001d, May 24). Cop resigns and avoids charges. *The Montclair Times*. Retrieved July 22, 2004, from http://www.montclairtimes.com/page.php?page=1929.

Isenberg, D.J. (1981). Some effects of time-pressures on vertical structure and decision-making accuracy in small groups. *Organization Behavior and Human Performance*, 27, 119–134.

Janis, I.L. (1982). *Groupthink* (2nd ed.). Boston: Houghton Mifflin.

Jessup, H.R. (1990, November). New roles in team leadership. *Training and Development Journal*, 79–83.

Kerr, N.L. (1983). Motivation losses in small groups: A paradigm for social dilemma analysis. *Journal of Personality and Social Psychology*, 45, 819–828.

Komacki, J.L., S. Zlotnick & M. Jenson (1986). Development of an operant based taxonomy and observational index of supervisory behaviour. *Journal of Applied Psychology*, 71, 260–269.

Kozlowski, S.W.J. (1998). Training and developing adaptive teams: Theory, principles and research. In J.A. Canon-Bowers & E. Salas (Eds.), *Making decisions under stress: Implications for individual and team training* (pp. 115–153). Washington, DC: American Psychological Association.

Larson, J.R., Jr., P.G. Foster-Fichman & T.M. Frantz (1998). Leadership style and the discussion of shared and unshared information in decision-making groups. *Personality and Social Psychology*, 24, 482–495.

MacKenzie, A. (1969). The management process in 3D. *Harvard Business Review*, 47, 80–87.

Montclair, New Jersey (n.d.). Retrieved July 22, 2004, from http://www.city data.com/city/Montclair-New-Jersey.html.

Nahavandi, A. (2003). *The art and science of leadership, 3rd ed*. Upper Saddle River, NJ: Prentice Hall.

Salas, E., T. L. Dickinson, S.A. Converse & S.I. Tannenbaum (1992). Toward an understanding of team performance and training. In R.W. Swezey & E. Salas (Eds.), *Teams: Their training and performance* (pp. 3–29). Norwood, NJ: Ablex Publishing.

Sugiman, T. & J. Misumi (1988). Development of a new evacuation method for emergencies: Control of collective behavior by emergent small groups. *Journal of Applied Psychology*, 73, 3–10.

Tannenbaum, S.I., K. Smith-Jentsch & S.J. Behson (1998). Training team leaders to facilitate team learning and performance. In J.A. Cannon-Bowers and E. Salas (Eds.), *Making decisions under stress: Implications for training and simulations* (pp. 247–270). Washington, DC: American Psychological Association.

Tesluk, P.E. & J.E. Mathieu (1999). Overcoming roadblocks to effectiveness: Incorporating management of performance barriers into models of work group effectiveness. *Journal of Applied Psychology*, 84, 200–217.

Thorbourne, K. (2001, August 16). Homegrown recruits enhance police diversity. *The Montclair Times*. Retrieved July 22, 2004, from http://www.montclairtimes.com/page.php?page=2280.

_____ (2002, November 29). Civil Rights Commission gives housing crisis a look-see. *The Montclair Times*. Retrieved July 22, 2004, from http://www.montclairtimes.com/page.php?page=4169.

_____ (2003, February 26). Rights board looks at police hiring and student gap. *The Montclair Times*. Retrieved July 22, 2004, from http://www.montclairtimes.com/page.php?page=4742.

Toche, H. & J.D. Grant (1991). *Police as problem solvers*. New York: Plenum Press.

Weinkauf, K. & M. Hoegl (2002). Team leadership activities in different project phrases. *Team Performance Management: An International Journal*, 7/8, 171–182.

Zaccaro, J.J. & M.C. McCoy (1988). The effects of task and interpersonal cohesiveness on performance of a disjunctive group task. *Journal of Applied Social Psychology*, 18, 837–851.

Zaccaro, S.J., A.L. Rittman & M.A. Marks (2001). Team leadership. *Leadership Quarterly*, 12, 451–483.

Zadrozny, A. (2004, March 10). Chief retiring after 25 years on the force: David Harman moving to Georgia. *The Montclair Times*. Retrieved July 22, 2004, from http://www.montclairtimes.com/page.php?page=7166.

# 4

# In-Groups and Community-Oriented Policing

## *Leader-Member Exchange Theory*

### OVERVIEW OF THE THEORY

The leader-member exchange theory can be understood through the examples of Commissioner Lee P. Brown, whose career developed in Houston, Texas, and culminated in the New York Police Department, and Chief Darrel Stephens, whose career spanned many departments and ended in the Charlotte-Mecklenburg, North Carolina, Police Department. Their careers, particularly their relationships with what are conceived as the in-groups and out-groups, illustrate some of the key principles of the theory.

According to leader-member exchange theory, leadership does not necessarily involve leaders treating each subordinate under their command in the same fashion.[1] This theory puts forth the notion that leaders form different relationships with different subordinates, known as

---

[1]According to LeBlanc et al. (1993), the assumption that leaders have a uniform way of treating all their employees may be a key reason as to why studies of leadership style have had inconsistent results.

**TABLE 4–1   DYAD AS ANALYSIS UNIT**

| In-Group | Middle Group | Out-Group |
|---|---|---|
| *High-Quality Relationships* | | *Low-Quality Relationships* |
| • Have more influence over decision making<br>• Have extra benefits and status | | • Merely fulfill job requirements<br>• Receive the standard benefits |

(Graen and Cashman, 1975)

vertical linkages (Liden & Graen, 1980). The unit of analysis implied by this theory is the dyad in the form of the particular relationship between the manager and employee (Schriesheim et al., 2001).[2] A study of dyadic relationships in service departments within a university revealed that 90 percent of 41 dyads exhibited superiors who have differential relationships with subordinates (Liden & Graen, 1980).

Initial leader-member exchange theory involved the formation of two groups of subordinates under the leader: those in the in-group and those in the out-group (see Table 4–1). The in-group employees enjoy a high-quality relationship with the manager, characterized by more influence over decisions, extra benefits, and greater status, in exchange for higher expectations, task commitment, and loyalty. Contrastingly, the out-group is defined as employees who have a low-quality relationship to the leader. Out-group employees merely fulfill the formal job requirements and receive the standard benefits (Graen & Cashman, 1975). According to Graen and Cashman (1975), a middle group can also be identified that falls between the in- and out-groups, thus forming an exchange trichotomy of in-groups, out-groups, and middle groups. In addition, these researchers posit that supervisors have high-quality relationships with only a few of their subordinates (in the in-group) because it is more efficient for them. However, in subsequent theory, Graen and Uhl-Bien (1991) state that the theory suggests that managers should form high-quality relationships with all of their subordinates, thereby making everyone a part of the in-group. In one study, by manipulating the quality of dyadic relationships in a quasi-

---

[2] Schriesheim et al. (2001) have shown that there is a statistical problem with all of the work testing leader-member exchange theory: Researchers have used an individual unit of analysis when a dyadic one is appropriate. They suggest, therefore, that the stream of research is fundamentally flawed and that little is actually known about the theory's applicability.

experiment, there was a reported improvement in productivity when managers improved the quality of their dyadic relationships, saving the sample company an estimated $5 million (Graen, 1983).

In a later development of leader-member exchange theory, each dyadic relationship was considered unique and not dependent on other relationships of the group (in other words, there does not necessarily have to be an out-group or middle group). Emphasizing individuals over in- and out-groups, the individualized approach explores the differential levels of empowerment per subordinate under a particular leader (Yammarino et al., 2001),[3] suggesting a continuum stretching from in-relationships to out-relationships that is entirely circumstantial, not structural or inevitable.

## MEASUREMENT OF THE QUALITY OF THE DYADIC RELATIONSHIP

The quality of the leader-member exchange has been measured through the Leader Member Exchange (LMX) instrument (see Northouse, 2004). Early studies of the theory used a median-split procedure to define who was in the in- and out-groups in a particular organization. Employees with LMX results above the median were considered in the in-group; those below were placed in the out-group. Criticisms of the dichotomous approach were mounted by some scholars who instead suggested that the quality of dyadic relationships should be considered a continuous variable (LeBlanc et al., 1993; Vecchio & Gobdel, 1984; Yammarino et al., 2001). A higher-quality LMX score reportedly correlated with more job satisfaction, less turnover (Vecchio & Gobdel, 1984), a more positive review of the environment of the organization in general (Kozlowski & Doherty, 1989; LeBlanc et al., 1993), and salary raises and promotions (Erdogan et al., 2002).

The LMX instrument provided researchers with a composite score intended to summarize the quality of the dyadic relationship. LeBlanc et al. (1993), however, believe that two aspects of the relationship described in the original theory should be disaggregated: 1) personal attention to the employee and 2) assistance for the leader by the employee. Some have seen these two categories as synonymous

---

[3] It is noted, however, that Yammarino et al. (2001) do not merely discuss the leader-member exchange theory but place it within the framework of a multidimensional approach that includes style theory and team leadership.

with the leadership style and situational approaches, which involve the factors of consideration and initiation of structure (Norris & Vecchio, 1992). Regardless, the LeBlanc et al. study of nurses in Dutch hospitals found that the disaggregated factors were both positively related to the quality of the leader-member exchange. Furthermore, there was evidence that the theory was better able to be empirically supported when the LMX score is not considered unidimensionally.

## THE DYADIC RELATIONSHIP AND EFFECTIVENESS

Liden and Graen (1980) link high-quality dyadic relationships to increased effectiveness, operationalized as high-performance ratings of subordinates by leaders.

Results from other studies both support and disagree with the correlation between the quality of the relationship and job performance (Dunegan et al., 1992).

As Dunegan et al. (1992) explain, "[A]lthough there may be a certain intuitive appeal in expecting subordinate performance to be linked with the quality of leader-member exchange, the empirical evidence is such that the relationship remains inconclusive" (p. 60). Their test of the theory suggests that the relationship between the two variables can be predicted only after introducing the moderating variables of task analyzability and variety. In their study, as in previous studies, they measured subordinates' job performance as the performance rating given by supervisors.[4] Task analyzability is operationalized as the degree to which the subordinate's task involves a particular process or whether the task can only be accomplished through creative problem solving. Task variety refers to the degree to which the subordinate's task is routine or repetitive. The results point to the conclusion that when employees worked on tasks that were routine and unchallenging or when the tasks had a high level of uncertainty, the quality of their performance was based on the quality of the leader-member exchange. When the tasks had a more moderate level of uncertainty and challenge, there was no relationship between the leader-member exchange and performance (see Table 4–2). This suggests that the

---

[4] One of my doctoral students suggested that this can represent a tautology. If the dyadic relationship is positive, this could be because the subordinate performs well, necessitating a good evaluation, and the positive relationship may not necessarily be the reason the subordinate performs well. In other words, the independent and dependent variables may be measuring the same thing.

**TABLE 4–2   QUALITY OF EXCHANGE**

|  | Yes | No |
|---|---|---|
| **Routine/ Unchallenging Task** | Quality of performance is based on LMX. | No relationship exists between LMX and performance. |
| **High Degree of Uncertainty** | Quality of performance is based on LMX. | No relationship exists between LMX and performance. |

(Dunegan et al., 1992)

leader-member exchange theory could benefit from the addition of moderating agents, which would develop more of a contingency approach to the dyadic relationships (Dunegan et al., 1992).

Communication researchers have used leader-member exchange theory to explore how workplace communication patterns may reflect the quality of the dyadic relationship. Yrle et al. (2003) used a psychometric communication instrument to explore the communication style related to three factors (degree of coordination, participation, and freedom of expression) in the relationship. The findings suggest that relationships that score high on the leader-member exchange scale are correlated with high scores on the degree of coordination of work activities and participation of the subordinate in decision making. In contrast, low-quality relationships were correlated with only a high degree of coordination of work activities via effective communication. The authors conclude that in low-quality relationships there may be coordination of activities through effective communication, but this does not lead to true participation in decision making, suggesting that participation is a key component in the health of the relationship (Yrle et al., 2003).

Maurer et al. (2002) explored whether subordinate-perceived level of organizational support and the leader-member exchange dyadic relationship acted as a backdrop to the success of the subordinates' overall career development. Thus, leader-member exchange was treated as one antecedent to employee development. By reviewing the literature on leadership, the authors propose that when the dyadic relationship is weak, or the perceived level of organization support in general is weak, only personal benefits (salary, etc.) will motivate the subordinate. This may limit career development of the employee and limit the type of work activities the employee is willing to undertake. The authors suggest that ideally subordinates would be motivated by benefits both for themselves and for the organization.

Although the research is entirely theoretical and does not provide a test of the proposal, it suggests the prescriptive notion that managers must tap into each employee's individual talents and work styles in order to draw out loyalty and enthusiasm for the organization as a whole and not merely be satisfied with employees who work entirely for their own self-interest.

Managers must tap into each employee's individual talents and work styles in order to draw out loyalty and enthusiasm for the organization as a whole, and not merely be satisfied with employees who work entirely for their own self-interest (Maurer et al., 2002).

## ANTECEDENTS TO HIGH-QUALITY DYADIC RELATIONSHIPS

Leader-member exchange theorists emphasize that one of the key components in the quality of the exchange between the employee and the subordinate is the degree to which the employee has influence over decisions within the organization. Five typologies of the degree of decision-making influence, forming a continuum, are postulated by Scandura et al. (1986): autocratic, minimal involvement, consultation, collaboration, and delegation.

---

### High-Quality Dyadic Relationships

1. *Autocratic.* The leader makes decisions without the input of the subordinate.
2. *Minimal involvement.* The leader asks for the subordinate's opinion but makes the decision on his/her own.
3. *Consultation.* The leader meets with the subordinate and seeks information, ideas, and suggestions and incorporates the subordinate's input into the decision making as much as possible.
4. *Collaboration.* The leader and subordinate analyze the problem together, and there is near equal input into the process by both.
5. *Delegation.* The leader permits the subordinate to make the final decision after sharing his/her perspective on the problem.

High quality: Shared decision making or formal affirmation of a positive performance evaluation

(Scandura et al., 1986)

---

In essence, Scandura et al. consider decision-making influence as an antecedent to effective leader-member exchanges. Findings from their study of dyadic employee-manager relationships in a manufacturing setting suggest that subordinates who feel that they have a high degree of influence over decisions (approaching delegation on the continuum) are reported as having higher-quality leader-member exchanges. This would occur regardless of the superior's ratings of the subordinate's performance. However, where the leader-member exchange is weak, superior ratings are critical to the performance of the subordinate. Conversely, managers are most satisfied with employees with whom they share a high-quality leader-member exchange and for whom they give strong performance ratings (Scandura et al., 1986). This model suggests that for the dyadic relationship to work, subordinates need either informal positive feedback in the form of shared decision making or the formal affirmation of a positive performance evaluation. In turn, superiors need to foster relationships with employees, yet they also need to surround themselves with high-performance employees.

Another antecedent proposed to factor into a high-quality relationship is the degree to which the leader and subordinate share demographic characteristics and values. Duchon et al. (1986) found that gender matching partially explained a high-quality exchange. Steiner (1988) measured shared work-related values using the Survey of Work Values (SWV) instrument. Staging a simulation of dyadic relationships with samples of French and American students, Steiner found that high-quality relationships correlated with perceived similarity of values, as evaluated by the subordinate. This suggests that leaders could emphasize commonalities with subordinates in order to build a high-quality relationship.

## LEADER-MEMBER EXCHANGE THEORY AND BIAS

An ethical question has surfaced as to whether it is acceptable for a leader to treat employees differently and whether the theory actually describes and/or promotes discrimination. Research has suggested that designation to in- and out-groups occurs early in the life of a particular dyad and may be resistant to change (Dinesh & Liden, 1986; Graen & Cashman, 1975). From this, some theorists have posited that perhaps the quality of the relationship is based on demographic similarities rather than on any objective measure of subordinates' capacity in the workplace (Yrle et al., 2002). Yet at least three studies have reported that demographic similarity (race, gender, age) does not influence the effectiveness of the dyadic relationship (Steiner, 1988; Yrle et al., 2002, 2003). However, one study has found gender similarity to factor into the quality of the relationship (Duchon et al., 1986).


## LMX Theory and the Cases of Commissioner Lee P. Brown and Chief Darrel Stephens

The leader-member exchange theory highlights the very essence of human relationships, and more specifically the fact that we do not treat everybody the same way. We have our favorite people, those to whom we are indifferent, and those whom we dislike. On the other end of the spectrum, we are also somebody's favorite person, some people are indifferent toward us, others don't really like us, and sometimes someone really, really dislikes us. Is it possible to elevate oneself above these feelings and emotions and treat everybody equally? The answer to this question is pretty straightforward—no. Is it possible to interact, to trust, and to support people equally in a work environment? The answer to this question is even more straightforward—no. Thus any work environment will involve what LMX theorists refer to as in-group and out-group relations. In police environments, where emotional and physical trust has paramount importance, this classification into in- and out-groups will be more pronounced than in other organizations.

Police work is about reliance on others. It cannot be a one-man or one-woman operation. This does not mean that it will be easy or even possible to identify a true team environment in police organizations (see Chapter 3); however, the prevalence of the in- and out-group phenomenon is something that makes the subculture of policing so different from other organizational subcultures. From both the vantage point of policing as the vanguard of a democratic society and the perspectives of individual police officers on the beat, members of the public, police chiefs, and local politicians, the stakes in police work are very high. When the stakes are high, so are emotions. One of the better-known aspects of police subculture is the prevalence of suspicion and very limited trust. To be able to trust subordinates, one must know them quite well and have a common history; to gain trust or maintain it, one frequently must be prepared to compromise principles.

   Graen and Uhl-Bien (1991) posit that effective leaders, according
to the LMX theory, should develop in-group exchanges with all subordinates if possible. In police environments, several prevailing factors
make it impossible to develop in-group exchanges with all subordinates. Chief among them is the political nature of police organizations,
both within the police department and within the governmental and
civilian bodies to which they are ultimately responsible. Police unions,
however, are very powerful entities that traditionally are at odds with
the upper echelon of police organizations, and more specifically police
chiefs and commissioners. The reasons for this tradition are numerous
and beyond the scope of this chapter, but for the sake of this argument,
this will be accepted as an existing fact in most, if not all, police organizations that are indeed unionized, regardless of their size and shape.
The cases of the two police chiefs discussed in this chapter focus on their
inability to include unions in the in-group category. The consequences
of this inability led to criticism of their leadership as partially ineffective,
however untrue or unfair this characterization of their abilities is.

   One must accept the fact that it is simply impossible to make
everybody a part of one huge in-group. Clashes with the out-group
members are not necessarily a testimony to poor leadership skills but
rather a reflection of reality. The way one creates in-groups and maintains them, on one end of the spectrum, and the way one deals with
the out-groups on the other end are a true measure of successful leadership when one uses the LMX approach to police leadership. The
two chiefs profiled in this chapter, Commissioner Lee P. Brown and
Chief Darrel Stephens, illustrate these difficulties, particularly with
regard to implementation of community-oriented policing. They both
have long illustrious careers; the examples and situations described
here are merely highlights to illustrate the in-group/out-group concept and how it applies to policing.

## CAREER HIGHLIGHTS

**Commissioner Lee P. Brown**
*Houston Police Department, Texas, and New York Police Department, New York*

Lee P. Brown was born in Wewoka, Oklahoma, in 1937 (Belkin, 1989a).
He received a bachelor's degree in criminology from Fresno State
University in 1961 and a master's degree in sociology from San Jose
State University in 1964. In 1970, Brown earned his doctorate in crimi-
nology from the University of California at Berkeley ("Biography,"
n.d.). In 1972, he became an associate director of the Institute of

Urban Affairs and Research at Howard University in Washington, D.C. (Belkin, 1989a).

Brown entered policing in 1960 as a patrolman in San Jose, California. In 1968, he relocated to Portland, Oregon, where he founded the Department of the Administration of Justice at Portland State University. In 1975, he served as sheriff of Multnomah County, Oregon. The following year he became the director of justice services, heading the county's criminal justice agencies ("Biography," n.d.).

In 1978, Brown became the public safety commissioner in Atlanta, Georgia, where he oversaw the Atlanta Police and Fire Departments and the Departments of Correctional Services, Emergency Management Services, and Taxis and Limousines. He was noted for starting neighborhood policing in the city by setting up a number of police substations (Belkin, 1989a). In addition, as public safety commissioner, Brown led the investigation into the serial killings of 28 young African Americans. He set up a special task force in 1980 after the first 2 killings, which over the course of the investigation handled 200,000 pieces of information. When the task force closed in March 1982, he was able to provide evidence that the killer, Wayne B. Williams, was responsible for 23 of the 28 killings to which he had been linked (Harris, 1982). It was this investigation that earned Brown a national reputation as an effective law enforcement leader (Balz, 1982; Balz & Harris, 1982). He was nicknamed "No Rap" because of the limited amount of information he gave to the public during the investigation (Kurtz, 1989).

In 1982, Brown was appointed chief of the Houston Police Department, where he served until 1989. Brown was Houston's first black police chief. At that time, the force numbered 3,200 officers (Balz, 1982). The force complained that it was spread thin due to population growth and the large geographic area over which Houston is stretched (Balz & Harris, 1982). Brown inherited a department plagued with low morale and a reputation for excessive use of force. The week before the start of Brown's tenure, seven officers were dismissed and six suspended for harassing and beating black occupants of a local hotel. Mayor Kathy Whitmire indicated that she hired Brown because he was a "good manager" (Balz, 1982). However, some within the police force and city government were concerned about Brown's status as an outsider since he was not hired from within the department (Balz, 1982).

Brown's seven years in Houston were characterized as improving race relations and being in the vanguard in the use of community policing. He aimed to have each citizen know at least one patrol officer (Belkin, 1989a). As he had done in Atlanta, Brown set up police substations in order to facilitate neighborhood policing. He also instituted single-officer patrol cars in order to cover all of Houston (Belkin, 1989b; Blumenthal, 1989a). The force increased to 4,500 officers during his

(continued)

tenure (Kurtz, 1989). In addition, Brown increased the percentage of black police officers in the department to 14.1 percent from 8.5 percent (Belkin, 1989a). However, the union was often at odds with Brown, claiming that he lowered standards for recruitment, resulting in the hiring of irresponsible officers. In fact, when Brown left the department, three cases of police abuse overshadowed his departure. One involved the rape of a woman by an officer in a patrol car; that officer was sentenced to four months in prison. Another incident involved the arrest of an officer who was accused of telling several prostitutes he would release them from detention in exchange for sexual favors. A third incident involved the fatal shooting by police of a black motorist pulled over for speeding. However, according to Representative Craig Washington (Democrat, Texas), "[Brown] was the most popular police chief ever," and that criticism of the police was "directed at the institution, not at him personally" (Kurtz, 1989, p. A3).

After Houston, Brown was appointed commissioner of the New York Police Department in 1990, where he served until 1992. According to Mayor David Dinkins, Brown was hired because of his reputation of improving police-community relations and race relations (Purdum, 1989). In New York City, according to media accounts, the top policing issue of the day was controlling drugs. Likewise, at the time Brown considered drugs to be the biggest problem facing the nation and believed making officers "a part of the community—not apart from the community" could have an impact on the crisis (Blumenthal, 1989b, p. B3). Brown stated:

> We can't just rely on the police. We've been doing what we've been doing since we've had America, relying on the police to address the crime problem, but it's not going to happen. We should stop responding to incidents and start solving problems. (Blumenthal, 1990a, p. B1)

In 1990 he instituted Operation Take-Back, which aimed to stem the tide of murders and robberies associated with the drug trade by paying 200 officers overtime pay each day to increase patrols, including foot patrols, in seven crime-prone neighborhoods. In addition, the Tactical Narcotics Team (TNT) was shifted to focus primarily on these seven high-risk areas (McKinley, 1990). Despite these initiatives, crime rates continued to rise and Brown was criticized. At a press conference on September 24, 1990, Brown defended his approach by saying that he could not change the fact that citizens allowed drug dealers to operate in their midst and that "the presumptions that cops are not doing their job" were frustrating (Blumenthal, 1990b, p. B1). He also stated:

> People know who the drug dealers are, but all too often we don't get the cooperation that we need to address that as a major concern. We don't want people to do police work. We want them to be our eyes and ears. (Blumenthal, 1990b, p. B1)

Despite his public criticisms of citizen apathy, Brown was known for sharing his vision of community policing with citizens at a variety of gatherings. In his first year as chief, Brown attended hundreds of religious and civic meetings to explain citizen involvement in policing (James, 1991b).

In addition, budget freezes had required the police to do more with less (Blumenthal, 1989a). The force in 1990 numbered 26,300 officers, down by approximately 5,000 officers since 1974 (Blumenthal, 1990a). An initial hiring freeze accompanied Operation Take-Back (McKinley, 1990); however, by late 1990 a class of 500 entered the force, receiving six months of field training in community policing. Brown also hired civilian workers in order to relieve from desk jobs those officers who could be in the field (Purdum, 1990). Brown also believed that officers were "overspecialized" and that more officers needed to be deployed in a generalized community-policing capacity (Blumenthal, 1990b). In 1991, the department eliminated 14 specialized units, putting an additional 242 officers on patrol (McKinley, 1991).

As a nationally renowned police chief, Brown assumed a leadership role after the Rodney King beating in Los Angeles. Brown urged police chiefs across the country to focus on the problem of excessive use of force. He also held a "chiefs' summit" on April 16, 1991, in which chiefs from Atlanta, Baltimore, Boston, Bridgeport, Chicago, Dallas, St. Petersburg, San Diego, Tulsa, and other cities discussed the King incident and its ramifications (James, 1991a).

However, Brown's force was not immune from criticism. In the Crown Heights area of Brooklyn, riots broke out on August 19, 1991, after a Hasidic Jew, Yoseph Lisef, caused a fatal car accident, killing Gavin Cato, an African-American child. Subsequently, approximately 250 Crown Heights residents, mostly black youths, began rioting both against Hasidic Jews in the area and against police. In the first night of violence, bottles were thrown, a 17-year-old fired a gun at an officer, and a Yeshiva van was set on fire (McQuiston, 1991a). The next day, 12 police officers were injured during disturbances. In retaliation for Cato's death, Nelson Lemerick, Jr., an African-American man, stabbed Yankel Rosenbaum, a Hasidic student from Australia. During the second day of riots, rocks and debris were thrown at police and police had to separate black and Jewish protesters ("Child's death," 1991). On the third day, several hundred black youths hurled rocks and bottles primarily against the police, who were accused of colluding with the Hasidim for failing to arrest Lisef (Kifner, 1991). According to the press, the focus of the riotous anger shifted from the accident to a generalized expression of anger at racism and the history of blacks in this country ("Three nights," 1991).

Brown seemed to take a backstage position to Mayor Dinkins during the crisis. One of his rare public appearances was at a public meeting

*(continued)*

on August 21, 1991, in which Brown explained to citizens why Lisef had not been arrested, although all witnesses agreed that he had run a red light prior to the accident. Citizens criticized Brown for quickly arresting Lemerick, a black man, while no arrest of Lisef was made after the accident. According to media reports, Brown's explanations did not quell a gasping crowd (Kifner, 1991; McQuiston, 1991b).[1] In a city report about Crown Heights released in 1993, Brown was characterized as making appropriate efforts to reach out to the community by galvanizing community leaders. However, he was criticized for failing to adequately direct field operations during the disturbances. Reportedly, he unnecessarily decentralized command, leaving decisions to field commanders. He also allegedly did not monitor ongoing developments or challenge and question field commanders ("Crown Heights report," 1993).

In a minor controversy in November 1991, Brown was criticized for dispatching two police arson specialists to Long Island to advise a friend of Mayor Dinkins about a fire on his property. Brown told reporters that he did not believe he acted unethically, although he admitted that it was not common to send out officers for such missions. In addition, he stated that the same service would be offered to the average citizen. Brown also emphasized that Mayor Dinkins's friend, though not residing in New York City, worked there (James, 1991c).

In 1992, Brown added corruption spot checks and surveillance to the arsenal of Internal Affairs procedures. Internal Affairs investigators, whose numbers were increased, began after-hours surveillance of officers going to restaurants, bars, and their homes, even targeting those officers not specifically suspected of corruption. In addition, sting operations stashed bags of cash in crime-prone areas to see if officers who discovered them vouchered all of the money. The program was instituted as a response to the uncovering of a cocaine ring operated by six police officers who were arrested in May 1992. Although Brown did not believe the corruption problem was systemic, he admitted that the drug trade could be tempting to officers because of the cash involved (Wolff, 1992a).

In a second riotous event during Brown's service as police chief, on July 6, 1992, a disturbance broke out in the Washington Heights section of Manhattan during a demonstration against the fatal police shooting of Jose Garcia, a Dominican immigrant. Groups of 50 to 100 people overturned garbage cans and lit fires; a police helicopter was hit by gunfire. There were 11 arrests for charges ranging from arson to disorderly conduct (Dao, 1992a). A man throwing bottles fell five stories and died after being pursued along rooftops by police (Dao 1992a; Rein, 1992).

---

[1]A grand jury subsequently decided not to bring charges against Lisef because they believed the crash was an accident and not a criminal act ("Justice," 1991).

A second day of violence occurred when a police officer was shot in the foot; gunfire was heard and people threw jugs of water off rooftops (Rein, 1992). Riots ensued on a third day, and 2,000 police officers in riot gear descended on the neighborhood. On a sixth day, a firecracker injured two officers, including a captain; 14 people were arrested. In six days of violence, there were 139 arrests, 74 police officer injuries, 16 civilians injuries, and 121 car fires (Dao, 1992b).

As during the Crown Heights situation, Brown appeared to take a backseat to Mayor Dinkins in addressing the community and the press about the riots and was rarely mentioned in press accounts at the time. Yet Brown visited Washington Heights throughout the crisis, meeting with local community leaders. He indicated that he planned to institute community sensitivity training at the local precinct (Dao, 1992b). The Patrolmen's Benevolent Association criticized the mayor for not visiting officers in the Washington Heights precinct and offering them a morale boost, but they did not lodge a complaint against Brown's leadership (Finder, 1992).

Civilian complaints were up 19 percent in the first six months of 1992 compared to the same period the year before, according to the Civilian Complaint Review Board (CCRB). Brown told the press that it was due to the increase in new officers who tended to be "more aggressive." However, *The New York Times* reported that most complaints were lodged against officers who had been on the force for five and six years (Wolff, 1992b).

Brown's legacy in New York City extols his implementation of community policing, although only one precinct had completely adopted the model (Wolff, 1992c). Yet the commitment to the policy was deep; Mayor Dinkins said about community policing, upon Brown's resignation, "[I]t's no longer a program. This is how we do business" (Blumenthal, 1992, p. B4). Despite this success, the press characterized Brown as a reserved, not charismatic, leader (Wolff, 1992c).

While NYPD commissioner, Brown served also as the president of the International Association of Chiefs of Police from 1990 to 1991 (Blumenthal, 1989a). After leaving the job as NYPD commissioner, Brown returned to Houston to teach at Texas Southern University (Blumenthal, 1992) and directed the university Black Male Initiative program. From 1993 to 1996, he served on President Clinton's cabinet as the director of the White House Office of National Drug Control Policy ("Biography," n.d.). In 1998, he was elected as the first black mayor of Houston, serving until January 2004. While mayor, Brown negotiated a pay package for the Houston Police Department, making it one of the highest-paid police forces in the nation. According to a journalist who interviewed city administrators, Brown's leadership was characterized as problematic in that he

*(continued)*

overly relied on his subordinates and was perceived as being unable to make decisions. He also was described as favoring a conservative bureaucratic method (Fleck, 2003).

The fact that Brown had "no love affair" with the unions can be traced to his tenure as chief of the Houston Police Department. Accused by the union of lowering the standards of recruitment and hiring irresponsible officers who were later involved in egregious cases of police misconduct, Brown left the police department stigmatized by a lack of integrity rather than celebrated for his innovations. The truth of the matter is that, as identified by the pentagon of police leadership model (in Chapters 1 and 2), recruitment and selection are of paramount importance for effective police leadership. Nevertheless, it is frequently the case that recruitment and selection are informed by political considerations and that the potential recruit who is sought by a given department represents more the "flavor of the month" requirements rather than an embodiment of the true qualifications for police work. The whole idea of identifying true competencies for effective policing, though hardly novel, was never really researched and investigated well enough to provide a standard to be modeled and replicated by police organizations. Finally, even if such competencies were fully identified, the dictates of reality end such idealistic notions. People who are attracted to the police profession are not always the ones who should be attracted to it, and recruiters often must compromise; frequently the decision is based on who is available, not on who is desired. Regardless of these factors, the selection of some and not others always results in an out-group pointing an accusatory finger at the police chief, or any chief for that matter.

Brown's later appointment as police commissioner of the NYPD did not endear him to the local unions there either. His innovative approach to implementation of the ideas of community-oriented policing, and more specifically his priority of reducing police misconduct, was not something that the unions were willing to swallow easily. During the riots of Crown Heights and the second wave of riots in Washington Heights, Brown did show an overreliance on in-groups, whether within the organization itself or outside (by taking a backseat to Mayor Dinkins). Although Brown was not overtly criticized by the unions, which chose to criticize Mayor Dinkins instead, it was clear that Brown's preoccupation with the community members and their well-being, and his low profile as far as the police response to the riot was concerned, did not win much love from the local unions.

A police commissioner who attempts to clean up a police force on one hand and is overly preoccupied with the local community (to the point that the community is perceived as his in-group rather than the officers on the force) on the other will rarely gain real support from the unions. For better or worse, he will be perceived as an in- /out-group leader.

## CAREER HIGHLIGHTS

Chief Darrel Stephens
*Newport News, Virginia; St. Petersburg, Florida;*
*and Charlotte-Mecklenburg, North Carolina*

Darrel Stephens earned a bachelor's degree in administration of justice from the University of Missouri at Kansas City and a master's degree in public administration from Central Missouri State University ("Chief Darrel W. Stephens," n.d.). Stephens began his policing career in the Kansas City, Missouri, Police Department. He was the assistant police chief in Lawrence, Kansas, from 1976 until 1980. From 1980 to 1983, he was the chief of police in Largo, Florida ("Chief Darrel W. Stephens," n.d.).

In 1983, Stephens was hired as chief of police in Newport News, Virginia, to confront corruption in the department (Rogers, 1999b). However, he is most well known for initiating community-oriented policing in the city. In the mid-1980s, Stephens recommended the demolition of the New Briarfield Apartments, a housing project that was notorious for drug use and that had the highest rate of burglaries in the city. Police interviews with residents revealed that people lived in fear of criminal activity and were concerned that physical deterioration of the buildings and vacant housing units attracted criminals. The police worked with members of other city agencies to pick up trash, dispose of abandoned cars, remove potholes, and sweep streets in order to reduce low-level crime before the project's eventual demolition. According to the Police Executive Research Forum (PERF), the burglary rate dropped 35 percent after these improvements (Wilson & Kelling, 1989).

From approximately 1986 to 1992, Stephens served as executive director of the Police Executive Research Forum in Washington, D.C. ("Chief Darrel W. Stephens," n.d.). From 1992 until 1997, Stephens was chief of police in St. Petersburg, Florida. In assuming the job in St. Petersburg, Stephens inherited a 500-officer force in which infighting was common: blacks versus whites, union versus management, and managers versus civic leaders. In addition, police-community relations were tense. Stephens targeted community-oriented policing as a solution, which appeared to succeed in reaching out to the community but ultimately did not solve the divisions within the department (Roche, 1996a).

In pursuit of community-oriented policing, Stephens increased the visibility of police in the city, a move he believed would reduce citizens' fear of crime. This strategy involved creating three police substations in the city. Stephens also decentralized headquarters and permitted officers to police consistently in the same neighborhoods in order to build police-citizen partnerships. In addition, he proposed a program that would allow officers to take their patrol cars home. He hoped to

*(continued)*

spend $13 million on additional cars in order to assign them to specific officers. "I see the value of the cars to increase the visibility in the community and the neighborhoods. They will provide heightened sense of safety. My reason for proposing it has to do with increasing our visibility and decreasing fear, hopefully" (Roche, 1996a, p.1). However, the city council ultimately rejected the proposal (Roche, 1996a).

The most controversial event while Stephens served as chief occurred on October 24, 1996, when a white police officer, Jim Knight, killed an 18-year-old black motorist, Tyrone Lewis, the sixth victim of police shootings that year. Lewis had refused to roll down his tinted windows or follow any commands at a traffic stop for speeding. According to police accounts, the car lurched forward and nearly hit Officer Knight, who fired shots at Lewis. Minutes after the shooting, crowds took to the streets, burning buildings and throwing rocks and bottles in a 25-block area. Additionally, a patrol car was firebombed, two media vans were burned, and fires were set at a police substation and a post office; 11 people were injured, including a police officer and a photojournalist who were beaten. A total of 28 buildings were burned and 20 people were arrested (Flores, 1996).

Stephens responded by defending Officer Knight's conduct in the shooting of Lewis but placed Knight on administrative leave pending an investigation. City council member Ernest Filayu told the press that the frustrations exhibited by the riots went "deeper than a shooting" and that police come into black neighborhoods "with their guns cocked and their attitudes cocked. We have a legal harassment system" (Williams, 1996, A3). On October 27, 1996, 500 citizens attended a school desegregation meeting called by community leaders, but it quickly became an outpouring of frustration at the police department about the Lewis killing and the rioting. At another meeting that night, called by the Community Alliance, Stephens and the mayor attended and took notes. Many called on them to get to the bottom of the issue of police brutality that sparked the riot. Stephens spent the Monday after the riots praising his officers for the job they did during the disturbance. The Police Benevolent Association, however, criticized the department for not having enough portable radios and riot gear. Stephens later acknowledged that equipment arrived late on the scene (Landry, 1996).

A second disturbance in St. Petersburg occurred after a grand jury cleared another officer involved in the shooting of Lewis, rejecting the findings of a civilian review board that had found that Officer Knight had violated department policy in responding to the incident. Stephens responded in a memorandum to his officers stating that the policy allows officers to shoot to protect themselves if they have done everything in their power to get out of harm's way. He indicated that although Lewis's car was slow-moving, Knight was bumped by it several times and could not get out of the way (Howard et al., 1996). During the unrest, there were 78 reported fires and an armed robbery. A drive-by shooting injured one person; three additional people were injured in another shooting. An officer was shot but not seriously injured (Thompson, 1996a). There were 21 burglaries and 6 thefts and assaults (Roche, 1996c).

The disturbance geographically centered in the blocks near the house of the black militant group National People's Democratic Uhuru Movement, where youths roamed during the eight-hour disturbance. The Uhuru philosophy is one of violent resistance against a judicial system the Uhuru view as fraudulent (Thompson, 1996a). Earlier in the day, police arrested three Uhuru members on outstanding charges, reportedly in order to prevent these militants from stirring up trouble during any unrest that was likely to follow the grand jury verdict. In one demonstration prior to the second riot, the Uhurus held a mock tribunal and ordered the execution of Stephens and the mayor, Dave Fisher, by electric chair because they were allegedly guilty of genocide (Rogers, 1999a). Later in the evening, police pulled up in front of the headquarters and were fired on by Uhurus and supporters gathered around the station house. The police used tear gas to dispel the crowd, causing a stampede. In the following unrest, an officer and a citizen were shot, a motorist's jaw was broken by an object hurled into his window, and 33 fires were caused by Molotov cocktails. Near the headquarters, a man opened fire with an automatic on four police officers. The police fired back; there were no injuries in the exchange (Thompson, 1996a).

Black church and civic leaders criticized the arrest of the Uhuru leaders as being heavy-handed and complained that it exacerbated already troubled police-minority relations. Stephens indicated, however, that he had reasons for believing that the Uhurus were planning to react violently if Officer Knight was not charged and so used the preventive strategy of arresting some of them who had outstanding warrants (Roche, 1996b). Police intelligence reports indicated that the Uhurus had stockpiled bricks and bottles in neighborhood trash cans to use in a riot if the grand jury decided in favor of Officer Knight (Thompson, 1996a). Furthermore, complaints about the use of tear gas were also made. Stephens defended the actions of the police officers against the tear gas complaints, saying they were following his strategy of isolating the unrest and holding instigators accountable. He also said that the demonstrators were given a five-minute warning to disperse before the tear gas was set off. Yet he also revealed that the specific decision to use tear gas was made by police supervisors in the field. Police union leaders criticized Stephens for not having provided officers with extensive riot training. Stephens responded that there had not been a major disturbance in the area for two decades before the riots sparked by the killing of Lewis (Roche, 1996b).

*(continued)*

After the riots and criticism, Stephens admitted publicly in November 1996 that he was not sure he would survive as chief. He stated, "Any police chief that encounters a situation like we've encountered, people ought to be asking 'Is this guy doing the sorts of things he should have done the last several years?'" (Thompson, 1996b, p. 1). However, he also highlighted his department's accomplishments, including decreasing crime and increasing a sense of security among citizens. He reiterated his commitment to community policing despite the unrest, saying that approximately 20 percent of the black community supported the concept. He also stated that everyone in the city would need to address the socioeconomic conditions and racial tensions that act as barriers to effective policing (Thompson, 1996b).

A month later, the police union released survey results indicating that out of 307 officers who responded, 76 percent viewed Stephens as weak and ineffective. They called for an investigation into the chief's actions during the riots. Stephens responded by welcoming the outside review, indicating that his job was not about meeting the expectations of his officers but serving the interests of the community. Union President Jack Soule underscored the criticism, "[Stephens] is a sensitive person when it comes to dealing with issues in the community. Where we feel he has failed is with his building a foundation of a partnership with the employees" (Roche, 1996d, p. 1B). A subsequent State Advisory Board to the U.S. Commission on Civil Rights investigated the police response to the riots. Mary Frances Berry, the commission chairwoman, questioned Stephens for not personally leading the officers who were to arrest the Uhuru leaders on outstanding charges, suggesting that the tactic had inflamed the black community and been counterproductive. Stephens later acknowledged that the arrest of the Uhurus was a mistake in judgment (Smith, 1996). Despite the riots and subsequent controversy, press reports indicate that the black community generally credited Stephens with trying to calm racial tension (Rogers, 1999a).

Throughout his tenure as chief, Stephens struggled with low officer morale. A 1995 survey of 58 percent of officers in the Police Benevolent Association indicated that 93 percent of them felt officer morale was low or very low. More than half criticized police managers and Stephens regarding safety issues, retirement plans, and promotions. Between 1993 and 1995, four reverse discrimination suits were filed with the U.S. Equal Opportunity Commission. In response to the survey, Stephens told reporters that he was unsure what to do about the morale problem but that he would look into it (Thompson, 1995).

In June 1997, the St. Petersburg city administrator resigned and the mayor offered the position to Stephens. Struggling with the police department after the riots, Stephens indicated that he took the job at a "soul-searching" moment in his career (Ryan, 1998, p. 1B). The mayor did not expressly remove Stephens because of the racial tension and riots, but this was the public perception of his departure (Thompson, 2001). Stephens remained as city administrator until September 1999 when he left to become the chief of the Charlotte-Mecklenburg Police Department (Ryan, 1998).

Charlotte had a force of 1,500 sworn officers. In continuing his efforts at community-oriented policing, Stephens maintained advanced police technology and equipment in the department (Stephens, n.d.). He also focused on other city functions, such as swimming pool and park hours, and analyzed how these might affect the crime rates. Graffiti elimination and landscaping were also employed to reduce low-level street crimes (Rogers, 1999b).

In addition, Stephens formed a cold case team in February 2003 to investigate over 360 unsolved homicides spanning 40 years. Homicide detectives admitted that they rarely had time to look at old files. The team consisted of two experienced detectives, an FBI agent, two retired NYPD detectives, and a criminal justice professor. They were to review the cases first to find out which were the most solvable, with particular focus on which cases might have DNA evidence that could be analyzed using new technology ("Police designate," 2003).

One controversy Stephens confronted as chief in Charlotte began on May 8, 2002, after a bungled sting operation meant to capture a man who had previously assaulted and kidnapped his girlfriend. The girlfriend, a 33-year-old woman, was used as "bait" but was missing for 16 hours after the sting operation failed and she had left with the suspect without the officers' knowledge. Stephens immediately admitted that the sting operation was a mistake and that the detective who devised the plan, although he was well-meaning, had used the wrong methods to apprehend the suspect. Stephens also mentioned, however, that there was no department policy against using victims in sting operations (Whitmore, 2002).

Stephens was one of the main pioneers/proponents of community-oriented policing. It is likely that it was that approach which alienated local police unions from being an ideal in-group category. He was accused by the Police Benevolent Association of not providing enough radios and riot gear after the Lewis shooting; 76 percent of respondents to a union-initiated survey identified him as a weak and ineffective leader. Finally there came a point-blank accusation by the union president who blamed Stephens for failing to build a partnership with his employees at the expense of building a stronger and more sensitive partnership with the local community. This last accusation was, practically speaking, an affirmation of the in-out group concept, when the larger community becomes an in-group for the police chief and the prevailing perception among the union leaders is that, as a result, the officers become the out-group.

*(continued)*

The LMX theory of leadership's recommendation of creating an in-group of all is unrealizable in a democratic policing environment, in which there is a competing pull on police leaders to be accountable both to their own officers and to the community at large. One interesting parallel between these two chiefs is their endorsement of community-oriented policing. Yet their careers were both stigmatized by accusations that they favored groups outside the police organization. Their experience raises the question of whether full commitment to or an orientation toward community-oriented policing makes leaders prone to accusations of in-group/out-group polarity. Does it increase the chances that a police department's union will perceive that officers have become scapegoats, one large out-group for the police chief in charge, whose in-group has become the external community?

### Exercise

The police chief and commissioner detailed in this chapter have been examined through the prism of leader-member exchange theory. Using what you have learned from other theories in this book or from the summaries (as indicated in the Introduction) you have read thus far, it is possible to consider their approaches through the lens of different theories. What other theories can you find applicable to these leaders? Are there lessons to be learned from those applications, or do those theories indicate alternative paths or approaches that might have yielded a more successful outcome?

## REFERENCES

Balz, D. (1982, March 10). Atlanta official hired by Houston as police chief. *The Washington Post*, p. A24.

_____ & A. Harris (1982, April 20). Atlanta's troubleshooter is installed as Houston chief to clean up police. *The Washington Post*, p. A7.

Belkin, L. (1989a, December 19). Man in the news: A chief known for turning strife into calm. *The New York Times*, p. B9.

_____ (1989b, December 21). For new police commissioner, towering challenges: Stranger to New York, Brown says first act will be to "reach out." *The New York Times*, p. B1.

Biography of Lee P. Brown (n.d.). Office of National Drug Control Policy. Retrieved August 7, 2003, from http://clinton1.nara.gov/White_House/EOP/ondcp/html/Lee_Brown.html.

Blumenthal, R. (1989a, December 21). For new police commissioner, towering challenges: Rampant drug abuse and record murder toll compete with 911 calls and budget freezes. *The New York Times*, p. B1.

_____ (1989b, December 22). Police dept. is praised by next commissioner. *The New York Times*, p. B3.

_____ (1990a, August 3). Crime and commissioner: Pressure mounts for results. *The New York Times*, p. B1.

_____ (1990b, September 25). Head of police assails media on job image. *The New York Times*, p. B1.

_____ (1992, August 6). Brown says community policing will endure. *The New York Times*, p. B4.

Chief Darrel W. Stephens (n.d.). Retrieved July 17, 2003, from http://www.cicp.org/ Boardmembers.htm.

Child's death sparks outrage, riot, slaying (1991, August 21). *The Record*, p. A3.

Crown Heights report: From the report on police actions and Commissioner Brown (1993, July 21). *The New York Times*, p. B7.

Dao, J. (1992a, July 7). Angered by police killing, a neighborhood erupts. *The New York Times*, p. A3.

_____ (1992b, July 10). Washington Heights calm shattered by disruptions. *The New York Times*, p. B3.

Dinesh, R.M. & R.C. Liden (1986). Leader-member exchange model of leadership: A critique and further development. *Academy of Management Review*, 11, 618–634.

Duchon, D., S.G. Green & T.D. Taber (1986). Vertical dyad linkage: A longitudinal assessment of antecedents, measures, and consequences. *Journal of Applied Psychology*, 71, 56–60.

Dunegan, K.J., D. Duchon & M. Uhl-Bien (1992). Examining the link between leader-member exchange and subordinate performance: The role of task analyzability and variety as moderators. *Journal of Management*, 18 (1), 59–76.

Erdogan, B., M. Kraimer & R.C. Liden (2002). Person-organization fit and work attitudes: The moderating role of leader-member exchange. *Academy of Management Proceedings*, F1–F6.

Finder, A. (1992, July 9). Tension in Washington Heights: Dinkins, amid crowd, nurtures fragile peace. *The New York Times*, p. A1.

Fleck, T. (2003, May 15). Parting shots: Foes of Mayor Brown want to see him gone. And a lot of his friends feel that way, too. *Houston Press*, News Section. Retrieved November 3, 2004 from http://www.houstonpress.com/ issues/2003–05–15/news/feature.html.

Flores, I. (1996). St. Petersburg police restrict gun, gas sales day after rioting. *Chattanooga Free Press*, p. A1.

Graen, G. (1983, May–June). Bias in management research? A defense. *Business Horizons*, 42–45.

_____ & J.F. Cashman (1975). A role making model of leadership in formal organizations: A developmental approach. In J.L. Hunt & L.L. Larson (Eds.), *Leadership frontiers* (pp. 143–165). Kent, OH: Kent State University Press.

_____ & M. Uhl-Bien (1991). The transformation of professionals into self-managing and partially self-designing contributions: Toward a theory of leader-making. *Journal of Management Systems*, 3 (3), 33–48.

Harris, A. (1982, March 2). Atlanta ends special probe into killings. *The Washington Post*, p. A1.

Howard, P.E., S. Thompson & D. Sommer (1996, November 14). Jury report sparks unrest. *The Tampa Tribune*, p. 1.

James, G. (1991a, April 9). Brown sponsors a police summit on excess force. *The New York Times*, p. B2.

_____ (1991b, August 14). Brown's gospel: Community policing. *The New York Times*, p. B1.

_____ (1991c, November 14). Brown defends sending officers to Dinkins's L.I. friend. *The New York Times*, p. B3.

Justice in Crown Heights (1991, September 7). *The New York Times*, p. 22.

Kifner, J. (1991, August 22). Tension in Brooklyn: Clashes persist in Crown Heights for 3d night. *The New York Times*, p. B1.

Kozlowski, S.W.J. & M.L. Doherty (1989). Integration of climate and leadership: A neglected issue. *Journal of Applied Psychology*, 6, 546–553.

Kurtz, H. (1989, December 19). Texan to head N.Y. police: Brown's term marred by 2 recent killings. *The Washington Post*, p. A3.

Landry, S. (1996, October 29). Anger comes out at forum. *St. Petersburg Times*, p. 1A.

LeBlanc, P.M., R.D. deJong, J. Geersing, J. Furda & I.H. Komproe (1993). Leader member exchanges: Distinction between two factors. *European Work and Organizational Psychologist*, 3 (4), 297–309.

Liden, R.C. & G. Graen (1980). Generalizability of the vertical dyad linkage model of leadership. *Academy of Management Journal*, 23 (3), 451–465.

Maurer, T.J., H.R. Pierce & L.M. Shore (2002). Perceived beneficiary of employee development activity: A three-dimensional social exchange model. *Academy of Management Review*, 27 (3) 432–444.

McKinley, J.C. (1990, July 19). Extra patrols to be added for 7 precincts. *The New York Times*, p. B1.

_____ (1991, February 9). Anti-crime plan will curb violence, commissioner says. *The New York Times*, p. 27.

McQuiston, J.T. (1991a, August 20). Fatal crash starts melee with police in Brooklyn. *The New York Times*, p. B1.

_____ (1991b, August 22). Tension in Brooklyn: Case weighed in car accident that killed boy. *The New York Times*, p. B3.

Norris, W.R. & R.P. Vecchio (1992). Situational leadership theory: A replication. *Group and Organizational Management*, 17, 331–342.

Northouse, P.G. (2004). *Leadership: Theory and practice*, 3rd ed. Thousand Oaks, CA: Sage.

Police designate investigators for unsolved killings (2003, February 11). *The Associated Press*, state and local wire.

Purdum, T.S. (1989, December 19). Dinkins names Houston's chief to be his police commissioner. *The New York Times*, p. A1.

_____ (1990, September 19). Police chief wants to add more civilians. *The New York Times*, p. B1.

Rein, L. (1992, July 8). Violence flares anew: Cop is shot in fallout from killing. Unrest in Washington Heights. *The Record*, p. A1.

Roche, T. (1996a, March 31). Chief wants to make officers more visible. *St. Petersburg Times*, p. 1.

_____ (1996b, November 15). Police had not planned for immediate violence. *St. Petersburg Times*, p. 1A.

_____ (1996c, November 20). Unrest adds up to large expense. *St. Petersburg Times*, p. 1B.

_____ (1996d, December 4). Union president calls for police chief's ouster. *St. Petersburg Times*, p. 1B.

Rogers, D.K. (1999a, August 26). Stephens to head Charlotte force. *St. Petersburg Times*, p. 1B.

_____ (1999b, September 19). Stephens anxious to begin new post. *St. Petersburg Times*, p. 1.

Ryan, K. (1998, June 14). City administrator Darrel Stephens: From top cop to city bureaucrat. *St. Petersburg Times*, p. 1B.

Scandura, T., G.B. Graen & M.A. Novak (1986). When managers decide not to decide autocratically: An investigation of leader-member exchange and decision influence. *Journal of Applied Psychology*, 71, 579–584.

Schriesheim, C.A., S.L. Castro, X. Zhou & F.J. Yammarino (2001). The folly of theorizing "A" but testing "B": A selective level-of-analysis review of the field and a detailed leader-member exchange illustration. *Leadership Quarterly*, 12, 515–551.

Smith, A. (1996, December 5). Rights panel grills mayor, police chief. *St. Petersburg Times*, p. 1A.

Steiner, D.D. (1988). Value perceptions in leader-member exchange. *Journal of Social Psychology*, 128 (5), 611–618.

Stephens, D. (n.d.). Message from the Charlotte-Mecklenburg police chief. Retrieved on July 17, 2003, from http://www.charmeck.nc.us/Departments/Police/About+Us/Command+Staff/home.htm.

Thompson, S. (1995, August 11). Union survey finds cop morale low. *The Tampa Tribune*, p. 1.

_____ (1996a, November 15). Uhuru black militants thrust into spotlight with new unrest. *The Tampa Tribune*, p. 12.

_____ (1996b, November 27). Stephens admits his job could be in jeopardy. *The Tampa Tribune*, p. 1.

_____ (2001, December 23). Tenuous race relations haunt police chiefs. *The Tampa Tribune*, p. 1.

Three nights, three moods in the streets (1991, August 25). *The New York Times*, p. 37.

Vecchio, R. & B. Gobdel (1984). The vertical dyad linkage model of leadership: Problems and prospects. *Organizational Behavior and Human Performance*, 34, 5–20.

Whitmore, T. (2002, May 8). Police chief: Sting operation a mistake. *The Associated Press*, state and local wire.

Williams, M. (1996, October 27). St. Petersburg searches its soul: Riot highlights racial tension belying progress. *The Atlanta Journal and Constitution*, A3.

Wilson, J.Q. & G.L. Kelling (1989, February). Making neighborhoods safe. *Atlantic Monthly*, 46–52.

Wolff, C. (1992a, July 1). Brown to add inquiry power in police graft. *The New York Times*, p. B1.

_____ (1992b, July 30). Police review board says public complaints are up. *The New York Times*, p. B2.

_____ (1992c, August 4). Brown's resignation. Brown legacy: Community policing. *The New York Times*, p. B2.

Yammarino, F.J., F. Dansereau & C.J. Kennedy (2001). A multiple-level multidimensional approach to leadership: Viewing leadership through an elephant's eye. *Organizational Dynamics*, 29 (3), 149–163.

Yrle, A.C., S.J. Hartman & W.P. Galle, Jr. (2003). Examining communication style and leader-member exchange: Considerations and concern for managers. *International Journal of Management*, 20 (1), 92–100.

_____, S. Hartman & W.P. Galle (2002). An investigation of relationships between communication style and leader-member exchange. *Journal of Communication Management*, 6 (3), 257–268.

# 5

# When the Chief Becomes the Force

## *Transformational Theory*

## OVERVIEW OF THE THEORY

Transformational leadership is a style in which the personality of the leader stimulates change because he or she raises consciousness, motivation, and morale. Here it is illustrated through the examples of Chief Reuben Greenberg of the Charleston, South Carolina, Police Department and Chief Daryl Gates of the Los Angeles Police Department. Although both had careers with many facets, the key for both was the degree to which their personalities succeeded in creating desired change.

The theory of transformational leadership was first articulated by Burns (1978), who identified a process by which leaders affect the attitudes and motivations of followers. According to Burns, transformational leadership involves leaders who tailor their leadership to the needs of their followers in an effort to move them into a state of elevated goals and performance that transcends the implicit or explicit demands of the task. Burns refers to two developmental continua: follower motivation and moral development. *Follower motivation* involves inspiring followers to meet self-actualization needs and to perform at their highest potential. Leaders must also have *moral development*, or the ability to be inspirational and uplifting to the extent that they can move followers to a higher moral stage. This involves urging followers to transcend their own self-interest for the sake of the organization (Bass, 1985). According to Bass and Avolio (1994), transformational leadership can range in style from democratic and participative to directive and authoritarian.

Burns contrasts transformational leadership with transactional leadership, characterized as exchanges between leaders and followers that remain within the limits of self-interest. Under this model, followers are motivated only by what they personally will gain from the task (e.g., salary, bonuses), and leaders are satisfied with the mere fulfillment of contractual obligations, referred to as *contingent reward*. Transactional leadership can also take the form of *laissez-faire management*, when leaders are passive and avoid taking any action. Thirdly, transactional leadership may also be *management-by-exception* in which the leader monitors followers, intervening only if a corrective action is required (Bass, 1999).

The transformational/transactional distinction represents the difference between mere management and true leadership. Burns (1978) originally conceptualized the two as opposite ends along a spectrum of leadership. Bass (1985), however, believes the two are separate concepts, and a leader could be both transactional and transformational. Regardless, the distinction between mere management and leadership appears to be rooted in historical trends. In the 1970s and 1980s, leadership researchers were responding to the inability of American companies to cope with changing economic demands. This was diagnosed as a problem of too much management and too little leadership (Conger, 1999). Bennis and Nanus

---

### Ethics and Leadership

- Leaders are to encourage followers to develop a set of values that emphasizes justice, liberty, and equality.
- These values give transformational leadership its moral purpose.
- Transactional leadership lacks a moral center because it is inherently uncritical of the people involved in the leadership exchange.

(Burns, 1978)

---

## Ethics and Transactional Leadership

Giampetro-Meyer et al. (1998)
- Transactional leadership can lead to ethically questionable behavior on the part of leaders.
- Due to "craft ethics," leaders do not reflect on what they personally think is right but merely follow what those on the job or in the workplace believe is ethical.

Turner et al. (2002)
- Leaders who use the transactional style of leadership do not become more effective regardless of whether they have the capacity to reason morally.
- This is because, by definition, transactional leadership is merely a dyadic exchange to satisfy individual needs.

(1985) define this crisis as a lack of leadership skills and talents on the part of industry managers.[1]

Transformational leadership can be broken down into four factors: idealized influence (charisma), inspirational leadership, intellectual stimulation, and individualized consideration. *Idealized influence* (charisma) and *inspirational leadership* occur when followers want to identify with leaders because of their ability to define goals, to state how they can be accomplished, to set high standards, and to exhibit confidence and determination. *Intellectual stimulation* involves tapping into followers' creativity. *Individualized consideration* refers to a coaching style of leadership in which leaders concern themselves with the career development of their followers (Bass, 1999; Bass & Avolio, 1994).

## IMPORTANCE OF CHARISMA IN LEADERS

Max Weber conceptualizes charismatic leadership as the followers' belief that their leader has extraordinary qualities. Likewise, House (1976) stresses the significance of charisma within the transformational

---

[1]See my review of trait theory (Chapter 12) for a synopsis of Bennis and Nanus (1985). According to their conception of transformational leadership, transforming leaders have vision, act as social architects, create trust, and use creative deployment of self through positive self-regard. Although Bennis and Nanus believe that these strategies of leadership are skills that can be learned, the skills appear to also operate much like traits in that they describe what characteristics a transforming leader should possess.

framework. He identifies indicators of charismatic leadership, including follower perceptions and leader traits and behaviors. Charismatic leaders are associated with self-confidence and a need for power. Their typical behaviors include the ability to manage their image, articulate visions, communicate high expectations, and instill confidence in followers (De Vries et al., 1999). House's model originally focused on the dyadic relationship between leaders and followers rather than on collectives. Criticism of House's conception includes that the charismatic leaders who can be identified historically are too varied to identify specific traits (Bryman, 1992; De Vries et al., 1999). In subsequent theory development, House and Shamir (1993) moved from the dyadic to the collective, proposing that charismatic leadership occurs when leaders link their followers' sense of identity to the larger goals of the organization. By doing this, followers internalize the larger goals of the organization as part of their self-identity.

The relationship between personality and transformational leadership was tested by Judge and Bono (2000) using the five-factor model of personality, providing empirical support for the centrality of charisma in the transformational model (see Figure 5–1). The five factors are extroversion, agreeableness, conscientiousness, emotional adjustment, and openness to experience, all of which are theoretically positively related to the likelihood that a leader will be a transformational one. According to this study, the sample of 223 Midwestern community

**FIGURE 5–1    FIVE FACTOR MODEL OF PERSONALITY**

*Source:* Adapted from Judge and Bono, 2000.

leaders revealed that agreeableness was the strongest predictor of transformational leadership behaviors, particularly that of charisma. Extroversion and openness to experience were also positively related. Conscientiousness was not correlated with transformational leadership. Emotional adjustment was operationalized using measures of its opposite, neuroticism. There was no correlation between neuroticism and the absence of transformational leadership. Although as a whole the five-factor model was not an ideal predictor of transformational leadership behavior, this study's importance rests on the empirical finding that charisma as a measure of agreeableness is the best predictor of transformational behavior, as suggested by the approach of House (1976) and those who follow his paradigm.

Others have hypothesized that charisma is not a trait that resides in a person but is a behavioral phenomenon (Conger & Kanungo, 1998). According to this model, charisma is based on followers' perceptions of leader behavior. Leaders first evaluate the talents and needs of subordinates. They then expose the weaknesses of the status quo within the organization, followed by the formulation of new goals. Conger and Kanungo (1998) characterize charismatic leadership as leading toward radical change. This is similar to the Tichy and DeVanna (1990) approach, which emphasizes that recognizing the need for change is a key characteristic of transformational leaders. They also propose that the charismatic vision is based on the circumstances of the external environment and may not entirely be the product of the needs of the organization internally. Leaders may articulate new processes and goals that are necessary due to pressures mounting from outside the organization (Conger, 1999).

## Need for Charismatic Leadership

In a follower-centered approach, De Vries et al. (1999) tested the notion that followers differ in their need for charismatic leadership. They define the need for leadership as the extent to which followers desire the leader to outline the path toward individual, group, or organizational goals. *Subjective needs* for leadership are those associated with individual goals; *objective needs* for leadership characterize group and organizational goals. In a random sample of Dutch households, participants responded to a survey about their relationship with their employer. The researchers found that subordinates who reported having charismatic bosses also exhibited a higher need for leadership. Need for leadership acted as a moderator variable between level of leaders' charisma and measures of performance. The researchers conclude that subordinates are more

## Charismatic Leader's Effect on Subordinates

Subordinates are more dependent rather than empowered when under a charismatic leader (De Vries et al., 1999).

*or*

Charismatic leaders empower their followers to greater independence and career development (Bass & Avolio, 1994).

dependent rather than empowered when they are under a charismatic leader. This contradicts the traditional transformational theory (Bass & Avolio, 1994), which holds that charismatic leaders empower their followers to greater independence and career development.

# META-ANALYTIC STUDIES
# ON TRANSFORMATIONAL LEADERSHIP

Two meta-analytic studies have been done on the vast research on transformational leadership. A study found that transformational leadership behaviors are correlated with subjective and objective measures of leadership effectiveness and that this can be generalized across types of organizations and levels of management. Furthermore, individualized consideration, intellectual stimulation, and idealized influence (charisma) not only are correlated with effectiveness but also are strongly correlated with each other (Lowe et al., 1996). A second meta-analytic study also showed that transformational leadership is related to leader effectiveness (Fuller et al., 1996).

## Transformational Leaders and Moral Reasoning

- Transformational leaders transcend self-interest goals to a more mature set of values, culminating in a sense of universalistic ethical principles of fairness, equality, and justice. These values form ends in themselves for mature leaders.
- Moral reasoning has been empirically connected to leadership effectiveness, using a measure of moral reasoning and subordinate ratings of leaders in a sample of managers.
- Moral reasoning is considered a cognitive function that can develop over a life span.
- Leaders with the cognitive capacity to reason morally will use this higher degree of transformational leadership and will be more likely to behave in a way that serves the collective good.

(Kuhnert and Lewis, 1987)

## TRANSFORMATIONAL LEADERSHIP
## IN MILITARY CONTEXTS

Several studies testing transformational leadership using samples of military leaders and subordinates have been undertaken. Transformational leadership, operationalized using the Management Leadership Questionnaire (MLQ instrument) developed by Bass and Avolio that tests the four factors of this style of leadership (individualized consideration, intellectual stimulation, inspirational leadership, and idealized influence), was empirically related to subjective and objective performance evaluations in a sample of U.S. Navy leaders and followers. Measures of transactional leadership were not found to be significantly related to performance (Yammarino et al., 1993).

Masi (2000) studied transformational leadership among recruiting units of the U.S. Army, hypothesizing that transformational leadership behavior leads to high levels of subordinate motivation, commitment to quality, and productivity. A sample of 2,596 personnel associated with 18 randomly selected recruiting battalions were surveyed using the MLQ instrument as well as other instruments. Results showed significant relationships between transformational leadership behaviors and motivation of subordinates; however, there was a negative relationship between transformational leadership behaviors and commitment to quality and productivity. Masi concludes that in structured settings such as the military, leaders have only a marginal impact on the norms of their units, suggesting that structural changes (job redesign, revised human resources practices) would be needed to effect change in commitment to quality and productivity.

Shamir et al. (1998) tested the House and Shamir (1993; see above) conception of charisma and self-identity on a sample of leaders and subordinates in the Israeli Defense Forces. They suggest that the theory did not appear to be supported by their empirical findings. The only factor relating to measures of subordinate trust of the leader, identification with the leader, increased motivation, and willingness to sacrifice themselves for their military unit (measures of the success or failure of the charismatic leadership) was emphasis on collective identity. The researchers feel that soldiers were alienated from the larger military system. Charismatic traits (ideological approach, high devotion, high motivation, and high role involvement) on the part of leaders were cynically interpreted by subordinates as reflecting the interests of the military at large rather than the subordinates' own interests.

Dvir et al. (2002) conducted a field experiment involving 54 military leaders within the Israeli Defense Forces, their 90 direct followers (immediate subordinates; for example, for a lieutenant, his/her sergeant), and 724 indirect followers (for example, for a lieutenant, the officers commanded by his/her directly subordinated sergeant). Direct followers have been the primary consideration of studies of transformational leadership. Here, indirect followers are also being studied, although the researchers offered no hypothesis as to what may be different about indirect followers. The experiment subjected seven squads of platoon leaders and cadets to transformational leadership training. Five squads were assigned to the control group and received no transformational leadership training. In this study, a critical-independent approach, extra effort, and collectivist orientation were the dependent variables, all of which increased with the experimental group over time and decreased with the control group, regarding both direct and indirect followers, thus supporting the efficacy of transformational leadership. However, transformational leadership was not significantly related to direct followers' active engagement, internalization of moral values, and self-actualization needs. Regarding indirect followers, results suggested that transformational leadership creates a stronger relationship between direct and indirect followers, thereby improving the performance of indirect followers.

Dvir and Shamir (2003) continued studying the Israeli Defense Forces by testing whether followers' developmental characteristics predicted transformational leadership. The sample was the same as for the above study. However, in this study the organization's moral values, collectivist orientation, critical-independent approach, active task engagement, and self-efficacy were independent variables, measured using various survey instruments. The researchers hypothesized that the independent variables positively predicted transformational leadership over time. Results showed that the hypothesis was supported among indirect followers. However, direct followers showed a negative relationship. The researchers suggested three mechanisms to explain the unexpected outcome regarding direct followers. According to a threat explanation, the empowerment of direct followers acts as a threat to the power of their leaders; therefore, direct followers may suppress their level of development. The indirect followers, however, pose no threat to their leader's status, so their initial development level can be high. A compensatory explanation involves leaders perceiving direct followers as weak and thereby asserting their transformational leadership to a greater extent. This relationship does not exist between the leader and indirect followers because indirect followers do not share leadership responsibilities as leaders and direct followers do. A third explanation involves the potential disillusionment of direct followers who have daily face-to-face interactions with their leader.

## TRANSFORMATIONAL AND TRANSACTIONAL LEADERSHIP STYLES AND THE CASES OF CHIEF REUBEN GREENBERG AND CHIEF DARYL GATES

Scholars define transformational leadership as an approach that differentiates between management and true leadership. It romanticizes the notion of a leader as someone who fully transforms the organization he/she heads to the extent that the agency is identified more with the leader's personality and his/her impact on subordinates and the organization than with the actual changes he/she creates and implements. Leadership techniques and philosophies and their results are emphasized less than the one individual who represents the culture of a given police organization. It frequently goes even a step further: The transformational leader *is* the organization that he/she leads.

The romanticized notion of a transformational leader as portrayed by Kuhnert and Lewis (1987)—who depict transformational leaders as those who transcend self-interest goals to a more mature set of values that culminates in a sense of universalistic ethical principles of fairness, equity, and justice—does not necessarily fit the environment of policing. It is hard to envision the truly altruistic police chief who elevates himself/herself above and beyond self-interest goals; it is indeed hard to envision anybody who can truly reach such heights of moral development. One wants to transform an organization, a police organization or any other organization, based on one's personal vision of what is right; this personal vision does not necessarily transcend self-interest goals. After all, if one believes that a certain vision should be implemented, it is based on the fact that this particular vision appears to be what projects one's values and beliefs, and it is self-serving, by default, when one implements that dream.

**CAREER HIGHLIGHTS    Transformational Approach**

Chief Reuben Greenberg
*Charleston Police Department, South Carolina*

This phenomenon of personal vision and transformation appears to be the case with Chief Reuben Greenberg of the Charleston, South Carolina, Police Department. He introduced his values and beliefs to the Charleston Police Department and that, combined with his long and unprecedented tenure in this organization, enabled him not only to introduce change but also to make it happen and maintain it for long enough that the organization became identifiable with him and his personality rather than with the function that it serves in the community.

Since 1982, Greenberg has been chief of police of the Charleston Police Department, a force with approximately 350 officers ("Greenberg hinting," 1999).[1] He officially retired in 2002 but has kept working as chief under a program that allows state employees to work past their retirement and earn both their salary and retirement benefits ("Like he never left," 2002). By most accounts, Greenberg is a popular police chief with national prominence (Bauer, 1999; Munday, 2002; Stevens, 2001). A Charleston synagogue even dedicated a stained-glass window to the chief, likening his qualities of strength and protection to the biblical Reuben (Munday, 2002). In a snapshot of his policing philosophy in *Fast Company* magazine, Greenberg stated that he runs a service organization, the success of which he measures by complaints and compliments: "Ultimately, we don't just want to fight crime—we want to make life better for people. So all of our officers can make on-the-spot decisions to help citizens" (McCauley, 1999, p. 97).

Greenberg received his bachelor's degree from San Francisco State University in 1967 and continued on to receive two master's degrees from the University of California at Berkeley: public administration (1969) and city planning (1975). He has taught as an assistant professor at California State University and has been an instructor at University of North Carolina[2] and Florida International University ("Reuben M. Greenberg," n.d.).

He has held the positions of undersheriff of the San Francisco County Sheriff's Department; chief of police in Opa Locka, Florida; chief deputy sheriff of Orange County, Florida; director of public safety in Mobile, Alabama; and deputy director of the Florida Department of Law Enforcement ("Chief Reuben M. Greenberg," n.d.). He was considered for the chief of police in Atlanta (Blackmon, 1994) and the NYPD Police Commissioner (Stevens, 2001). Greenberg belongs to the National Association of Black Law Enforcement Executives and the International

---

[1]Greenberg was still chief as of August 2004.
[2]While teaching at UNC, Greenberg was a mentor figure to Charles A. Moose, encouraging him to consider a career in policing ("Greenberg mentored," 2002).

Association of Chiefs of Police. He has received several national awards and is the author of a 1989 book titled *Let's Take Back Our Streets* ("Chief Reuben M. Greenberg," n.d.).

Greenberg's accomplishments during his 22-year career in Charleston are numerous. He ended the city's open-air drug markets by effectively placing uniformed police officers on street corners where the drugs were sold ("Adding police," 1997). However, he has expressed frustration at the courts' response to drug crimes, especially in high-crime areas such as the East Side neighborhood of Charleston. Greenberg implemented foot and horseback patrols in the area, along with drug-sniffing dogs, which have been successful in making 900 arrests a year for narcotics possession or resale (Hicks, 2000). He also introduced advanced technology to better respond to firearms offenses, in particular, acoustic sensor technology, which uses computers and phone lines to pinpoint where guns have been fired in the city (Smith, 2003). Yet he has realistically pointed out that such community-oriented efforts probably did not eliminate such crimes but merely displaced them to other jurisdictions. "Displacing crime means displacing it from here to somewhere up north. How far north it goes is no concern of ours," he was reported as saying in 1999 (Menchaca, 1999, p. A1).

Hiring practices also reportedly improved under Greenberg. Five police officers were unable to read or write when Greenberg became chief of police. Since then, he has raised recruitment standards, accepting only college graduates for officer positions. He has also emphasized military discipline in training new officers by requiring recruits to have excellent physical fitness (Menchaca, 1999). In addition, he has also maintained a ratio of black officers that reflects Charleston's population: Half of the officers on the force are black; in Charleston, 41 percent of the citizens are black (Jacobs, 1999).

Initiatives related to juveniles have also characterized Greenberg's approach. In 2001, he established an informal curfew to protect youths during a summer spike in crime. Police were instructed to escort home anyone under age 17 found outside after 11 p.m. (Hardin, 2001; Lundy, 2002). A truancy policy has officers pick up juveniles and take them home before they commit a crime (Bauer, 1999). Moreover, the Charleston Police Department has teamed up with the Charleston Yacht Club to provide sailing memberships and instruction to disadvantaged youths. The program was designed to promote an interest in sailing and provide an alternative to delinquent activities (McCormack, 2002).

Among his controversies, Greenberg has been criticized for his approach to issues of importance to the black community. A police officer shot a black schizophrenic man during a confused struggle in a dark hallway of the victim's house on May 21, 1999; a white officer accidentally shot and killed a black officer who had also responded to the call. The Southern Christian Leadership Conference called their deaths an

*(continued)*

example of police racism and held Greenberg accountable. The officer involved, however, was cleared of any wrongdoing in a subsequent police investigation (Fennell, 1999). Charleston has no civilian review board (Jacobs, 1999).

Greenberg's positions on racial profiling are also controversial. Greenberg told the press that most police stops of blacks are reasonable because blacks commit an inordinate amount of violent crime, although he stated that blacks are also the most often victimized. According to Greenberg, the problem is how innocent blacks are treated when they are stopped. "The problem is we don't know how to disengage. Most officers, once convinced that they have the wrong guy, just tell the citizen, "Hey, beat it; get out of here'" (Jacobs, 1999, p. A1). This response failed to improve his public relations because critics pointed out that in 80 percent of stops for a felony offense, the stopped person turns out not to be the suspect (Jacobs, 1999). Greenberg continued to minimize the importance of racial profiling when the department was accused of the practice in subsequent forums, including forums hosted by black and progressive groups (Brazil, 2001), and at a Cato Institute debate where he stated, "So-called racial profiling . . . does not have any appreciable impact on our criminal justice system" (Piacente, 2001, p. A1). He also accused opponents of racial profiling of being more interested in weakening drug laws and not augmenting the rights of blacks. The comment angered both liberals and conservatives. Greenberg had hoped to reframe the debate in terms of the problem he believes is more relevant: black-on-black crimes (Piacente, 2001). In addition, Greenberg opposed federal hate crimes legislation and told a congressional panel that the existing laws adequately provide for arrest and prosecution of offenders involved in bias-related incidents (Piacente, 1999).

In other conflicts, a protracted dispute between the police department and residents of James Island led to an accusation of harassment against Greenberg personally. A regular at the Riverland Terrace Boat Landing filed an incident report against Greenberg for allegedly harassing him for drinking beer at the park. Greenberg contended that he was not harassing people at the boat landing but was enforcing city codes prohibiting alcohol consumption in public places (Rucker, 1995).

Another controversy ensued when Greenberg made a comment, reported in the press, that the family of a 71-year-old Alzheimer's sufferer who wandered from his home was not properly caring for him. "You ought to get a warrant and have those SOBs arrested," he was reported as saying. The following day Greenberg declined State Senator Robert Ford's request for an apology on behalf of the family ("Greenberg's remarks," 1995).

Greenberg has also had differences with Charleston's county sheriff. An impasse between the two law enforcement agencies began in December

1992 when the two were observed in an angry dispute over a hazardous chemical leak. In addition, they have had some jurisdictional arguments stemming from the city's attempt to annex unincorporated parts of the county, thereby shrinking the territory patrolled by the sheriff's officers ("Charleston chief," 1995). However, the two reportedly agree on Greenberg's stance on racial profiling (Porter, 2002).

Greenberg publicly endorsed Elizabeth Dole during her 2000 presidential election campaign. He indicated that her gun-control position was appealing because it neither infringed on Second Amendment rights nor ignored the need to protect cops and children. Dole's plan included mandatory trigger locks on guns, background checks for gun-show purchases, and bans on assault rifles (Kropf, 1999). In addition, Greenberg started a program offering $100 to anyone who turns in someone with an illegal firearm (Bauer, 1999). However, the endorsement of Dole's gun-control policies seemed to be contradicted later when Greenberg implied to Charleston business owners that they could best protect themselves by procuring firearms, calling burglaries and robberies "a fact of life" (Walker, 2003, p. B1).

Transformational leadership can be truly implemented only through a long-lasting tenure and influence on all aspects of an organization. This influence, as in the case of Greenberg, frequently extends from selection and recruitment through training and changes both in the organizational structure and in the subculture of the employees. Within the rigid environment of police organizations, such profound changes can be achieved only through a long and uninterrupted "reign." On this author's first visit to research the Charleston Police Department, the taxi driver from the airport commented on my destination of the police department. His reaction was indeed very telling: "Yes, I know Reuben. Please say hello from me—Reuben *is* the Charleston Police Department." No other statement can characterize better a truly transformational police leader.

On the other end of the spectrum is transactional leadership, defined as an exchange between a leader and a follower wherein the leader is satisfied with an outcome that fulfills the particular contractual obligation. Transactional leadership emphasizes the interdependence between reward and punishment. As long as a task is performed according to expectations, there is a reward; if the subordinate deviates from expectations, the response is punishment. Transactional leadership presumes little, if any, understanding or desire to know why things are done or not done in a particular manner. There is very little emphasis on the needs of the followers or their personal development.

## Transformational and Transactional Leadership

- Transformational and transactional leadership can both be ethically based.
- They reflect two different value systems and motives.
- Transformational leaders possess an organic worldview characteristic of a deontological perspective. Such a perspective asserts that leaders' actions have a morally intrinsic value. An act is moral when it, as a means to an end, is executed with a sense of duty to others guided by Kantian pure reason; this is referred to as genuine or moral altruism.
- Transactional leaders reflect teleological ethics in which ends or outcomes are emphasized. The leader has an atomistic worldview, meaning that he/she feels separate from others and emphasizes independence rather than interdependence.

(Kanungo, 2001)

---

**CAREER HIGHLIGHTS** Transactional Approach

Chief Daryl Gates
*Los Angeles Police Department, California*

Daryl Gates was born on August 30, 1926, and was raised in Glendale, California. In 1945, he served in the U.S. Navy in World War II. Upon returning home after the war, he attended college at the University of Southern California on the GI Bill but did not finish (Gates & Shah, 1992). He served as the chief of police of the Los Angeles Police Department (LAPD) for 14 years, from 1978 to 1992.

Gates joined the LAPD in September 1949. After going to the academy, he worked in accident investigation and then was transferred to patrol (Gates & Shah, 1992). Gates was mentored by then-LAPD Police Chief William H. Parker. In 1950, he became Parker's chauffeur, and their relationship blazed a trail for Gates's career in policing (Shapiro, 1992). In 1965, as a patrol commander when the Watts riot erupted, Gates personally led lines of officers through the upheaval in order to resume control. After the riot, he was critical of the department for not providing officers with the tools and leadership to deal with civil unrest (Shapiro, 1992).

Gates became chief of the LAPD in 1978 at a time when the department's budget was particularly slim. By 1985, the department had only 6,900 sworn personnel, a ratio of 1 for every 429 inhabitants (New York and Chicago, at the time, had ratios of approximately 1 officer for every 242 inhabitants).[1] At the same time, the population of the city was exploding due to the immigration of hundreds of thousands of Hispanics and Asians to Los Angeles ("History," n.d.).

---

[1]New York had a force of 28,700 and a population of approximately 7 million; Chicago had a force of 12,399 and a population of approximately 3 million.

Among Gates's accomplishments was the master plan he developed for security at the 1984 Olympic Games held in Los Angeles ("Former Los Angeles police chief," 2003), which elevated the LAPD to being perceived as one of the top police forces in the country (Stone, 1991).

Moreover, Gates created the first Special Weapons and Tactical Team (SWAT), now a common feature of most urban police departments (Stone, 1991). Whereas in the context of SWAT, Gates's aggressive police style was praised, this style was also viewed suspiciously in the context of the battle against gangs in the city. For example, in 1988, a drug raid in south Los Angeles involving more than 80 officers turned into a rampage on four apartments where residents were harassed and beaten. The raid turned up only one ounce of cocaine and six ounces of marijuana. Subsequent lawsuits led to city settlements of $3.5 million (distributed among 52 litigants). A report on the incident, released to the public in 1991, revealed that the gang unit operated without discipline. Officers assigned to the gang task force were uncertain about who was in charge, and commanders were unsure about how to operationalize their authority. None of the operations devised were routinely reviewed by senior officers, nor were the supervisors subject to performance evaluations. Furthermore, the report documented that the war on gangs was set up in a guerrilla-like military fashion and promoted a warlike mentality among officers ("Report," 1991).

Gates founded the Drug Abuse Resistance Education (DARE) program in cooperation with the Los Angeles public schools in 1983 ("Former Los Angeles police chief," 2003). The program involved 17 one-hour sessions with a police officer who provided information about illegal drug use and its consequences as well as strategies to resist drugs. The program eventually was adopted in 70 percent of schools across the United States and has spread to 44 countries. However, empirical evaluations of the program suggest that there has been no significant reduction in actual drug use as a result of the program (Walker & Katz, 2002; Wyson et al., 1994).

Gates is credited with initiating community policing in Los Angeles. However, Goldstein (1990) indicates that one initiative in 1985 in the Wilshire area, the Community Mobilization Project (CMP), eventually reverted to traditional policing. Pressure to respond to calls for service undercut the problem-oriented approach (Goldstein, 1990), perhaps because the LAPD was stretched thin. However, media sources in the early 1990s reported that Gates's community-policing programs appeared to be effective in combating crime. As a result, during this time, Gates was a favorite of Washington politicians and was often mentioned by then-President George H. W. Bush as an effective crime fighter ("Beating crime," 1991).

Gates was known throughout his career as being prone to making inflammatory, discriminatory, and racist remarks. Within the first few weeks of his tenure, Gates stated that Hispanic officers were not being promoted at

*(continued)*

the same rate as others because they were "lazy" (Stone, 1991). In 1982, he justified the use of now-banned police choke holds that had led to the deaths of several black suspects, saying, "We may be finding that, in some blacks, when [the choke hold] is applied, the veins or arteries do not open up as fast as they do in normal people" (Domanick, 1991, p. 39). He told reporters in 1988 that a victim of a police beating was "probably lucky that's all he got." In 1990, he stated that casual drug users should be shot. The following year he called an immigrant cop killer "an El Salvadoran drunk—a drunk who doesn't belong here" (Stone, 1991, p. A9).

The most notorious incident during Gates's tenure as chief was the March 3, 1991, police beating of black motorist Rodney King, which ultimately ignited the April 29, 1992, Los Angeles riots. King, who was on parole after being convicted of robbery, was beaten 56 times with clubs and stunned with a 50,000-volt dart gun while being arrested for drunk driving The beating was caught on videotape that showed 4 officers attacking King while another 21 watched, despite a crowd of citizen onlookers ("Beating crime," 1991). Gates's initial response to the incident was to order a review of all recent police brutality complaints and to have department psychologists reinterview officers involved in such cases ("Probes," 1991, A3). However, he refused to accept any responsibility in the King incident and insisted that it was an "aberration" despite the fact that the city was then paying at least $10 million in claims to blacks and Hispanics who had been brutalized by LAPD officers (Kramer, 1991).

Pressure mounted for Gates to resign ("Probes," 1991, A3). Mayor Tom Bradley, a former police officer, initially was cautious about placing blame on Gates, but within weeks of the incident, he called for Gates to step down (Cannon, 1991). Gates was then ordered by the LA Police Commission (which includes the city council and the mayor) to take a 60-day paid leave of absence while an investigation was conducted into his potential mismanagement of the department. Gates complied but also said he would sue the commission ("The chief," 1991). Thus ensued a political battle to force Gates to resign. Legally, Gates could not be directly fired by the police commission absent proof of corruption or criminal behavior.[2]

The beating of King had a dramatic effect on public opinion in Los Angeles and around the country. Prior to the episode, 70 percent of whites in Los Angeles approved of the LAPD, but between March 1991 and May 1992, this approval rating dropped to 40 percent. The approval of blacks fell to only 14 percent in late March 1991 (Walker & Katz, 2002). According to the American Civil Liberties Union (ACLU), complaints of police

---

[2]A 1937 amendment to the city charter provided for a virtual lifetime appointment of the police chief, who could not be fired barring serious malfeasance. This policy was created as a way of insulating the police chief from the whims of politicians. At that time, police officers were dependent on political patronage (Witkin & Tharpe, 1992).

brutality in Los Angeles rose from 75 per week before King's beating to 350 weekly (Cannon, 1991). Celebrities residing in the city joined with black groups in denouncing Gates specifically. For example, actress Kim Basinger proclaimed that Gates had lost the moral authority necessary to continue as police chief. However, it appears that a majority of cops within the department supported Gates ("Beating crime," 1991). It also had a national effect; the congressional black caucus and then-Attorney General Dick Thornburg initiated two federal inquiries into police brutality on March 14, 1991 ("Beating crime," 1991).

On July 9, 1991, the Christopher Commission released a 228-page report criticizing Gates and the LAPD for a pattern of brutality, including the King beating (Orlov, 1991). Officers were routinely not disciplined for excessive use of force; 63 cops had 20 or more civilian complaints. An officer who dragged a handcuffed suspect by his feet down a hallway was recommended for a position of training recruits (Turque & Foote, 1992). The commission also discovered transcripts of racist messages between patrol-car computers (Orlov, 1991), the sheer volume of which indicated that such talk was commonplace on the job. Blacks were derided as "monkeys" and gays as "bun boys." One officer described a police helicopter "attack" of Watts in which officers were reenacting the film *Apocalypse Now* and playing "Ride of the Valkyries" from patrol-car loud speakers (Turque & Foote, 1991). There was also extensive testimony from top brass that was critical of Gates's leadership (Orlov, 1991). In an indictment of Gates, Assistant Chief David Dotson told the commission that Gates "failed miserably" in holding supervisors accountable for officers' conduct. The report recommended the replacement of Gates for—at the very least—tolerating a department saturated in racism and brutality (Turque & Foote, 1991). A subsequent Amnesty International report indicated that police brutality by the LAPD could be classified as torture as it commonly rose to the level of shootings, beatings, and electric stun-gun shocks. The report conveyed that such conduct was evident even against suspects who posed little or no threat to officer safety ("Criticism mounts," 1992).

Despite calls for his removal by citizens, celebrities, interest groups, the Christopher Commission, the mayor, and the city council, Gates soldiered on. He only reluctantly agreed to retire at the end of June 1992, not before he was the focus of even more outrage following riots on April 29, 1992. Despite assuring the city that his force was ready to deal with any unrest stemming from the King verdict, the LAPD failed to control the riots, which occurred after the officers who beat King were found not guilty. After four hours of unrest by mobs of looters and arsonists, the police had lost control of South Central Los Angeles; motorists trapped in one intersection were dragged from their cars and assaulted (Shapiro & Curry, 1992). Four days of violence led to 55 deaths and 2,000 injuries ("LAPD has changed," 2002). At the time

(*continued*)

the riots broke out, Gates was attending a political fund-raiser in Brentwood to raise money to challenge a ballot initiative that would make the police chief more accountable to elected officials ("L.A. officials," 1992; Shapiro, 1992; Shapiro & Curry, 1992). Dotson described to reporters Gates's lack of leadership in preparation for the verdict and the potential unrest. Gates reportedly refused to clarify issues around the chain of command and claimed to have a plan for dealing with unrest, yet none was shared with his commanding officers. During the first 90 minutes of the riot, Gates indicated he was in touch with his commanding officers, but this was contradicted by other accounts. In addition, there was no communication in the first hour with fire department crews waiting for police escorts (Shapiro & Curry, 1992). A report released by former FBI and CIA Director William Webster in November 1992 concurred that there was no real evidence of a workable plan to respond to the crisis. Most of the criticism in the report was leveled at Gates for misleading city officials to believe the city was ready for the verdict. Reportedly Gates, even before reading the report, called Webster and his team "liars" ("Caught off guard," 1992).

After the riots, the police commission pursued disciplinary action against Gates in order to force him out ("L.A. officials," 1992). They also secured a new police chief to follow Gates: Willie Williams, then police commissioner in Philadelphia (Tharp & Friedman, 1992; Yang, 1992). Although Gates had agreed to the June resignation, early in that month he threatened to stay on in order to spite the commission ("L.A. officials," 1992). That move would have jeopardized the appointment of Williams (a delay, due to the city charter, would effectively nullify Williams's appointment and force a new chief selection process) (Yang, 1992). Gates told the *Los Angeles Times*, "I said I was going to retire at the end of June and my feeling is now, 'Screw you. I'll retire when I want to retire'" ("L.A. officials," 1992, p. A3). A couple of days later, he denied that he was serious about the threat, stating that although he wanted to hurt the city officials, he had given his word to Williams that he was retiring (Yang, 1992).

In August 1992, Gates's autobiography, *Chief: My Life in the LAPD*, was released. It was written after the King beating but before the riots (Shapiro, 1992). Since his departure from the LAPD, Gates has maintained a public voice in criminal justice issues. At a 1996 pro-police rally in Los Angeles (following a police beating of undocumented immigrants who led police on an 80-mile chase), he spoke about the need for aggressive policing (Babwin, 1996). Gates continues to deny wrongdoing in the King beating, telling *ABC News* in 2001 that King "got whacked a few extra times" but "brought it on himself" (Werner, 2001). In a 2002 *Frontline* interview, he did concede that the King beating "looked horrible, no question about it" but claimed that it was not a racially motivated incident ("Interviews," 2001). Gates continues to defend the LAPD as the best police department in the world, but one thwarted by vindictive city politicians (Werner, 2001).

Since 1992, Gates has worked as a law enforcement consultant (Werner, 2001). In March 2003, he was named senior advisor of SAFKEY Corp., which produces a security system to prevent car theft, carjacking, and drunk driving ("Former Los Angeles police chief," 2003).

Gates, a driven leader, had a vision of what was right and wrong for the LAPD; however, this vision was implemented through assignments of tasks to individuals without particular attention given to the match between the people and these tasks. As long as the tasks were performed and accomplished, the officers were rewarded. When the tasks were not performed according to the vision, the officers were punished, but this exchange was based more on the classical transactional approach of cost-benefit exchange process than on the analysis of the real price of this exchange. A transactional leadership style can lead to ethically questionable behavior on the part of a leader. Gates's lack of sensitivity toward minorities exhibited itself in the fact that officers accused of inflammatory and racist remarks remained on the force instead of being swiftly reprimanded, disciplined, and (if necessary) removed. His lack of sensitivity toward minority communities was one of the biggest mistakes of his career, particularly when he underestimated the reaction of minority communities in the aftermath of the Rodney King incident.

But for Gates it was about a transactional exchange. Transactional leaders frequently engage in a laissez-faire type of behavior, not interfering with subordinates and empowering them in the decision-making process—as long as they deliver the desired results. His overreliance on the transactional approach led to too much empowerment of the commanding officers during the Rodney King incident and to the eruption of the riots. Leaders who use the transactional style of leadership do not become more effective regardless of whether they have the capacity to reason morally. This is because, by definition, transactional leadership is merely a dyadic exchange to satisfy individual needs (Turner et al., 2002). Gates's individual needs were closely tied to his view of what the right thing was for the LAPD; however, he never took a larger or more collaborative view of what it was that the force really needed and ultimately demanded the transaction without a more in-depth understanding of the outcomes.

## Exercise

The police chiefs detailed in this chapter have been examined through the prism of transformational theory. Using what you have learned from other theories in this book or from the summaries (as indicated in the Introduction) you have read thus far, it is possible to consider their approaches through the lens of different theories. What other theories can you find applicable to these chiefs? Are there lessons to be learned from those applications, or do those theories indicate alternative paths or approaches that might have yielded a more successful outcome?

# REFERENCES

Adding police is a priority (1997, January 28). *The Atlanta Constitution*, p. 10A.

Babwin, D. (1996, April 16). Deputies defended by Gates, crowd: The former LA police chief blasts media's handling of the beatings of undocumented immigrants. *The Press Enterprise*, p. A1.

Bass, B.M. (1985). *Leadership and performance beyond expectations*. New York: Free Press.

_____ (1999). Two decades of research and development in transformational leadership. *European Journal of Work and Organizational Psychology*, 8 (1), 9–32.

_____ & B.J. Avolio (1994). *Improving organizational effectiveness through transformational leadership*. Thousand Oaks, CA: Sage.

Bauer, T. (1999, February 23). Forum tackles policies. *The Augusta Chronicle*, p. C8.

Beating crime (1991, March 23). *Economist*, 318 (7699), p. 28.

Bennis, W.G. & B. Nanus (1985). *Leaders: The strategies for taking charge*. New York: Harper & Row.

Blackmon, D.A. (1994, November 17). Harvard's rivals? None came close. *The Atlanta Constitution*, p. C2.

Brazil, B. (2001, February 27). Minority residents accuse officers of racial profiling. *The Post and Courier*, p. B3.

Bryman, A. (1992). *Charisma and leadership in organizations*. London: Sage.

Burns, J.M. (1978). *Leadership*. New York: Harper & Row.

Cannon, L. (1991, April 8). Anti-police atmosphere as thick as smog over L.A. *Seattle Post-Intelligencer*, p. A9.

Caught off guard: A report on the L.A. riots singles out the city's former top cop as culprit (1992, November 2). *Time*, 18, p. 140.

Charleston chief, sheriff feuding over just about everything (1995, October 1). *The Herald*, p. 4B.

Chief Reuben M. Greenberg (n.d.). Retrieved May 29, 2003, from www. lsrcl.org/ Bios/greenburgbio.htm.

Conger, J. (1999). Charismatic and transformation leadership in organization: An insider's perspective on these developing streams of research. *Leadership Quarterly*, 10 (2), 145–179.

_____ & R. Kanungo (1998). *Charismatic leadership in organizations*. Thousand Oaks, CA: Sage.

Criticism mounts as Gates leaves police force: King arrested (1992, June 27). *Seattle Post-Intelligencer*, p. A3.

De Vries, R.E., R.A. Roe & T.C.B. Taillieu (1999). On charisma and the need for leadership. *European Journal of Work and Organizational Psychology*, 8 (1), 109–133.

Domanick, J. (1991, July/August). Field marshal Daryl Gates. *Mother Jones*, 16 (4), 39.

Dvir, T. & B. Shamir (2003). Follower development characteristics as predicting transformational leadership: A longitudinal field study. *Leadership Quarterly*, 14 (3), 327–344.

Dvir, T., E. Dov, B.J. Avolio & B. Shamir (2002). Impact of transformational leadership on follower development and performance: A field experiment. *Academy of Management Journal*, 45 (4), 735–744.

Fennell, E.C. (1999, June 29). Officer won't face charges. *The Post and Courier*, p. A1.

Former Los Angeles police chief Daryl Gates has a new gig (2003, March 11). *City News Service*.

Fuller, J.B., C.E. Patterson, K. Hester & D.Y. Stringer (1996). A qualitative review of research on charismatic leadership. *Psychological Reports*, 78, 271–287.

Gates, D. & D.K. Shah (1992). *Chief: My life with the LAPD*. New York: Bantam Books.

Giampetro-Meyer, A., S.J.T. Brown, M.N. Browne & N. Kubasek (1998). Do we really want more leaders in business? *Journal of Business Ethics*, 17, 1727–1736.

Goldstein, A. (1990). *Problem-oriented policing*. New York: McGraw-Hill.

Greenberg hinting at departure (1999, November 17). *The Post and Courier*, p. A1.

Greenberg mentored police chief (2002, October 11). *The Post and Courier*, p. A9.

Greenberg's remark sparks angry letter (1995, December 10). *The Post and Courier*, p. A27.

Hardin, J. (2001, July 17). Cops, city want teens off streets. *The Post and Courier*, p. A1.

Hicks, B. (2000, April 12). East Side seeks more police. *The Post and Courier*, p. B7.

History of the LAPD (n.d.). Retrieved July 7, 2003, from www.lapdonline.org/ general_information/history_of_the_lapd/gen_history_lapd.

House, R.J. (1976). A 1976 theory of charismatic leadership. In J.G. Hunt & L.L. Larson (Eds.), *Leadership: The cutting edge* (pp. 189–207). Carbondale: Southern Illinois University Press.

_____ & B. Shamir (1993). Toward the integration of transformational, charismatic, and visionary theories of leadership. In M. Chemers and R. Ayman (Eds.), *Leadership: Perspectives and research directions* (pp.81–107). New York: Academic Press.

Interviews: Daryl Gates (2001, February 27). *Frontline*. Retrieved on July 1, 2003, from www.pbs.org/wgbh/pages/frontline/shows/lapd/interviews/gates.html.

Jacobs, D. (1999, September 14). S.C. police chief: Racial profiling not the problem. *Knoxville News-Sentinel*, p. A1.

Judge, T.A. & J.E. Bono (2000). Five-factor model of personality and transformational leadership. *Journal of Applied Psychology*, 85 (5), 751–765.

Kanungo, R.N. (2001). Ethical values of transactional and transformational leaders. *Canadian Journal of Administrative Sciences*, 18 (4), 257–265.

Kramer, M. (1991, April 1). Gates: The buck doesn't stop here. *Time*, 137 (13), 25.

Kropf, S. (1999, July 29). Greenberg endorses Mrs. Dole. *The Post and Courier*, p. B3.

Kuhnert, K.W. & P. Lewis (1987). Transactional and transformational leadership: A constructive/developmental analysis. *Academy of Management Review*, 12, 648–657.

L.A. officials want police chief dismissed (1992, June 8). *Seattle Post-Intelligencer*, p. A3.

LAPD has changed in decade since rioting (2002, April 29). *USAToday.com*. Retrieved July 7, 2003, from www.usatoday.com/news/nation/2002/04/28/riots.htm.

Like he never left (2002, July/August). *Law Enforcement News*, vol. XXVIII, nos. 581, 582. Retrieved August 10, 2004, from http://www.lib.jjay.cuny.edu/len/2002/ 07.08/p & p.html.

Lowe, K.B., K.G. Kroeck & N. Sivasubramaniam (1996). Effectiveness correlates of transformation and transaction leadership: A meta-analytic review of the MLQ literature. *Leadership Quarterly*, 7, 385–425.

Lundy, S. (2002, March 17). More of a police presence appreciated by residents. *The Post and Courier*, p. 10A.

Masi, R.J. (2000). Effects of transformational leadership on subordinate motivation, empowering norms, and organizational productivity. *International Journal of Organizational Analysis*, 8 (1), 16–47.

McCauley, L. (1999, May). Measure what matters. *Fast Company*, 24, p. 97.

McCormack, F. (2002, June 6). Program teaches kids adventures of sailing. *The Post and Courier*, p. B1.

Menchaca, R. (1999, February 25). Greenberg praises department. *The Post and Courier*, p. A1.

Munday, D. (2002, June 28). Synagogue window honors chief. *The Post and Courier*, p. B3.

Orlov, R. (1991, July 21). L.A. chief Gates reportedly agrees to quit under fire. *The Seattle Times*, p. A1.

Piacente, S. (1999, August 5). Greenberg says hate crimes laws are not needed. *The Post and Courier*, p. B1.

_____ (2001, May 20). Racial profiling remarks set off Washington buzz. *The Post and Courier*, p. A1.

Porter, A. (2002, April 21). Charleston county sheriff defends use of racial profiling. *The Post and Courier*, p. A1.

Probes of police brutality: In L.A., pressure grows on chief to resign (1991, March 21). *Seattle Post-Intelligencer*, p. A3.

Report of command breakdown in police war on LA gangs (1991, June 24). *The San Francisco Chronicle*, p. A15.

Reuben M. Greenberg (n.d.). Retrieved May 29, 2003, from www.charlestonpd.org/rmgbio.html.

Rucker, A. (1995, August 9). Greenberg accused of harassment. *The Post and Courier*, p. A1.

Shamir, B., E. Zakay, E. Breinin & M. Popper (1998). Correlates of charismatic leadership behavior in military units: Subordinates' attitudes, unit characteristics, and superiors' appraisal of leader performance. *Academy of Management Journal*, 41, 387–409.

Shapiro, J.S. (1992, August 20). The law and Daryl Gates: No hail to this chief. *The Recorder*, p. 9.

Shapiro, W. & T. Curry (1992, May 18). Lessons of Los Angeles. *Time*, 139 (20), 38.

Smith, B. (2003, March 14). New gunfire detection system to begin in Charleston. *The Associated Press*, state and local wire.

Stevens, K. (2001, October 8). Greenberg considered for top job at NYPD. *The Post and Courier*, p. B3.

Stone, K. (1991, July 10). Conflict has marked Gates' tenure. *Seattle Post-Intelligencer*, p. A9.

Tharp, M. & D. Friedman (1993, August 2). New cop on the block. *U.S. News & World Report*, 115 (5), 22.

The chief takes a walk—For now (1991, April 14). *U.S. News & World Report*, 110 (14).

Tichy, N.M. & M.A. DeVanna (1990). *The transformational leader* (2nd ed.). New York: John Wiley.

Turner, N., J. Barling, O. Epitropaki & V. Milner (2002). Transformational leadership and moral reasoning. *Journal of Applied Psychology*, 87 (2), 304–311.

Turque, B. & D. Foote (1991, July 22). Damned—but defiant: A scorching report of a violent and racist LAPD. *Newsweek*, 118 (4), 22.

Walker, S. & C.M. Katz (2002). *The police in America* (4th ed.). New York: McGraw-Hill.

Walker, T. (2003, January 24). Chief suggests arms can keep businesses safe. *The Post and Courier*, p. B1.

Weber, M. (1947). The theory of social and economic organizations (T. Parsons, trans.). New York: Free Press.

Werner, E. (2001, March 3). Ex-chief still defiant: A decade later, Gates said Rodney King "brought it on himself." *ABCnews.com*. Retrieved July 1, 2003, from abcnews.go.com/sections/us/DailyNews/Rodney_king_gates010303.html.

Williams, M.P. (2000, October 27). Profiling called minor problem. *The Richmond Times Dispatch*, p. B3.

Witken, G. & M. Tharpe (1992, June 8). Police chiefs at war. *U.S. News & World Report*, 112 (22), 33–34.

Wyson, E., R. Aniskiewicz & D. Wring (1994). Truth and DARE: Tracking drug education to graduation as symbolic politics. *Social Problems*, 41, 448–471.

Yammarino, F.J., W.D. Spangler & B.M. Bass (1993). Transformational leadership and performance: A longitudinal investigation. *Leadership Quarterly*, 41, 81–102.

Yang, J.E. (1992, June 9). Chief Gates says his threat was a bluff. *The Houston Chronicle*, p. A2.

# 6

# Parameters
# for Empowerment and Trust

## *Style Theory*

## OVERVIEW OF THE THEORY

The style theory focuses on what leaders do, not who they are. Leader behavior, plus intervening variables, leads to end result variables (Yukl, 1994). In this chapter, the example of Chief Earl Sanders of the San Francisco Police Department is used to illustrate the choices one chief made in managing a scandal when his department was accused of covering up officer misconduct. The other case study focuses on Chief Dennis Nowicki; he has also faced numerous challenges during his career at the Charlotte-Mecklenburg Police Department, but his method of handling them differed significantly from Sanders's.

## OHIO STATE UNIVERSITY LEADERSHIP STUDIES

Studies first conducted by a group of researchers at Ohio State University explored the behavior of leaders rather than traits. The researchers compiled a list of approximately 1,800 types of leadership behavior and then narrowed it down to an essential 150 leadership functions. A sample of military and civilian personnel was then surveyed; the personnel rated their supervisors as to these functions.

Subsequent factor analysis of the questionnaire reflected that person-nel identified two broad dimensions of behavior: having considera-tion and initiating structure (Yukl, 1994). As described in Northouse (2004), having consideration refers to the degree to which the leader is concerned for the well-being of subordinates; this is often referred to as being relationship-oriented. Initiating structure addresses the extent to which the leader focuses on goal attainment; this is referred to in subsequent literature as task-oriented behavior.

Having consideration and initiating structure were seen as independent behavior categories, meaning that leaders could fall anywhere on the spectrum of high to low in respect to having consid-eration, irrespective of their orientation relative to initiating structure (Misumi, 1985; Yukl, 1994).

## MICHIGAN UNIVERSITY LEADERSHIP STUDIES

Another group of leadership studies was carried out by Michigan University researchers, who focused on the effect of leaders on meas-ures of group performance. A series of field studies with leaders, partic-ularly in insurance companies and railroad section gangs, compared the behavior of effective and ineffective leaders in terms of productivity (Yukl, 1994). The study led to the formulation of two main dimensions of leadership behavior: task-oriented behavior and relationship-oriented behavior.

Cartwright and Zander (1960) refer to these two functions as 1) leaders' concern with the achievement of a group goal and 2) leaders' maintenance and strengthening of the group itself. Task versus relation-ship behavior was conceptualized along a continuum (and therefore

---

### Style Theory

- What leaders do (not who they are)
- Task-oriented behavior vs. relationship-oriented behavior
- Universal theories of leadership: Most effective leaders earn a 9,9 (the highest possible score on a grid).
- Both task-oriented and relationship-oriented: Most effective leaders change the situation rather than adapt to it.

---

being high on one dimension meant being low on the other), as described in Northouse (2004). A third dimension of leadership often cited in this literature is participative leadership.

## Participative Leadership

In addition, the Michigan University studies proposed a third style category called participative leadership. This category encompasses the leader using group supervision rather than merely supervising each employee separately (Kahn, 1956; Yukl, 1994). With participative leadership, the supervisor instills in the employees a sense of responsibility as to the organizational goals and does not micromanage each small specific task. Ostensibly, this approach is better fostered when the group also has high peer loyalty. Using group meetings to solve problems and giving the employees a sense of ownership of the problems (and a hand in their solution) are also important facets of this approach (Likert, 1961).[1] The joint decision-making aspect of participative leadership can be seen as a continuum with four main categories (Yukl, 1994):

1. *Autocratic*. The leader makes decisions without soliciting any feedback from the subordinates.
2. *Consultation*. The leader solicits subordinates' opinions but makes the decision alone.
3. *Joint*. The leader discusses the decision with subordinates, and collectively the group makes the final choice, with the leader having no more influence on the choice than subordinates.
4. *Delegation*. The leader gives the group authority to make the decision, specifying only the outer limits on the choice. Prior approval in this case may not be required before implementing the decision.

Kahn (1956) places particular emphasis on delegation, noting that delegation affords the leader greater respect from subordinates. However, as Yukl (1994) notes:

> Sometimes what appears to be participation is only pretense . . . a manager may solicit ideas and suggestions from others, and then ignore them when making a decision. Likewise, the manager may ask subordinates to make a decision, but do so in such a way that the subordinates are

---

[1]In the Ohio State University studies, this dimension was incorporated within the notion of consideration (Yukl, 1994).

afraid to show initiative or deviate from the choice they know the boss prefers. (p. 84)

Bowers and Seashore (1966) came to a similar conclusion as the Michigan researchers that some form of participative leadership style correlates with effectiveness:

> [B]usiness growth is high when the agent force does *not* hold classical business ideology; when regional managers, by accepting the opinions and ideas of their agents, encourage professional development; and when managers reduce rivalries among agents by encouraging their interaction. (p. 261)

Further, unlike prior leadership studies, Bowers and Seashore did not limit their exploration of leadership to people who have formal vested authority. Attention was also given to informal leaders, making leadership independent of position in the organization.

## HARVARD UNIVERSITY STUDIES

Researchers at Harvard University have also uncovered two leadership styles. They conceptualized two types of leaders: task leaders and social-emotional leaders. The types were derived from explorations of both small groups and family units in 56 countries (Reddin, 1967), and they parallel the task-oriented and relationship-oriented styles postulated by the Michigan researchers. In one study by Zelditch (1955), the male adult in families often specialized in providing task leadership while the female adult functioned as the maintenance, or social-emotional, leader (Reddin, 1967). This distinction seems to parallel the paternalism/maternalism dichotomy often discussed in relation to the managerial grid.

## THE MANAGERIAL GRID

The managerial grid, as summarized by Northouse (2004), was designed by Blake and McCanse (1991) as a tool for leaders to assess their strengths and weaknesses. It maps behavior along two axes: concern for production (task orientation) and concern for people (relationship orientation) (Northouse, 2004). These factors are mapped on intersecting axes, where minimum concern receives the score of 1 and maximum concern receives a score of 9. Therefore, a score of 1,9 would reflect a manager with a low concern for production and a high concern for relationship.

## Managerial Grid

*1,1 (low task, low relationship) Impoverished management.* Exertion of minimum effort to get required work done is appropriate to sustain organization management. It may indicate fear of termination (negative) or desire to please (positive).

*1,9 (low task, high relationship) Country club management.* Thoughtful attention to the needs of the people for satisfying relationships leads to a comfortable, friendly organizational atmosphere and work tempo. It may indicate fear of rejection (negative) or desire to please (positive).

*9,1 (high task, low relationship) Authority-compliance management.* Efficiency in operations results from arranging conditions of work in such a way that human elements interfere to some degree. It may indicate fear of failure (negative) or desire for control, mastery, and domination (positive).

*5,5 (middle task, middle relationship) Middle-of-the-road management.* Adequate organizational performance is possible through balancing the necessity to get work out with maintaining morale of people at a satisfactory level. It may indicate fear of humiliation (negative) or desire to belong (positive).

*9,9 (high task, high relationship) Team management.* Work accomplishment is from committed people; interdependence through a common stake in organizational purpose leads to relationships of trust and respect. It may indicate fear of selfishness (negative) or desire for fulfillment through contribution (positive).

(Blake and McCanse, 1991 [as summarized by Northouse, 2004])

The managerial grid also provides a framework for understanding one's personal motivations, adding a third dimension to the task versus relationship grid, to show the positive or negative motivations that lead to that style. For example, a leader who is high in both task and relationship (9,9) may be motivated along a continuum of fear of selfishness (negative) to desire for fulfillment through contribution (positive). Furthermore, Blake and McCanse (1991) envision a grid for leaders' subordinate counterparts. The vertical and horizontal dimensions for subordinates are concern for the boss and concern for task accomplishment, respectively.

Finally, Blake and McCanse (1991) suggest that several factors are determiners of leadership style. First, organizational culture may force the leader to shift or adapt styles. Second, a leader's style corresponds to personal values he/she holds. Third, deep-rooted personal history may also dictate a leader's predisposition toward a particular style. Fourth, antiquated assumptions of there being no choice but to operate in a certain way may also lock a leader into a particular style (Blake & McCanse, 1991).

## STYLE AS A UNIVERSAL THEORY

According to Yukl (1994), the style approach led to universal theories of leadership behavior. These theories stated that the same style of leadership is effective in all situations. Most deem the high-high leaders (9,9) the most effective because they are both relationship-oriented and task-oriented (Misumi, 1985; Yukl, 1994). Blake and Moulton (1982) and Dainty (1986) also argue for one style being the most effective, a style in which the leader changes the situation rather than adapting to it. This style is again one that is high in both task and relationship orientations. Leaders who integrate both fundamental orientations can effectively use the full range of requirements in any managerial position (Bass, 1990; Stogdill, 1974).

Other researchers have considered possible situational antecedents to leaders' adoption of one or both of the fundamental styles. Managers who have immediate external pressure to produce desired outcomes are more likely to be task-oriented and less likely to nurture relationships. These theories begin to blend with situational and contingency theories (see Chapters 7 and 8), which emphasize environmental variables over the leaders' behavior style. Similarly, Stogdill (1974) concludes from a research review of tests of the style theory that the two dimensions of behavior (consideration and structure) are significant "not because they are exhibited by the leader, but because they produce differential effects on the behavior and expectations of the followers" (p. 141).

Likewise, personal antecedents to behavior have also been posited, which blend into trait theory (see Chapter 12). Some have argued that people with different temperaments differentially gravitate toward either the task or the relationship orientation (Bass, 1990).

## STYLE THEORY AND MILITARY LEADERSHIP

The Leader Behavior Description Questionnaire (LBDQ), developed by the Ohio State University researchers to gauge style, was given to military personnel in several studies in the 1950s and 1960s, as cited in Stogdill (1974) (see Table 6–1). Christner and Hemphill (1955; cited in Stogdill, 1974) found that Air Force crews in which the commander was high in consideration exhibited more friendliness, mutual confidence, conversation on duty, and willingness for combat. If the commander was high in structure, however, crew members tended to exhibit only friendliness and confidence (out of the above considerations).

**TABLE 6–1    STYLE THEORY IN MILITARY ENVIRONMENTS**

| During Training | During Combat |
|---|---|
| • Crew members' satisfaction with their commanders during training was positively related to consideration and negatively related to structure. | • Crew members felt more effective when their commanders scored high in both consideration and structure. |
| • Supervisors viewed the commanders more positively if they were high in structure and low in consideration. | • Supervisors of the commanders remained more positively oriented toward commanders high in structure. |
| • Military groups tend to be more cohesive when their leaders score high in both consideration and structure, but does cohesion translate to greater effectiveness in accomplishing organizational goals? | |

(Halpin, 1954 [as cited in Stogdill, 1974])

A study by Halpin (1954; cited in Stogdill, 1974) found that crew members' satisfaction with their commanders during training was positively related to consideration and negatively related to structure. However, superiors viewed the commanders more positively if they were high in structure and low in consideration. During combat, crew members felt more effective when their commanders scored high in both consideration and structure. Superiors of the commanders again were more positively oriented toward commanders high in structure in combat situations.

Giving the LBDQ to cadet flight members who were asked to describe 48 flight leaders, Newport (1962; as cited in Stogdill, 1974) showed that leaders who were equally high in consideration and structure differed from those who exhibited low levels of each style in the following ways. The high-high leaders desired individual freedom of expression, little resistance to social pressure, strong desire for power, and high levels of cooperativeness, and they were strong in aggressive attitudes. Fleischman (1957; as cited in Stogdill, 1974), applying the LBDQ to peer ratings of ROTC leaders, found that emergence of a leader in a leaderless group task was negatively related to consideration and positively related to structure.

Stogdill (1974) concludes that military groups tend to be more cohesive when their leaders score high in both consideration and structure. However, he remains skeptical that either measure is highly related to the groups' effectiveness of accomplishing organizational goals, whether in military or civilian organizations.

---

**Style Theory and Police Leadership**

- They studied relationships between police dispatchers and their supervisors.
- Effective communication was best facilitated when subordinates felt they received social support from their supervisors. Therefore, they responded better to managers whose style was high on the relationship-oriented continuum.

(Kirmeyer and Lin, 1987 [as cited in Bass, 1990])

---

## STYLE THEORY AND POLICE LEADERSHIP

Thus far, the only study located that relates to policing and leadership styles is the Kirmeyer and Lin study (1987; as cited in Bass 1990), which examined the relationship between police dispatchers and their supervisors. In the sample, the researchers chose 60 randomly selected dispatchers and recorded 107 face-to-face interactions between dispatchers and their bosses. Effective communication was best facilitated when subordinates felt they received social support from their supervisors, thereby suggesting that police dispatchers responded better to managers whose style was high on the relationship-oriented continuum (Bass, 1990).

## STYLE THEORY AND THE CASES OF CHIEF EARL SANDERS AND CHIEF DENNIS NOWICKI

The style leadership theory posits that leadership effectiveness is dependent on the behavior of the leader. The two broad categories that inform such behaviors are tasks and relationships, in other words, the concern for the structure of the organization and the concern for people. According to Blake and Moulton (1982), the intersection of the two behavior dimensions forms a grid of styles of management. Each leader has a style that is used in all situations. In many aspects, it is indeed sort of a universal theory of leadership due to the fact that in all leadership situations, one must consider the task to be accomplished and the people who are part of the implementation. Aspects of the careers of Chief Earl Sanders and Chief Dennis Nowicki are good examples to illustrate the style approach; however, each of them exhibits a different spectrum. Of course, it is important to remember that the purpose of this exercise is to illustrate the theories and that the career of each chief has varying facets that may not fall in line with these depictions. But to illustrate the theory, for Sanders the major consideration is relationships, or the people in his organization; for Nowicki it is tasks, or his police organization.

Although researchers contend that the high-high leaders (9,9) are the most effective leaders because they are high on both relationship orientation and task orientation, high-high (9,9) ratings are extremely unlikely (if not impossible), at least in police environments due to the inherent conflict between being relationship-oriented and meeting the demands of a critical public. It is probably possible to witness such orientation in for-profit environments, where the leaders of the organization are motivated, first and foremost, by the profit margin and where the limited level of accountability is skewed toward the interests of owners or shareholders. Such accountability does not approach the transparency and high standards demanded from police. Events of various natures and intensities are not just scrutinized and criticized internally by the Internal Affairs mechanisms; they are also frequently brought to light by members of the concerned communities and the ever-powerful media. Accountability leaves no room for cover-up, nor can a discretionary approach have even a hint of misconduct.

Traditionally, and in popular thought, police leaders who choose a relationship orientation are considered to be "cops' cops," who gain the respect and trust of the organization, but often at the expense of perpetuating a code of silence. In the cases presented, the chief who responded to allegations of misconduct with task-oriented behavior appeared more ethical, insofar as he responded to scandals with the action demanded by public and media pressure. Neither style orientation has a greater inherent moral authority, but task-oriented policing may be more conducive to the accountability demands when considered through the prism of a police leader's tremendous contribution to a healthy democratic society.

**CAREER HIGHLIGHTS**    Relationship-Oriented Style

**Chief Earl Sanders**
*San Francisco Police Department, California*

Earl Sanders was born in Nagodoches, Texas, in 1938. He moved to San Francisco alone as a teenager after his mother died. In the 1950s, he lived in a rooming house and washed dishes at night, attending high school during the day (Reiterman & Glionna, 2003c). He joined the police department in 1964 after serving in the Army (Zamora & Lelchuk, 2002).

He earned his bachelor's and master's degrees in public administration of justice (Reiterman & Glionna, 2003c).

In 1971, Sanders became a homicide detective and subsequently worked more than 300 cases (Reiterman & Glionna, 2003c). He and his partner, Napoleon Hendrix, were considered to be the best homicide investigators in the city's history. They investigated a number of prominent murders in the city (Zamora & Lelchuk, 2002).

Sanders is the founder of Officers for Justice, which initiated a lawsuit against the city on civil rights and discrimination grounds. In 1979, he testified in a federal discrimination trial about the racist jibes directed against him throughout his career by members of the department (Zamora & Lelchuk, 2002). His testimony in the federal case reportedly helped to weaken the old-boy network that had previously controlled the department ("Chief Sanders," 2003).

Sanders became the first African-American police chief in San Francisco history when he was appointed in 2002 (Reiterman & Glionna, 2003c). He inherited a 2,300-officer force, which was among the nation's worst at solving violent crime. At that time, on average, 28 percent of violent crimes were solved ("An officer," 2002). According to a *San Francisco Chronicle* investigative report, the homicide unit solved only half of its cases, compared to an average of 61 percent solved in other urban departments. Police solved less than 40 percent of murders involving black victims between the years 1997 and 2001. Murders involving white victims were solved 60 percent of the time (Van Derbeken, 2002). As a result of this report, Sanders made solving violent crime his top priority. He hired his retired partner from his days as a homicide detective, Napoleon Hendrix, to work on cold cases. He also attempted to transform promotions in the homicide unit by making them merit-based rather than seniority-based (Van Derbeken, 2002).

Sanders also increased the number of officers involved in community policing in hopes of reaching out to citizens who had become skeptical of overzealous policing ("An officer," 2002). He began a recruitment drive in order to raise the number of officers to the highest the budget allowed, 2,450 ("S.F.'s new chief," 2002).

Sanders's short term as police chief was overshadowed by a police scandal that became known as "fajitagate." The scandal stemmed from an incident that occurred on November 20, 2002. Three off-duty cops, Alex Fagan, Jr. (the assistant chief's son), David Lee, and Matt Tonsing, allegedly assaulted two men, Jade Santoro and Adam Snyder, outside a bar in the Pacific Heights neighborhood (Van Derbeken & Sward, 2002a). Santoro was beaten and required hospital treatment for a laceration on his head and a broken nose. According to the victims, the attack was unprovoked. Reportedly, the officers demanded that the victims hand over a bag of

*(continued)*

take-out food, steak fajitas. When they wouldn't comply, the officers assaulted them (Van Derbeken & Sward, 2002b).

The case, which became known as "fajitagate," evolved into an enormous scandal that reached far beyond allegations of misconduct of three off-duty officers. The nexus of the case became police protection of the offenders and cover-up of the case's mishandling. It damaged the relationship between police and prosecutors and exacerbated race relations in the city. It eventually resulted in Sanders's estrangement from the force, although he was not formally dismissed.

Initial problems with the case involved mishandling of evidence collected in the early stages of the scandal. Allegedly, investigators failed to seize the clothes the officers wore during the assault, nor did they test for blood. In addition, the two assaulted men were not permitted to make an on-the-scene identification of the officers involved. Instead, the officers were allowed to drive away without being detained, interviewed, or tested for alcohol content in their blood (Van Derbeken & Sward, 2002a). They subsequently changed clothes and were permitted to drink large quantities of water before their blood-alcohol level was tested, four hours later ("Police scandal," 2003). On November 22, 2003, District Attorney Terence Hallinan had a meeting with senior police officials during which the police were unable to explain the problems with evidence collection during the early investigation (Van Derbeken & Sward, 2002a); later press reports alleged that these problems were a deliberate police cover-up (Van Derbeken, 2003a). Assistant Chief Alex Fagan, Sr., withdrew from the investigation as his son was one of the officers, but only after the initial evidentiary mishandling (Van Derbeken & Sward, 2002a). Internal investigators encountered a wall of silence, finding members of the department hesitant to give statements (Van Derbeken & Sward, 2002b). Lieutenant Joe Dutto, who headed the internal investigation into the incident, was transferred to a less prestigious vice assignment by top officials; although the official reason given was that it occurred as part of a large-scale transfer of mid-level officers, Dutto called the transfer evidence of retaliation because he had failed to clear the officers of wrongdoing ("Chronicle," 2003; Reiterman & Glionna, 2003a, 2003b).

On February 27, 2003, the district attorney eventually indicted Sanders and Assistant Chief Alex Fagan (for conspiring to reassign Dutto, the investigator), as well as Deputy Chief David Robinson, Deputy Chief Gregory Suhr, Lieutenant Edmund Cota, Captain Greg Corrales, and Sergeant John Syme, for conspiracy to obstruct justice (by playing a more direct hand in the cover-up) (Van Derbeken, 2003a). Less than two weeks later, the district attorney dropped the charges against Sanders and Fagan Sr. for lack of evidence, and the charges against the other accused conspirators were dismissed later that year ("Charges," 2003; Van Derbeken, 2003c).

Sanders responded to early criticism by defending his department's actions; rank-and-file officers also largely supported the chief and commanders ("Police scandal," 2003). In early public comments about the criticisms of the initial investigation, Sanders compared the unjustified accusations to the biblical experience of Jesus Christ and his persecutors (Van Derbeken & Sward, 2002b). After the indictment against him was dismissed, Sanders indicated in a statement that the charges reflected an attack against the criminal justice system itself and that it was one of the worst such attacks in California history (Glionna et al., 2003). In an interview a couple of days later, Sanders defended his department's internal investigation into the assault. He stated that he disagreed with the criticisms and that the behavior he was accused of did not constitute criminal conduct; he attributed the indictments to unspecified political motivations inside and outside the department (Reiterman & Glionna, 2003c).

In the early stages, Mayor Willie Brown, also an African American, was loyal to Sanders and the top commanders and did not demand a more thorough inquiry, nor did he ask the officers to step down ("Room," 2003). Mayor Willie Brown's response to the indictment, after an emergency meeting of the police commission, was that the charges were politically motivated ("Room," 2003; "San Francisco police chief," 2003). Eventually, the mayor's support for the police turned. Only weeks after the indictment, Mayor Brown expressed frustration at the scandal, criticizing Hallinan, Sanders, and Dutto (the officer who headed the Internal Affairs investigation). Brown expressed distress at the damaged relationship between the police and prosecutors. In addition, the mayor specifically attacked Sanders for asking the state attorney general to get involved (Glionna & Reiterman, 2003).

As public disquiet increased, the press revealed unsavory aspects of the department's history of handling misconduct under Sanders and exposed the personal records of some of the officers involved. *The San Francisco Chronicle* described the department as harboring a "permissive climate," which may have contributed to the scandal (Sward & Wallace, 2003). In Sanders's first six months at the helm, only one case had been referred to the police commission for a disciplinary hearing, compared to approximately a dozen cases under the former chief (Sward & Wallace, 2003). Assistant Chief Fagan was singled out by the press to indicate a larger problem with discipline in the department. In 1990 he had threatened California Highway Patrol officers during a roadside confrontation but was never disciplined after the incident. In addition, Fagan Jr. had 16 violent encounters with suspects on his record over a 13-month period ("Police scandal," 2003).

According to the media, the black community was split about Sanders and the scandal. To the black attorneys, civic leaders, and clergy of Bay Area Police Watch, the "fajitagate" case was another example of police brutality disproportionately affecting minorities. However, the

*(continued)*

NAACP reportedly defended the police in the case and did not credit claims of a cover-up. At least one black clergyman felt that the indictments represented an attack against a black high achiever because of his success (Asimov, 2003). This clergyman led a prayer session for the chief and command staff one Sunday. A citizen commented to the press at the prayer session that the indictment represented an attack by a white liberal district attorney against a black man of leadership (Morse, 2003).

Additional questions were raised about Sanders's conduct. When he accepted the job, the city attorney was investigating Sanders's involvement in a security contract proposal at the airport, which may have involved a conflict of interest (Matier & Ross, 2002). In addition, in June 2003 a federal lawsuit was filed by two men who say they were wrongly convicted of a 1989 gang murder due to false testimony encouraged by Sanders and his partner, Hendrix. The false testimony was given by a then-14-year-old girl who later indicated that she was not at the crime scene. According to her more recent account, Sanders and Hendrix pressured her into sticking to her original story (Rosenfeld, 2003b). Allegedly, Sanders and other members of the prosecution team also suppressed a confession from an individual other than the petitioners that would have proved their innocence. Sanders had previously indicated that he did not believe the suppressed confession and suspected it was part of a gang ploy to thwart the prosecution (Rosenfeld, 2003a).

After he was indicted, Sanders stepped down from day-to-day duties, as did the six top commanders who were also indicted ("Room," 2003). However, shortly thereafter, Sanders took paid medical leave for high blood pressure, exacerbated by the stress of the indictments. Acting Assistant Chief Heather Fong took over the department (Reiterman & Glionna, 2003a), the first woman in San Francisco history to act as chief (Van Derbeken et al., 2003a). After the charges were dropped, Fagan Sr. took over the job as acting chief (Van Derbeken et al., 2003b). The mayor also stated that Sanders was welcome to resume his role as chief when his health permitted. This decision was a rebuke to the district attorney who, at the time when he dropped the charges, had specifically recommended that Sanders and Fagan Sr. not return to work, citing that they would be supervising many of the officers who may have testified against them in the grand jury (Glionna et al., 2003). Sanders resigned at the end of the year.

Chief Sanders demonstrates the pitfalls of a people-oriented police leader, based on his management of the "fajitagate" scandal involving the three off-duty police officers. Looking at the Blake and Moulton (1991) leadership grid, it is rather easy to place Sanders in the category of the country club management style. This type of leadership style is characterized by focusing more on relationships than on tasks. The assumption is that if employees are treated well, they will accomplish the tasks set before them ("being treated well" is an ambiguous concept, but in this case it meant delegating investigation to upper management). The results hardly met demands for an unbiased investigation, not surprising given the lack of supervision over a situation in which suspects included the son of the assistant chief, who was part of the upper management conducting the investigation. Sanders should have immediately removed him from handling this investigation, despite his confidence in the deputy. The task (in this case, not just conducting an unbiased investigation but also maintaining the reputation and integrity of the department) had to be of paramount importance in the decision-making process, lest the department be accused of promulgating and encouraging the infamous code of silence. Instead, relationship orientation took precedence. It might have been a noble approach, putting trust in people ahead of the task; however, in this case trust was not adequately allocated, and this misguided allocation tainted Sanders's otherwise impressive law enforcement career.

## CAREER HIGHLIGHTS    Task-Oriented Style

### Chief Dennis Nowicki
*Charlotte-Mecklenburg Police Department, North Carolina*

Dennis Nowicki holds a bachelor's degree in personnel management from Northwestern University and a master's degree in public service from DePaul University (SimpliCity, n.d.). Nowicki began his police career in 1964 at the Chicago Metropolitan Police Department, rising through the police ranks to deputy superintendent of the Bureau of Administrative Services by the time he departed the force in 1989 ("Charlotte police chief," 1999). For the following three years, he served as police chief in Joliet, Illinois, which then had 230 employees ("Charlotte police chief," 1999). In 1992 he applied for the police chief position at the Chicago Metropolitan Police Department, but ultimately he was not selected for the job (Casey, 1992). From 1992 to 1994, he was executive director of the Illinois Criminal Justice Information Authority, where he worked on developing crime-mapping technology to focus on geographic risk factors ("Charlotte police chief," 1999; Wisby, 1992). Nowicki was police chief of the Charlotte-Mecklenburg Police Department from 1994 until 1999.

In 1994, Nowicki took over the helm at the Charlotte-Mecklenburg Police Department approximately a year after Charlotte and Mecklenburg Counties merged their police forces. He oversaw a force of 1,400 employees, which included 1,200 officers ("Charlotte police," 1994). Under Nowicki, the force operated in a relatively decentralized fashion, with four services areas each headed by a deputy chief. In each service area, there were three divisions led by a captain (Bostic, 1999).

*(continued)*

According to then City Manager Wendell White, Nowicki was selected as chief because of his experience with community-oriented policing in Joliet. Community policing was targeted as the solution to Charlotte's violent crime problem ("Charlotte police," 1994). In 1993, the city had 129 murders; by 1996, this rate dropped to 74.[1] Local media credited Nowicki with the reduction, citing such community-oriented programs as Right Moves for Youth, which consisted of 160 clubs that met with a police officer, a citizen, and a teacher twice a week in every school in the county ("Violent crimes," 1997). Nowicki procured a $4.1 million COPS MORE (Making Officer Redeployment Effective) grant in 1997 ("Congressman Waite," 1997). By 1999, the department had 80 specifically designated neighborhood officers (Bostic, 1999).

Nowicki has been credited with introducing innovative technology to the Charlotte-Mecklenburg Police Department (Bostic, 1999). He implemented a videoconferencing system to streamline the process of acquiring misdemeanor criminal warrants. Officers save time driving to see a magistrate by being hooked up to the court system via teleconferences. The system cost $65,000 and was paid for by a grant from the governor's crime commission ("New teleconferencing system," 1999). Nowicki also provided each officer with laptop computers. In addition, he utilized the Geographic Information Systems (GIS) and Future Alert Contact Network (FALCON), a proactive problem alert system, in developing crime-fighting strategies in communities. For example, Nowicki studied the pattern of streetlights in the Grier Heights area in order to show that street robberies occurred where lighting was the dimmest. He then worked with the local electric company to improve lighting. Subsequently, street robberies reportedly dropped in the area (Bostic, 1999).

At the end of his tenure, Nowicki, along with Robert Guy (head of the North Carolina Department of Corrections), created Combined Enforcement and Supervision Effort (CEASE). The program consisted of police departments sharing technology, information, and police beats with area probation officers. Probation and parole officers were assigned to specific police neighborhood districts. The cooperation permitted police to quickly learn who was wanted for a violation of probation or parole and who was ignoring court-ordered curfews ("Charlotte leaders," 1999; "Charlotte-Mecklenburg police," 1999).

Nowicki's primary challenge as chief was maintaining a positive police-citizen relationship with Charlotte's black community. The fight against violent crime provoked racially charged controversies throughout North Carolina, with similar police criticism cropping up in Winston-Salem, Lumberton, Asheville, and Greensboro (Ahear & Woodall, 1994).

---

[1]This same year violent crimes dropped by 7 percent nationwide, with an 11 percent drop in murders ("Violent crime," 1997).

Citizens speculated that cases with black victims were receiving lower priority than those of white victims (Ahear & Woodall, 1994). In 1994, a city council member called for an independent investigation into the reasons for the length of time that preceded the arrest of serial killer Henry Louis Wallace, who murdered 11 black women. Ultimately, the outside audit was not undertaken. The majority of city council members agreed with Nowicki, who argued that such a review would threaten the case against Wallace. He did, however, complete an internal investigation, the results of which were presented in a closed session of the city council ("Outside police probe," 1994).

A citizen community review board was created by the city council in the fall of 1997 in response to three controversial police shootings ("Family members," 1998), including the shooting of an unarmed black motorist, Windy Gail Thompson. Internal police investigation cleared Officer Mark Framer of wrongdoing in the shooting ("Outside police probe," 1994). The second shooting involved 19-year-old James Willie Cooper, a black teenager pulled over by police during a traffic stop. According to Officer Michael Marlow, who shot him, Cooper had reached into the back of his car as though he was going to pull out a gun. Police investigations cleared Marlow in the shooting. The third incident involved the shooting of a car fleeing a checkpoint. The car was shot 22 times and a shot killed passenger Carolyn Sue Boetticher, who was riding in the backseat. According to a police statement, the officers were a short distance from the roadblock interacting with another motorist when they were radioed to stop a white Chevrolet Corsica, which had been reported stolen. The car, in which Boetticher was traveling, swerved toward Officer Shannon Jordan. He and Officer Don Belz then opened fire as the car was speeding away (Burritt, 1997).

Nowicki's tenure continued to be plagued with controversy after the creation of the review board. In 1998, a Special Weapons and Tactical (SWAT) team drug raid led to the fatal shooting of Charles Irwin Potts. According to police, Potts brandished a gun at SWAT team member James D. Guard, who then shot him. Guard was subsequently placed on administrative duty pending an internal investigation. At the time of the drug raid, 10 people were in the house and 2 of them contradicted police, telling the press that Potts did not point a gun before he was killed. Press reports quoted Nowicki: "The Charlotte-Mecklenburg Police Department is well respected for its thorough and objective investigations of police use of force. There aren't any reasons to mistrust the police department" ("Family members," 1998).

In 1999, Nowicki left policing to become a law enforcement consultant and head of the Center for Public Service and Leadership at Pfeiffer University in Charlotte ("Deputy chief," 1999). At the center, Nowicki has continued developing crime-mapping technology. Along with the Carolina Institute of Community Policing, Nowicki trained neighborhood leaders in

*(continued)*

how to use GIS to track and fight crime ("The state/police," 1999). In 2001, he was a consultant to the National Center for Children Exposed to Violence (Horn & Prendergast, 2001). Nowicki has also been a consultant to the U.S. Department of Justice Civil Rights Commission, Yale University Child Study Center, and the National Institute of Justice (SimpliCity, n.d.).

Unlike Sanders (whose career was marked by one defining incident), Nowicki faced multiple challenges throughout his career in the Charlotte-Mecklenburg Police Department. His leadership style is very consistent with task orientation, particularly in the way he initiated the structure approach in response to these challenges.

Nowicki appears to exhibit the participative style of leadership, one that emphasizes the use of group supervision rather than the supervision of each individual employee. Although the joint decision-making aspect of participative leadership can be divided into four main categories, his style seems to match specifically the delegation category, whereby the leader gives the group authority to make decisions, delineating the outer limits of their choices. The author participated in one of Nowicki's briefings of his command staff during his tenure as chief, and she vividly recalls the chief addressing his deputies on a certain issue of concern and finishing the discussion by stating the following: "I am a big believer in delegation and empowerment, but I am the one who is going to define the outer perimeter of this empowerment." It was a very telling and powerful statement that is backed not just by the words spoken during this briefing but by the events described in his biography.

Indicators of this task orientation/participative style include implementation of community policing ideas, responses to various use-of-force incidents that plagued his tenure, decentralization of the force into four service areas and empowerment of the deputy chiefs to lead these areas (if closely supervised), and many innovations and technology-driven initiatives that emphasized cooperation and high accountability. His approach was not completely devoid of relationship orientation, of course, but the task to be accomplished remained the focus of his efforts. It is difficult to imagine a scandal of "fajitagate" proportions ever occurring in Charlotte with these safeguards and priorities.

### Exercise

The police chiefs detailed in this chapter have been examined through the prism of style theory. Using what you have learned from other theories in this book or from the summaries (as indicated in the Introduction) you have read thus far, it is possible to consider their approaches through the lens of different theories. What other theories can you find applicable to these chiefs? Are there lessons to be learned from those applications, or do those theories indicate alternative paths or approaches that might have yielded a more successful outcome?

# REFERENCES

Ahear, L. & B. Woodall (1994, June 26). Civilian boards: Mixed reviews. *News & Record*, p. A3.

An officer for justice (2002, July 15). *The San Francisco Chronicle*, p. B4.

Asimov, N. (2003, March 1). Race factor evokes complex responses from blacks: Center backs Sanders, but watchdogs wary of blue uniforms. *The San Francisco Chronicle*, p. A18.

Bass, B.M. (1990). *Bass and Stogdill's handbook of leadership: A survey of theory and research*. New York: Free Press.

Blake, R.R. & A.A. McCanse (1991). *Leadership dilemmas—Grid solutions*. Houston, TX: Gulf Publishing.

Blake R.R. & J. Moulton (1982). The uncertain future of the leadership concept: Revisions and clarifications. *Journal of Applied Behavioral Science*, 18 (3), 275–291.

Bostic, H., Jr. (1999, March 3). Meeting report. Retrieved May 21, 2003, from www.charlotterotary.org/march2_99.htm.

Bowers, D.G. & S.E. Seashore (1966). Predicting organization effectiveness with a four-factor theory of leadership. *Administrative Science Quarterly*, 11, 238–263.

Burritt, C. (1997, April 10). Charlotte police defend roadblock shooting. *The Atlanta Constitution*, p. 6A.

Cartwright, D. & A. Zander (1960). *Group dynamics research and theory*. Evanston, IL: Row, Peterson.

Casey, J. (1992, February 3). City gets 40 applicants for top police post. *Chicago Sun-Times*, p. 5.

Charges against San Francisco police chief dropped (2003, March 12). *CNN.com*. Retrieved July 23, 2003, from http://cnn.com.

Charlotte leaders praise CEASE initiative (1999, May). *North Carolina Department of Corrections News*. Retrieved May 25, 2003, from http://www.doc.state.nc.us/NEWS/1999/9905news/CEASE.htm.

Charlotte-Mecklenburg police to track 8,000 criminals on probation, parole (1999, April 5). *The Associated Press*, state and local wire.

Charlotte police chief announces resignation (1999, February 15). *The Associated Press*, state and local wire.

Charlotte police recruit Chicago veteran as chief (1994, March 8). *News & Record*, p. B2.

Chief Sanders deserves better (2003, March 11). *The San Francisco Examiner*, p. 12.

Chronicle of events leading up to SF police indictments (2003, March 9). *The Associated Press*, state and local wire.

Congressman Waite announces $4 million COPS MORE grant to Charlotte (1997, January 29). Press release. Retrieved May 25, 2003, from http://www.house.gov/watt/pr970129.htm.

Dainty, P. (1986). Leadership and leadership research. *Journal of Managerial Psychology*, 1 (1), 40–43.

Deputy chief among candidates for Charlotte-Mecklenburg police (1999, August 7). *The Associated Press*, state and local wire.

Family members of slain man vow to take case to review board (1998, September 7). *The Associated Press*, state and local wire.

Glionna, J.M. & T. Reiterman (2003, March 10). S.F. mayor angry about scandal: Willie Brown says he blames himself as well as others for the police controversy. *Los Angeles Times*, Metro, p.1.

_____, T. Reiterman & M. Dolan (2003, March 12). Case against chief, top aide dropped. *Los Angeles Times*, p. 1.

Horn, D. & J. Prendergast (2001, May 15). Justice Dept. to begin police review. *The Cincinnati Enquirer*. Retrieved May 25, 2003, from http://www.enquirer.com/editions/2001/05/15/loc_justice_dept_to.html.

Kahn, R.L. (1956). The prediction of productivity. Journal of Social Issues, 12, 41–49.

Likert, R. (1961). New patterns of management. New York: McGraw-Hill.

Matier, P. & A. Ross (2002, July 14). S.F. top cop: The story behind the badge. *The San Francisco Chronicle*, p. A21.

Misumi, J. (1985). The behavioral science of leadership: An interdisciplinary Japanese research program. Ann Arbor: University of Michigan Press.

Morse, R. (2003, March 3). S.F.'s indicted police chief joins in prayer for justice. *The San Francisco Chronicle*, p. A10.

New teleconferencing system saves officer time (1999, February 26). *The Associated Press*, state and local wire.

Northouse, P.G. (2004). Leadership: Theory and practice (3rd ed.). Thousand Oaks, CA: Sage.

Outside police probe vetoed in Charlotte: Serial killer investigation (1994, May 10). *News & Record*, p. B2.

Police chief promises fair investigation into police shooting (1998, September 8). *The Associated Press*, state and local wire.

Police scandal rocks San Francisco (2003, March 4). *CBSNews.com*. Retrieved July 23, 2003, from http://www.cbsnews.com/stories/2003/03/04/national/printable542678.html.

Reddin, W.J. (1967). The 3-D management style theory. *Training and Development Journal*, 21 (4), 8–18.

Reiterman, T. & J.M. Glionna (2003a, March 5). S.F. enters plea of innocent: He and six aides are arraigned in alleged cover-up. *Los Angeles Times*, Metro, p. 1.

_____ (2003b, March 6). S.F. chief says D.A. was invited to direct probe: In a brief filed with state attorney general, police leader says he met prosecutor twice. *Los Angeles Times*, Metro, p. 1.

_____ (2003c, March 13). S.F. police chief recounts "the worst day" of his life. *Los Angeles Times*, Metro, p. 1.

Room for leadership (2003, March 4). *The San Francisco Chronicle*, p. A20.

Rosenfeld, S. (2003a, April 6). SFPD in crisis: New bombshell in old homicide. *The San Francisco Chronicle*, p. A1.

_____ (2003b, June 19). Witness: DA, cops, coached me to lie; Sanders, partner accused in tainted murder testimony. *The San Francisco Chronicle*, p. A1.

San Francisco police chief, others indicted in connection with fight. *CNN.com*. Retrieved July 23, 2003, from http://cnn.com.

S.F.'s new chief wants to be fully staffed (2002, July 20). *The San Francisco Chronicle*, p. A16.

SF police chief asks state to investigate his indictment (2003, March 1). *MSNBC.com*. Retrieved July 23, 2003, from http://stacks.msnbc.com/local/kntv/a1514201.asp.

SimpliCity (n.d.). Simply connecting citizens to government. Retrieved May 21, 2003, from www.simplicity311.com/team.htm.

Something funny is going on in Charlotte police departments (1999, January 12). *News & Record*, p. B2.

The state/police, area leaders can learn system: University offers latest anti-crime technology (1999, December 14). *Wilmington Star-News*, p. 3B.

Stogdill, R.M. (1974). *Handbook of leadership: A survey of theory and research*. New York: Free Press.

Sward, S. & B. Wallace (2003, March 2). SFPD's dismal record battling misconduct: Lawsuits, complaints, jury awards no bar to promotions. *The San Francisco Chronicle*, p. A1.

Van Derbeken, J. (2002, August 11). Homicide shakeup at SFPD: New chief changes head of troubled unit. *The San Francisco Chronicle*, p. A1.

——— & S. Sward (2002a, November 23). Mayor, chief soft-pedal cop fracas. *The San Francisco Chronicle*, p. A1.

——— & S. Sward (2002b, December 12). D.A. sees holes in probe of cops. *The San Francisco Chronicle*, p. A25.

——— (2003a, January 23). Chief defends handling of beating case: SFPD smeared by media, he tells police commission. *The San Francisco Chronicle*, p. A15.

——— (2003b, July 15). Ailing S.F. police chief vows to return to duty. *The San Francisco Chronicle*, p. A17.

——— (2003c, July 24). D.A. to refile in fajita case. *The San Francisco Chronicle*, p. A19.

———, R. Gordon & J.H. Zamora (2003a, March 4). S.F. police chief, aides step aside: Sanders on sick leave; others suspended. *The San Francisco Chronicle*, p. A1.

———, R. Gordon & J.H. Zamora (2003b, March 12). Fagan put in charge: He'll be acting chief mayor says. D.A. drops case against top cops. *The San Francisco Chronicle*, p. A1.

Violent crime in U.S. falls a record 7%, local results mixed (1997). *The Virginian-Pilot*, p. A3.

Wisby, G. (1992, September 10). Plan fights gangs, domestic violence. *Chicago Sun-Times*, p. 11.

Yukl, G. (1994). *Leadership in organizations* (3rd ed.). Englewood Cliffs, NJ: Prentice Hall.

Zamora, J.H. & I. Lelchuk (2002, July 12). New chief paid his dues for decades. *The San Francisco Chronicle*, p. A17.

Zelditch, M. (1955). Role differentiation in the nuclear family: A comparative study. In T. Parsons, R.E. Bales and J. Olds (Eds.), *Family socialization and interaction process*. Glencoe, IL: Free Press, 307–351.

# When the Event Is Just Too Much to Handle

*Situational Leadership Theory*

## OVERVIEW OF THE THEORY

Situational leadership theory focuses on what leaders should do given the nature of their subordinates. In this chapter, Montgomery County Chief Charles A. Moose (an individual who had to manage the complex and high-profile sniper shootings in suburban Washington, D.C., in the autumn of 2002) illustrates the complexity of managing a diverse set of subordinates. Los Angeles Chief Bernard Parks (whose approach to a Los Angeles Police Department already riddled with allegations of misconduct then backfired when yet another scandal, Rampart, was exposed) demonstrates the other case study. The situational theory expects leaders to vary their approach depending on their subordinates. In essence, the level of maturity of the subordinates dictates the best leadership style, building on the 3-D leadership framework developed by Reddin (1967). The theory, however, adds an effectiveness dimension (Hersey & Blanchard, 1969). According to Stogdill (1974), a meta-analysis of 124 studies of leadership traits supports "the view that leaders tend to change certain aspects of their behavior in response to changes in group task demands" (p. 16). Bass (1990) explains:

> It is apparent that the kind of leader who emerges in an organization and the individual who is successful as a leader and is evaluated as effective as a leader depends on the philosophy of the larger organization in which the leader's group is embedded. (p. 571)

Subordinate maturity is an example of a situational moderator variable (Yukl, 1994), or the factor that varies and dictates the best leadership style (consideration versus structure, or directive behaviors versus supportive behaviors) in that particular situation. It is measured in regard to the specific task to be accomplished by the subordinate. There are two components to maturity: job maturity and psychological maturity (in a later model, it is referred to as "willingness"). The first refers to the subordinate's ability; the latter refers to the subordinate's self-confidence related to the task (Yukl, 1994). Both are composite variables of what Hersey and Blanchard take to be the main factors involved in maturity (Yukl, 1994). For example, job maturity focuses on the ability the subordinate has, which is a function of knowledge, experience, and skill. Willingness is operationalized as the extent to which the employee has confidence, commitment, and motivation for the work (Fernandez & Vecchio, 1997).

Northouse (2004) puts forth the broad outlines of the theory, originally conceptualized as life cycle theory; it was later modified and renamed situational leadership by Hersey and Blanchard. They start with the basic premise that there is no normative or best style of leadership. Successful leaders are those who are flexible enough to adapt and accommodate to their followers (Hersey & Blanchard, 1969). They also advocate thinking of the workplace structure as a team rather than a pyramid, in terms of the roles to be played. Thus, leaders exist to help the followers accomplish organizational goals. Implied by this are duties such as performance planning, day-to-day coaching and counseling, and performance evaluations based on measurable objective criteria. Goals are determined based on the criteria suggested by the acronym SMART (specific, measurable, attainable, relevant, and trackable) (Blanchard et al., 1985).

Moreover, underpinning the theory is the notion that organizations are open systems, meaning that what takes place outside a system is likely to affect what happens inside the system (Bass, 1990). Subordinate maturity, therefore, is a function of preceding experiences of subordinates that shape both their ability to complete task objectives and their psychological maturity.

Empirically, there seems to be more support for the notion that job maturity, rather than willingness or psychological maturity, is the critical follower attribute (Fernandez & Vecchio, 1997). However, the notion of maturity has been criticized as unduly ambiguous when researchers attempt to empirically test the theory (Graeff, 1983; Yukl, 1994). Furthermore, empirical testers have found that there is weak support for the validity of the theory, particularly because of a poor theoretical foundation for the hypothesized relationship among the variables (Graeff, 1997). In addition, the Leadership Effectiveness and Adaptability Description (LEAD) instrument used to match follower orientation with leadership style has been considered biased against the use of low task/low relationship style (Dainty, 1986; Graeff, 1997). Despite numerous criticisms, however, the theory survives primarily because it has strong intuitive appeal; it has also benefited from being a management fad in the 1980s (Graeff, 1997).

Chadbourne (1980) uses the notion of subordinate maturity to determine trainers' leadership styles when teaching trainees. She describes the organic development of a training group. In the beginning, "the leader takes initial responsibility for building a conducive learning climate through structuring, modeling effective behaviors and providing didactic input" (p. 55). In the middle stages of the training, the leader encourages team building through small-group activities (with less structure flowing directly from the leader), which provide time for reflection on the material to be learned. Finally, as the trainees gain job and psychological maturity related to the training material, the leader has effectively provided the trainees with the opportunity to pursue their goals and personal growth on their own.

In addition, the theory suggests that the reverse operation of the above schematic is possible. Leaders' behavior can hypothetically influence the subordinates' level of maturity. According to Hersey and Blanchard, they can utilize developmental interventions in order to create the level of maturity desired. In the event that the leader and subordinate disagree as to the subordinate's level of maturity, the leader may need to concede to the subordinate's view in order to maintain the task environment. As Bryman (1986) speculates: "This possibility forces one to question how far the maturity level of subordinates is a deterministic model, if the leader may have to adopt what he believes to be an inappropriate style in terms of his own assessment" (p. 148).

One developmental intervention is contingency contracting. This involves a negotiated agreement between the leader and the subordinate about the tasks and objectives and the leader's role in accomplishing the desired outcomes. By creating such a predetermined plan of attack, which challenges the subordinate within the realistic limitations of his/her abilities, the subordinate can reach a higher maturity level (Yukl, 1994).

Rewarding subordinates is implied by the theory as well. Blanchard and Nelson (1996) explain that the best managers not only provide the direction and support commensurate with maturity but also recognize employees for their efforts. This can assist the leader in communicating that the achievement of high maturity and task effectiveness, though requiring hard work, is not without reward. However, regardless of subordinates' stage of maturity, each stage has a corresponding best practice for providing recognition: S1 types (enthusiastic beginners with low maturity) need the attention of specific direction and redirection on a daily basis; S2 types (disillusioned learners) need feedback on their performance and face-to-face praise; S3 types (capable but cautious learners) need public praise and perhaps an award such as a photo on a "wall of fame"; and S4 types (self-reliant achievers with high maturity) require similar public rewards as the S3 but can also be rewarded by being given the task of training other, less mature workers.

## SITUATIONAL LEADERSHIP THEORY AND EMPLOYEE BURNOUT

Niehouse (1984) states that the theory has particular applicability when confronting employee burnout, the symptoms of which include chronic fatigue, job boredom, cynicism, lack of recognition, less commitment, moodiness, poor concentration, and physiological changes. Niehouse (1984) argues that leadership decisions can affect employees negatively when not applied in a way that is appropriate both to the situation and to the subordinates' level of maturity, creating a fight-or-flight syndrome which then leads to burnout. "Dealing with organizational causes [of burnout] is a function of managerial effectiveness through appropriate leadership behavior" (p. 85). Borrowing from situational leadership theory, Niehouse states that, for example, burnout can occur easily when a leader provides too much structure to a mature capable employee. However, besides appropriate style, Niehouse suggests that any leadership changes should be implemented gradually, without ambiguity and with realistic goals in mind.

## SIMPLIFIED SITUATIONAL LEADERSHIP THEORY

Van Auken (1992) proposes a simplified version of situational leadership theory. He puts forth four main leadership situations and the styles they demand:

1. *The political arena.* Issues such as vacation schedules and work design problems fall into this category because employees have a stake in the outcomes, although they are not the substantive issues of the work at hand. In this situation, the supervisor functions with a "politician" style in trying to keep "constituents" happy.

2. *The bureaucratic arena.* Routine operations, such as ordering inventory, require decisions best made without subordinate involvement in order not to needlessly waste subordinates' time.

3. *The technical arena.* Technical problems are an opportunity to solicit subordinate involvement in problem solving in an informal manner. Even if the problem has a minor effect on employees, they are flattered to be asked to weigh in on the issue.

4. *The professional arena.* Participative management is ideal when subordinates are affected by an issue and have the skills to handle it. Setting goals and creating deadlines are examples of issues in which the leader would be foolhardy not to involve employees. Consensus building on key issues keeps subordinates happy and functional.

## POLITICS AND SITUATIONAL LEADERSHIP THEORY

In the political realm, leadership style exists along a continuum from centralized authoritarian leadership to participative democracy. The leadership question then becomes under what societal conditions leaders should adopt one of the two styles. According to Korten (1962), the situational moderator variables are either high goal structure or low goal structure. In high goal structure, groups in society have specific goals that they have determined via consensus. In low goal structure, groups have fewer shared objectives; the emphasis is on individual rather than shared goals. From the above, Korten envisions a four-cell matrix with structural variables on one axis and leadership styles on the other. Intervening is also a stress variable. A group's perception of immediate threats, and the anxiety or stress caused by such

---

**Individuals vs. Group Subsystems**
- What happens is not as important as how you react to what happens.
- Police leaders are constantly confronted with conflict. How they manage it is their litmus test.

**Two dimensions to manage**
- Internal
- External

---

threats, determines shifts in the style. Political leadership that is particularly autocratic is more appropriate in situations in which there are stressful ambiguities, in which immediate reaction is deemed necessary, and in which there is consensus on society-wide goals. However, authoritarian leadership cannot maintain itself without stress. When the stress or crisis subsides, individual needs will be the priority, and participative democracy can better satisfy such needs. This political or crisis theory dovetails with aspects of this theory that might be most applicable to policing, discussed above.

## POLICING AND SITUATIONAL LEADERSHIP THEORY

Hersey and Blanchard (1969) indicate that a high task style is the most appropriate for crisis-oriented organizations. This is because success in stressful situations often depends on unequivocal responses to orders from leaders. Therefore, it is likely that Hersey and Blanchard would

---

| Types of Conflict | Conflict Factors |
|---|---|
| Intrapersonal | Power |
| Interpersonal | Control |
| Structural | Frustration |
| Strategic | |
| Community | |

**Conflict as a Dynamic Process**
- *Latent conflict.* Condition exists but is not recognized.
- *Perceived conflict.* Condition is recognized by both parties.
- *Felt conflict.* Internal tensions exist but are not apparent.
- *Manifest conflict.* Conflict is open and obvious to involved parties.
- *Conflict aftermath.* New conflict or cooperation results.

---

apply the high task style to police agencies. Bass (1990) similarly argues that unstable environments lead to organizational policies that are less uniform. Leadership styles will change to be flexible and to respond to the ever-changing reality. Crime-control agencies can also be said to operate in a world of shifting crime trends and crime-control strategies.

Consistent with the above and drawing from Hersey and Blanchard (1977), Kuykendall and Unsinger (1982) surveyed police supervisors and found that the most common management style was one that was high task and high relationship, as defined under style leadership (see Chapter 6) and situational leadership theories. The other frameworks that respondents could select from included "Great Man" (trait theory; see Chapter 12), environmental (time, place, and circumstance), exchange (of mutual rewards), humanistic (intersection of individual and organizational interests), and interaction-expectation (ability to interact to get a desired response in subordinates).

Kuykendall and Unsinger administered Hersey and Blanchard's LEAD instrument to 155 police managers during seven managerial training programs in Arizona and California in 1978, 1979, and 1980. The instrument measures managerial style range and adaptability; style range refers to the number of styles a leader uses, and adaptability refers to the ability of the manager to fit the style to the situation. Police managers were given the instrument at the beginning of the training program. The managers were asked to respond to the scenarios described, using the available task- or relationship-oriented styles, as they would in the workplace. There were four styles to choose from:

1. *Telling*. This style refers to high task, low relationship orientations.
2. *Selling*. This style is characterized by high task and high relationship approaches.
3. *Participating*. This encompasses high relationship, low task orientations.
4. *Delegating*. This reflects low relationship, low task approaches.

Descriptive information about the sample included that slightly less than one-half of the managers came from departments of 100 or more personnel. All but one manager had at least five years of police experience. All but 12 had some college education, and 72 indicated that they had four years or more of higher education.

Most managers indicated that they either had no dominant style or utilized a selling approach (high task, high relationship). None of the managers used all four possible styles, but 97 percent used two or three styles. The instrument also provides effectiveness scores. The scores reflected that 80 percent of the managers were somewhat to very effective. The instrument also measures to what degree the police managers were able to match the style to the situation. Results reflected that managers were most effective with a high task emphasis (selling and telling) and were least effective with low task approaches (participating and delegating). Delegating was the style that was rarely used (102 managers did not use it at all, and 31 managers used it only once). The analysis further showed that 78 percent of police managers tended to use participating/telling and telling/selling combinations. Selling was the most common management style employed. Hersey and Blanchard consider the selling style a safe approach because it is an effective style in most situations, even when it is not the most effective option.

The authors posit that the lack of delegation style may be unique to police environments. Delegation may counter the occupational emphasis on action over inaction. According to the authors, delegation is inactive. The factors that may contribute to the action imperative are 1) a self-perception about the role of policing, 2) the reform model of police thinking that dominated the 20th century, 3) a perception of behavior that is desirable under stressful situations, and 4) the consequences of "looking bad" in police work.

> Admittedly, the variety of situations in which police can become involved are, perhaps, unlimited. And the range of possible responses considered effective may be a function of the specific problem and its situational context. This, of course, means that providing definitive guidelines for what to do is extremely difficult. However, this often leaves the police in the position of being told they were wrong after a decision without previous guidance as to what was considered "right." Lacking such guidance, some police officers tend to "play it safe" while police managers come to believe that they must monitor the decisions made by their subordinates. (Kuykendall & Unsiner, p. 320)

Situational leadership continues to be a model advocated in police environments. The Community Policing Consortium (1997) presents situational leadership as the theoretical model underpinning the strategies it teaches as part of its training for police supervisors. Its advocacy of the model is based on its flexibility in getting others to act in accordance with organizational values. Citing Hersey (1985), the Community Policing Consortium provides training that encourages police supervisors to diagnose an officer's ability and willingness to perform a task (the employee's readiness, indicated by observable skills, experience, and training) and to assess the best level of relationship and task behavior to apply in that situation.

## Situational Leadership Theory and the Cases of Chief Charles A. Moose and Chief Bernard Parks

Situational leadership theory emphasizes the importance of a given situation or event that a leader faces. The way the leader chooses to behave is directly dependent on the assessment of the subordinates and their level of commitment and competence. The level of intervention within any given situation will depend on the level of willingness and readiness of the police officers involved.

The two chiefs identified for this chapter represent two different approaches to the situational leadership style. Chief Charles A. Moose

---

### Overview of Situational Leadership Theories

Situational leadership refers to the interaction between these factors:

- Amount of guidance and direction (task behavior) a leader gives
- Amount of socioemotional support (relationship behavior) a leader provides
- Readiness level that followers exhibit in performing a specific task, function, or objective

Four styles of situational leadership:

*Style 1 (S1).* Characterized by above-average amounts of task behavior and below-average amounts of relationship behavior

*Style 2 (S2).* Characterized by above-average amounts of both task and relationship behaviors

*Style 3 (S3).* Characterized by above-average amounts of relationship behavior and below-average amounts of task behavior

*Style 4 (S4).* Characterized by below-average amounts of both relationship and task behaviors

Effectiveness of each style is dependent on the given situation.

(Developed by Hersey and Blanchard, 1969 [later refined by Hersey and Blanchard, 1977, 1988, 1993; Blanchard et al., 1985, 1993])

---

exemplifies the style 1 (S1) level of leadership, exhibiting above-average orientation toward the task while little time is allocated to the supportive mechanisms. When achievement of the task becomes the primary orientation, subordinates can be prevented from providing input and their feelings are minimized. Chief Bernard Parks, on the other end, displayed the other extreme, the style 4 (S4) level of leadership. In this approach, also known as the delegating style, the leader is convinced that his/her involvement in both task and relationship can be minimized and in essence gives control over to the subordinates. Of course, as much as the situations chosen to illustrate the theory for each chief are very much defining aspects of their careers, their careers likewise contain many facets that may run contrary to situational theory. The point here is to illustrate the theory and should by no means be interpreted to mean that in all situations the chiefs used these methods.

**CAREER HIGHLIGHTS    Situational Leadership Style (S1)**

Chief Charles A. Moose
*Police Bureau, Portland, Oregon;*
*and County Police Department, Montgomery, Maryland*

Charles A. Moose was a celebrated and high-profile police chief even before the national spotlight focused on him in the fall of 2002 when he oversaw the investigation of sniper shootings in suburban Washington, D.C.

Moose was born in 1953 in New York City while his father was attending Columbia University. The family left the city for Lexington, North Carolina, when he was a toddler. Moose, an African-American, attended segregated schools through the sixth grade. He attended the University of North Carolina, Chapel Hill, earning a degree in U.S. history. While in college, he intended to go to law school, but a professor encouraged him to take a police exam to earn extra credit. During his senior year, he was offered a job as a police officer in Portland, Oregon, which he accepted. He intended to police for a few years before turning to law school but has remained in policing ever since (Fermino & Kranes, 2002).

Moose joined the Portland Police Bureau in 1975 (Bernstein, 1999a). While an officer, he attended the 154th session of the FBI National Academy in 1988 ("Vital Stats," n.d.). He later earned a master's degree in public administration in 1984 and a Ph.D. in urban studies and criminology in 1993 from Portland State University. He has one academic publication in a peer-reviewed journal about the impact of community-policing values on the implementation of a domestic violence reduction strategy in

*(continued)*

Portland, Oregon, which appeared in *Crime and Delinquency* in 1997. He was on the adjunct faculty in criminal justice at Portland State University from 1994 to 1995. From 2000 until the present, he has been on the adjunct faculty at Montgomery College ("Vital Stats," n.d.).

Racial issues have always been a point of tension for Moose. Between 1975 and 1992, he was disciplined four times for excessive anger at people he thought were discriminating against him while on the job (Bernstein, 1999c; Fermino & Kranes, 2002). In 1992, he blew up at a retail clerk he thought was not serving him and shouted, "Does my skin have to turn white to get help?" (Sisk, 2002).

## Chief of the Portland Police Bureau (1993–1999)

Moose served as chief of the Portland Police Bureau from 1993 to 1999. Among controversies in Moose's tenure as police chief in Portland was his decision to use shotguns loaded with beanbags to control crowds. The beanbag rounds are made of nylon sacks filled with lead shot that are designed to injure but not kill. The issue was brought to the fore on August 17, 1998, when approximately 40 people, protesting the closure of a park in the King neighborhood of the city (where Moose also lived) protested in front of his house. Police used the beanbag ammunition against the crowd. Moose justified the decision later by saying that the ammunition was more safe and effective than other options. He also stated in a public forum that he and his wife had made the wrong decision to live in the King section of Portland, an area with an African-American majority and a high crime rate (Greimel, 1998). Originally, in late 1993, he indicated that he bought the house in King to signal that he was committed to rebuilding the neighborhood and to promote community policing. He believed that community-policing ideals included the concept that officers should live in the communities they protect (Nkrumah, 1999).

In January 1999, Moose took over the school police in Portland, which had been operating independently of the police force. The impetus for the change was cutting administrative costs of policing schools by the city. The decision was unpopular among school officers who were concerned about internal upheaval and career paths ("Plan," 1999).

In a popular move, Moose and Portland-area police chiefs signed a joint resolution in April 1999 denouncing racial profiling by police conducting traffic stops. According to the U.S. Department of Justice, it was the first such resolution by law enforcement officials in the nation. The resolution, drafted by Moose, was a response to increased criticism that police target minorities disproportionately in automobile stops. Contemporaneously, Attorney General Janet Reno had called for increased data collection to identify the scope of the problem. Moose, in statements to the press, appeared ready to be accountable to the public for any future such profiling when he said, "If we're perceived to be engaging in this behavior, I expect to get this document back in my face" (Oshiro, 1999, p. A1).

The chief had been praised throughout his tenure for developing community policing (Bernstein, 1999a), receiving $26.6 million in federal and state money, some of which was used to hire 60 additional officers. For example, he had regular meetings with community leaders, called "Chief's Forums" (Bernstein, 1999c). He also raised the bar on the educational background required of new recruits to a four-year college degree (Bernstein, 1999a). Officers praised Moose for choosing to wear his uniform and not losing his connection to the street (Bernstein, 1999c).

However, he received criticism for his occasional angry outbursts (Bernstein, 1999a). One media source reported that he was ordered to take anger management classes while Portland's police chief (Duin, 2002). His style of management was described by the media as "heavy-handed" (Bernstein, 1999c). Charles Makinney, who headed the bureau's fiscal and records division from 1981 to 1994, told reporters, "[H]is ability to deal as a manager was horrendous. If he was able to deal with personnel better, I think he would have been a better chief" (Bernstein, 1999c, p. A1). The subsequent fiscal and records manager, Nancy Dunford, who resigned in 1997 after clashing with Moose, said, "He wasn't able to generate community spirit in his own bureau. People were attacked. It was dictatorial, not participatory" (Bernstein, 1999c, p. A1). During the city's investigation of the use of bean-bag-style ammunition, Moose yelled at the mayor and city commissioners, saying that the inquiry was a waste of time (Barnett, 2002; Bernstein, 1999c).

Moose was also criticized for his handling of internal police investigations (Bernstein, 1999a). In 1996, he investigated a central precinct commander over allegations the commander routinely hired male prostitutes. Although the commander was not indicted, Moose sought to terminate his career. The commander then filed a federal lawsuit against Moose, claiming he was investigated because he was gay. In addition, in April 1997, Moose disciplined two commanders for using their work-issue cell phones for personal calls; then he changed his mind and returned them to work without discipline. He subsequently disallowed all officers' use of city cell phones, angering officers and the community (Bernstein, 1999c).

On September 13, 1997, David Moose, the chief's then-17-year-old son (by his first wife), and his 16-year-old friend were arrested for possession and distribution of an undisclosed amount of crack cocaine. He was booked in juvenile detention but released the same day on bail. According to news reports, Moose praised his officers for making the arrest even though they were aware that the suspect was his son ("Son," 1997). The charges were subsequently dismissed in court because the drugs were discovered pursuant to an illegal search and seizure during a stop for jaywalking (Video Monitoring Service, 1997).

(continued)

Upon his departure from Portland to take the police chief job in Maryland, the governor declared June 28, 1999, Chief Charles A. Moose Day for his leadership in law enforcement and his commitment to community-oriented policing. The Oregon Association of Chiefs of Police gave Moose its President's Award for promoting a diverse police force and for reaching out to the community (Bernstein, 1999b).

## Police Chief of Montgomery County (1999–2003)

Moose had unsuccessfully sought a position as police chief in Washington, D.C. (Bernstein, 1999a). He took over the Montgomery County Police in suburban Rockville, Maryland, in August 1999, after Montgomery County Executive Douglas Duncan stated that Moose was "a natural leader" and recruited him (Sisk, 2002). Upon instatement, Moose indicated that he planned to confront racial issues. When his tenure began, the U.S. Department of Justice was conducting a review of deadly use of force in the county after several police shootings involving minorities (Holly, 1999).

In the fall of 2002, two snipers, John Lee Malvo and John Mohammad, held the public in fear for weeks as they carried out sniping attacks against random civilians. Moose headed the high-profile investigation involving thousands of law enforcement officers from local, state, and federal agencies. He was hailed by the public after the capture of the two snipers. President George Bush was compelled at one point during the investigation to say that the FBI would not be taking over the investigation for Moose, as they had hoped to do (Sisk, 2002). After the investigation, media coverage suggested that Moose had become "America's policeman" (Kennedy & Becker, 2002). As one source reported, "He was unprepared, unrehearsed and seemingly incapable of staying calm in the face of the growing carnage. . . . Moose then was the perfect metaphor for [the public's sense of] helplessness" (Duin, 2002, p. A1). On November 24, 2002, people wore moose antlers made of purple foam in his honor in a parade ("Parade," 2002). Subsequently, Moose was in high demand as a public speaker (Manning, 2003). He spoke at such venues as the American Leadership Forum of Oregon (Tsao, 2003); he was also featured in a national television interview by Barbara Walters (Terzian, 2003).

Despite the successful outcome in the sniper investigation, Moose was criticized for his handling of the case (Sisk, 2002). One of the criticisms revolved around the information he gave the public, which some have said incited fear rather than reassurance. For example, early on in the crisis he stated that the elusive sniper "may be gloating" nearby (Clines, 2002, p. A12). Furthermore, the police union formed a special committee to investigate his handling of lookout information during the manhunt.

Officials believe that Moose endangered patrol officers by withholding critical information, in violation of a recently signed labor contract in which Moose agreed to a safety provision involving the sharing of information with officers. In April 2003, testimony was heard from detectives who worked the sniper manhunt that indicated Moose may have held back information about the snipers' physical descriptions. There was also evidence that he had identified the suspects as early as October 22, 2002 (Sperry, 2003). However, Moose continued to allow the police and the public to search for unidentified white suspects in a white van instead of the allegedly then-identified black suspects in a blue Chevrolet Caprice (Malkin, 2003; Washington, 2002).

In addition, Moose's volatile temperament, cited throughout his career, returned, this time in the public spotlight. He cried in front of the media while reporting the sniper shooting of a 13-year-old. He also lashed out at the media for reporting about a note, "I am God," left by the sniper on a tarot card depicting the skeletal figure of Death (Barnett, 2002). In yet another emotional display, while debasing former cops and FBI profilers who had speculated about the killer on television, he threatened to turn the case over to the media: "[A]nd you can solve it" (Kennedy, 2002, p. 7).

In January 2003, *The Washington Post* reported that Moose signed book and movie deals based on his leadership role in the sniper investigation ("Top sniper cop," 2003; Tsao, 2003). One deal was made with E.P. Dutton publishers in which Moose was to write a first-person account of the sniper investigations. The second deal was for a television movie with a Hollywood production company. In addition, after the sniper investigation, he and his wife, Sandy Moose, started a crisis-management consulting company, which has not yet been profitable (Terzian, 2003). The deals and consulting company triggered a Montgomery County Ethics Commission hearing. According to the relevant county ethics law, a public employee is not permitted to intentionally use the prestige of a public office for private gain (Manning, 2003).

In late March 2003, the ethics panel ruled unanimously that Moose could not write a book or consult for a movie based on the sniper suspects while also serving as the county's police chief. His biggest supporter, County Executive Douglas Duncan, lobbied for the ethics panel to give him a waiver or to create legislation with an exception to the rule (Terzian, 2003). Losing the battle, Moose resigned from the force at the end of June 2003; in September 2003, he released his book about his career and the sniper investigations: *Three Weeks in October: The Manhunt for the Serial Sniper* ("Charles Moose," 2003; "Statement," 2003).

Throughout his career, Chief Moose has displayed a very low level of control over his emotional intelligence (EQ), for example, by shedding tears on national television and having characteristic angry outbursts.
*(continued)*

During times of crisis and fear, a chief of police must display to the public strength and reassurance, qualities which demand complete control over EQ. If a chief breaks down, then the message sent to the general public is vulnerability, the last emotion a person in a position of leadership should convey or want to convey.

However, this emotionalism was even more damaging given that his overall leadership is a style that Hersey and Blanchard would define as a directing style—high directive and low supportive. Indications of this style and its negative aspects emerged in Portland when his style was described as "dictatorial," and by his contradictory and confusing response to cell-phone usage policy. However, the style was particularly highlighted in the high-profile tense and fear-ridden period of the sniper crisis, in which directive was the least desirable style to adopt. Two factors are characteristic of his approach: the way he handled data information during the sniper investigation and the way this information was shared (or not shared) with the involved law enforcement parties. Especially telling were the accusations of his withholding a critical piece of information and (by doing so) endangering patrol officers who were searching for the suspects. Although his behavior was not malicious in nature but rather an error of judgment, such mistakes are highlighted by increased publicity and scrutiny. To some extent, the directive style is somewhat inevitable in the complex environment of this high-profile investigation, which involved numerous law enforcement bodies and competing jurisdictions. In order to be able to display a more confident style of leadership (for example, S2 or S3), one must have insight into one's subordinates and shine less of a spotlight on their every move.

The desire to keep subordinates on a tight leash, minimizing empowerment, is frequently an outcome of a particular necessity rather than an ego trip. This directing approach can only be received well coming from somebody who is perceived as very knowledgeable and experienced in a situation in which subordinates truly lack the readiness to complete a task. While Moose had the experience, he demonstrated a lack of knowledge with regard to the steps to be taken in order to solve the case. Less task direction and more coaching and delegation of the subordinates would have resulted in much more support for him and his way of leadership during this time of crisis of national proportion.

Lastly, in the case of the sniper investigation, the display of weakness on national television only exacerbated the shortcomings of Moose's S1 approach. The public are not the only ones who suffer from such a breakdown; police officers, who look to their leader for guidance and coaching, rather than just dry directions on how to do things, are also likely to be alienated by the directive style.

CAREER HIGHLIGHTS   Situational Leadership Style (S4)

Chief Bernard Parks
*Los Angeles Police Department, California*

Bernard Parks was born in Beaumont, Texas, on December 7, 1943 ("Full biography," 2003). He received a bachelor's of science degree from Pepperdine University ("Full biography," 2003). Parks then earned a master's degree in public administration at the University of Southern California in 1976. He entered the Los Angeles Police Department (LAPD) in 1965 and is a veteran of the department's Internal Affairs Division (Wilborn, 2002).

Bernard Parks served as chief of the Los Angeles Police Department from 1997 to 2002. Upon becoming chief, Parks outlined several goals for the department, including "moderately" reorganizing the command staff, increasing the budget to support officer fitness programs, improving the working relationship between the department and other city agencies, and launching a type of Command Accountability Strategies (COMPSTAT) program in order to develop better crime prevention strategies (McGreevy, 1997). Regarding the latter, the chief indicated a desire to focus on "quality-of-life" crimes and gang activity in order to improve neighborhood security (Stewart, 1997). Parks also persuaded the police commission to designate money to improve police facilities in order to make stations more attractive for citizens. Improvements included access ramps for the disabled and correction of unsafe building conditions (Berbeo, 1998e). Reportedly, the former police chief, Willie Williams, had refused to develop any of these community-policing techniques (Stewart, 1997).

Regarding the reorganization of command staff, Parks eliminated the department's three assistant chief positions in order to have more direct control over the rank and file (Morgan, 1997). He also implemented a mandatory four-hour training session on ethics and workplace violence in an effort to reduce lawsuits against the police (Berbeo, 1998a). In addition, Parks established a Financial Crimes Division to focus on white-collar crimes such as major fraud, trademark infringement, computer crime, and elder abuse. He indicated that he was able to devote officers to these crimes because the violent crime rate was lower than in many years. Parks also initiated a recruitment drive to increase the force by 1,000 officers (there were 9,500 officers on the force in 1998) using federal COPS MORE II funds (Berbeo, 1998b).

In 1998, Parks successfully urged the police commission to add automatic handguns and rifles to the arsenal of patrol weapons available to specially trained officers. According to Parks, the weapons would be more accessible to officers during critical events. The idea stemmed from the February 28, 1997, North Hollywood bank robbery shootout in which officers were outgunned by robbers; 10 officers were wounded in the incident ("Police commission," 1998).

*(continued)*

After his first year as chief, Parks received good reviews from community leaders. The human relations commission, a city reform panel founded after the Watts riots, indicated that community members largely approved of Parks. A similar opinion was expressed by members of the Los Angeles Urban League. Parks attributed the good reviews to his revision of use-of-force methods, training, and policies. In the 18 months preceding August 1998, only three use-of-force complaints had been entered against police (Berbeo, 1998c). At the same time, Parks supported the Special Investigation section of the department, an elite detective squad that was trained to use extreme force and was heavily armed. The unit had been criticized for threatening the safety of bystanders during their operations and was the subject of several federal lawsuits. *The Los Angeles Times* reported that the squad had wounded dozens of innocent people during its previous 33 years of operation, yet the unit made an average of only 45 arrests per year ("Critics question," 1998). Parks also defended LAPD's pursuit policy from criticism following an October 14, 1997, crash during a police chase that killed a woman and seriously injured her daughter. He indicated that to outlaw police chases in the city would allow criminals to run amok. He also stated that it would be irrational to make a change in policy based on the emotion evoked by a particular crash (Koval, 1997).

In addition, Parks raised the standards of conduct for officers, according to an independent report by the Los Angeles Police Commission. The improvements included policies that help to identify at-risk officers and a range of disciplinary responses to address poor conduct (Berbeo, 1998d). Parks focused on discipline as a way of addressing the recommendations of the 1991 Christopher Commission (sparked by the beating of Rodney King). He started a pilot program to put video cameras in patrol cars to discourage misconduct and to clear officers who may be wrongly accused of abuse (McGreevy, 1998).

Due to the above-noted focus on officer discipline, Parks struggled to keep good relations with the rank and file. Early in his tenure, officers were critical of his decision to end compressed work schedules ("Bernard Parks," 1997). Many negatively characterized Parks as a strict disciplinarian (Berbeo, 1998a). Conflict between the Los Angeles Police Protective League (LAPPL) and Parks over when and how officers should be punished plagued his tenure. The LAPPL claimed that officers were terrorized by the possibility that they would be disciplined or lose their job over minor infractions. The league backed reform that proposed an appeal process to a binding arbitration panel acting independently of Parks (Hutchinson, 1998). The morale problem was particularly evident in the results of a survey compiled by PriceWaterhouseCoopers for the city in December 2000. Officers from a variety of ranks indicated that they limited their response to radio calls because they felt that senior management would not support them if citizens made complaints.

The year's statistics supported this phenomenon: In 2000 arrests dropped 25 percent from the previous year. Parks was singled out by many respondents as the cause of morale problems, and 32.5 percent of respondents said the best response to the problems would be to oust senior management (Schodolski, 2000). A 2001 study by the University of California at Los Angeles and the University of Southern California showed that 57 percent of police officers would leave the department if they could. In January 2002, the LAPPL passed a vote of no confidence against Parks; according to the union, 93 percent of its membership did not support him. This vote led to demands for his resignation (Wilborn, 2002).

In 1999, one of the biggest scandals in Los Angeles history, Rampart, was exposed (Rogers, 1999). After pleading guilty to stealing cocaine from police evidence rooms in exchange for a lighter sentence, Rafael Perez revealed that officers at the Rampart Station of the LAPD routinely framed gang members for crimes, lied in court, and planted weapons on or shot unarmed people (Rogers, 1999). Perez said that officers awarded plaques to each other after wounding or killing people ("L.A.'s ungovernable," 2000). The scandal resulted in the city being sued for millions of dollars in civil liability lawsuits ("Key dates," 2002). Parks's early response consisted of suspending 10 officers and a supervisor at the Rampart Station (Rogers, 1999). The scandal, however, evolved to an investigation of 70 officers ("L.A.'s ungovernable," 2000). As a result, in over 100 cases, convictions were overturned or charges dropped. The scandal increased citizen mistrust ("Bratton calls for probe," 2003). Despite the scope of the Rampart affair, and the initiation of state and federal investigations, Parks defended his protocol for handling corruption ("L.A.'s ungovernable," 2000).

In 2002, Parks reluctantly signed a federal consent decree to address the problems exposed by the Rampart scandal ("LAPD complying," 2002). Specifically, the U.S. Department of Justice accused the LAPD of committing a pattern of civil rights violations that began before the Rampart scandal and of failing to initiate effective reforms ("Key dates," 2002). The required reforms consisted of improved officer training, a computer system to track officers' performance, new oversight of the antigang unit, and a ban on racial profiling during traffic stops. An independent monitor was hired who would have access to personnel documents until 2005 ("LAPD complying," 2002).

In February 2002, the year that Parks's five-year contract[1] was up, Mayor James K. Hahn announced that he was opposed to giving Parks

---

[1]After the 1992 riots, the Christopher Commission recommended, and voters approved, a change to the city charter that took away civil service protection for the chief of police. Instead, chiefs are limited to a five-year term, renewable at the police commission's discretion (Wilborn, 2002).

(continued)

a new contract. The mayor stated that he felt Parks was unable to address the insular culture of the department, racial profiling, recruitment, and community policing. According to Mark Ridley-Thomas, a black member of the city council, as well as civic and clergy leaders of the community, black constituents in general were angered by the announcement that Parks's contract should not be renewed (Almeida, 2002; Orlov, 2002a; Sterngold, 2002). The mayor's opinion also ran counter to reports issued by Chief Deputy City Attorney Terree Bowers and Councilwoman Cindy Miscikowski, who both indicated that the progress toward reform of the police initiated by the federal consent decree was on track ("LAPD complying," 2002). In response, Parks accused Hahn of lobbying the city council against him during contract talks (Orlov, 2002b). A *Los Angeles Times* poll in the spring of 2002 indicated that 50 percent of the residents supported the decision not to reappoint Parks. Hahn joined the LAPPL in claiming that Parks failed to address the problem of officer morale and was too resistant to necessary reforms. On April 22, 2002, Parks resigned, effective May 4, 2002, after the city council did not renew his contract. He could have stayed as chief until his term ended in August 2002 (Almeida, 2002).

In March 2003, Parks took office as a Los Angeles City Councilman for the 8th district. Among his priorities, he planned to address homelessness and housing problems (Villegas, 2003).

The overall motto and goal of Chief Parks appear to be the enhancement of the working conditions of police officers in an attempt to lower the crime rate and the improvement of the relationships between the police and the public. Those noble goals are no small vision for a department plagued by a history of officer-community tension as well as a real legacy of misconduct (given allegations made during the Rodney King and O.J. Simpson trials). In light of LAPD's past, it is rather naïve to assume that by replacing a number of high-ranking officers or by instituting some new modules of training, anyone would actually achieve a major change in the department and/or in the quality of relationships between the police and the public.

Furthermore, it is hard to achieve the desired level of integrity simply by instituting or introducing new mechanisms of control and new disciplinary sanctions. As addressed and discussed in Chapter 2, if one wants to maintain a department of integrity, first and foremost one must be aware of the way officers feel about mechanisms of control and sanctions before making them standard operating procedures. The Rampart scandal exemplifies, better than the overall dissatisfaction of officers and the unions, the low directive and low supportive style of Parks's leadership.

The major task during his tenure was the identification of priorities for the force and the identification of supervisors to enforce and supervise those priorities. This type of leadership would require the S2 type of situational leadership, coaching, in which a leader is highly involved in both the tasks and the socioemotional needs of subordinates. Instead,

Parks identified many tasks without assigning clear priorities. It was unclear from his laundry list of changes what was the first problem to target—officers' benefits, police-community relations, decreased crime rates, or police corruption. Although these are all interrelated, as the old adage goes, "You have to pick your battles." One cannot fight on all fronts at the same time; priorities have to be identified and then fully supported. In this case, success required less empowerment to senior command, a much higher degree of supportive involvement, and a higher directive approach to the problem of low morale and quite blatant misconduct. Parks's assessment of his command staff was erroneous and resulted in the choice of a wrong level of intervention. Instead of S2, a more laissez-faire type (S4) was chosen, for which his command staff was not ready. The consequences snowballed, resulting in the Rampart scandal and ultimately preventing the renewal of Parks's contract.

### Exercise

The police chiefs detailed in this chapter have been examined through the prism of situational theory. Using what you have learned from other theories in this book or from the summaries (as indicated in the Introduction) you have read thus far, it is possible to consider their approaches through the lens of different theories. What other theories can you find applicable to these chiefs? Are there lessons to be learned from those applications, or do those theories indicate alternative paths or approaches that might have yielded a more successful outcome?

## REFERENCES

Almeida, C. (2002, May 3). After bitter battle, police chief's last day in office Saturday. *The Associated Press*, state and local wire.

Barnett, J. (2002, October 10). Eyes turn to former Portland Chief Charles Moose, fills a difficult role in the search for Maryland sniper. *The Oregonian*, p. A1.

Bass, B.M. (1990). *Bass and Stogdill's handbook of leadership: A survey of theory and research*. New York: Free Press.

Berbeo, D. (1998a, July 24). LAPD officers get brush-up on ethics, workplace violence at training session. *Metropolitan News Enterprise*, p. 8.

——— (1998b, July 30). Parks says LAPD will bolster its efforts against white collar crime. *Metropolitan News Enterprise*, p. 10.

——— (1998c, August 20). Parks tells panel 80 percent of Christopher Commission reforms achieved. *Metropolitan News Enterprise*, p. 8.

——— (1998d, August 26). Parks says reforms proposed in two audits have been implemented. *Metropolitan News Enterprise*, p. 10.

——— (1998e, November 4). Police panel approves department's list of structural improvements needed. *Metropolitan News Enterprise*, p. 10.

Bernard Parks (1997, August 26). *City News Service.*

Bernstein, M. (1999a, May 27). Police chief resigns. *The Oregonian*, p. A1.

────── (1999b, June 29). Governor gives Moose a special day, praise for community policing work. *The Oregonian*, p. B2.

────── (1999c, July 28). Moose closes out 6-year tenure of achievement, pitfalls as chief. *The Oregonian*, p. A1.

Blanchard, K. & B. Nelson (1996). Where do you fit in? *Incentive*, 170 (10), 65–66.

Blanchard, K., P. Zigarmi & D. Zigarmi (1985). *Leadership and the one minute manager: Increasing effectiveness through situational leadership.* New York: William Morrow.

Blanchard, K., D. Zigarmi & R. Nelson (1993). Situational leadership after 25 years: A retrospective. *Journal of Leadership Studies*, 1 (1), 22–36.

Bratton calls for independent Rampart probe (2003, February 28). Retrieved June 22, 2003, from kcal9.com/topstories/topstoriesla_story05919851.html.

Bryman, A. (1986). *Leadership and organizations.* London: Routledge & Kegan Paul.

Chadbourne, J. (1980). Training groups: A basic life cycle model. *Personnel and Guidance Journal*, 59 (1), 55–58.

Charles Moose: Controversial police chief (2003, October 10). BBC News UK Edition (online). Retrieved July 9, 2004, from http://news.bbc.co.uk/1/hi/world/americas/3129388.stm.

Clines, F.X. (2002, October 7). Fear in sniper's wake: "This guy's our neighbor." *The New York Times*, p. A12.

Community Policing Consortium (1997). *Supervising the problem-solving process: A guide for supervision and supervisory instruction.* Facilitator's guide, version 2.0. Washington, D.C.: U.S. Department of Justice, Office of Community Oriented Policing Services.

Critics question whether police unit infamous for shoot-outs should be disbanded (1998, November 30). *The Associated Press*, state and local wire.

Dainty, P. (1986). Leadership and leadership research. *Journal of Managerial Psychology*, 1 (1), 40–43.

Duin, S. (2002, October 27). He frayed, fumbled, but chief Moose rose to the challenge of D.C. sniper case. *The Oregonian*, p. A1.

Fermino, J. & M. Kranes (2002, October 23). Maryland's Moose a New York kid. *The New York Post*, p. 5.

Fernandez, C.F. & R.P. Vecchio (1997). Situational leadership theory revisited: A test of an across-jobs perspective. *Leadership Quarterly*, 8 (1), 67–84.

Full biography for Bernard C. Parks (2003, February 23). Retrieved from http://www.smartvoter.org/2003/03/04/ca/la/vote/parks_b/bio.html.

Graeff, C.L. (1983). The situational leadership theory: A critical view. *Academy of Management Review*, 8 (2), 285–291.

────── (1997). Evolution of situational leadership theory: A critical review. *Leadership Quarterly*, 8 (2), 153–170.

Greimel, H. (1998, November 19). Police to keep using beanbag ammunition in crowd control. *The Associated Press*, state and regional.

Hersey, P. (1985). *The Situational leader.* Escondido, CA: Center for Leadership Studies, Inc., in Community Policing Consortium (1997). *Supervising the problem-solving process: A guide for supervision and supervisory instruction.* Facilitator's guide, version 2.0. Washington, D.C.: U.S. Department of Justice, Office of Community Oriented Policing Services.

——— & K.H. Blanchard (1969). Life cycle theory of leadership. *Training and Development Journal*, 23, 26–34.

——— (1977). *Management of organizational behavior: Utilizing human resources* (3rd ed.). Englewood Cliffs, NJ: Prentice Hall.

——— (1988). *Management of organizational behavior: Utilizing human resources* (5th ed.). Englewood Cliffs, NJ: Prentice Hall.

——— (1993). *Management of organizational behavior: Utilizing human resources* (6th ed.). Englewood Cliffs, NJ: Prentice-Hall.

Holly, D. (1999, August 2). Moose vows to take on all issues to build better Montgomery County Police Department. *The Associated Press*, Washington dateline.

Hutchinson, E.O. (1998, October 18). Chief effort to limit police violence. *The Daily News of Los Angeles*, Viewpoint.

Kennedy, H. (2002, October 10). Angry over tarot leak police chief rips media, ex-cops for taunting killer. *Daily News*, p. 7.

——— & M. Becker (2002, October 26). Moose is the toast of the beltway. *Daily News*, p. 6.

Key dates in LA police leadership (2002, April 10). *The Associated Press*, state and local wire.

Korten, D.C. (1962). Situational determinants in leadership structure. *Journal of Conflict Resolution*, 6, 222–235.

Koval, A. (1997, October 16). Chief: If chases weren't allowed, we wouldn't want to be in this city. *City News Service*.

Kuykendall, J. & P.C. Unsinger (1982). The leadership styles of police managers. *Journal of Criminal Justice*, 10, 311–321.

L.A.'s ungovernable police (2000, March 2). *The New York Times*, p. A26.

LAPD complying with federal consent decree reforms, city says (2002, February 14). *The Associated Press*, state and local wire.

Malkin, M. (2003, March 5). Don't ask Chief Charles Moose. *World Net Daily*. Retrieved May 16, 2003, from www.worldnetdaily.com/news/article.asp?ARTICLE_ID=31358.

——— (2003, March 3). Charles Moose remains a celebrity months after sniper probe, but faces ethics review. *The Associated Press*, domestic news.

McGreevy, P. (1997, August 13). Parks takes office: New chief says Los Angeles is "moving forward." *The Daily News of Los Angeles*, News.

——— (1998, September 26). Parks wants video cameras in all new police cars. *The Daily News of Los Angeles*, News.

Morgan, S. (1997, August 22). New Los Angeles police chief promises integrity. *Copley News Service*, state and regional.

Niehouse, O.I. (1984). Controlling burnout: A leadership guide for managers. *Business Horizons*, 27 (4), 80–85.

Nkrumah, W. (1999, May 28). Neighbors show range of opinion on Moose. *The Oregonian*, p. D2.

Northouse, P.G. (2004). *Leadership: Theory and practice* (3rd ed.). Thousand Oaks, CA: Sage.

Orlov, R. (2002a, April 25). Mayor defends decision on Parks. *The Daily News of Los Angeles*, p. N3.

—— (2002b, May 4). Parks out of LAPD at 5 p.m. *The Daily News of Los Angeles*, p. N4.

Oshiro, G.R. (1999, April 9). Portland-area chiefs denounce racist auto stops. *The Oregonian*, p. A1.

Parade honors officers who hunted sniper pair: Chief Moose in lead as grand marshal (2002, November 24). *The Record*, p. A11.

Plan puts Portland police chief in charge of school police (1999, January 20). *The Associated Press*, state and regional.

Police commission approves wider use of automatic weapons by officers. *Metropolitan News Service*, p. 11.

Reddin, W.J. (1967). The 3-D management style theory. *Training and Development Journal*, 21 (4), 8–18.

Rogers, J. (1999, September 18). Police corruption scandal expands in Los Angeles: Hundreds of cases could be tainted. *The Record*, p. A18.

Schodolski, V.J. (2000, December 31). LAPD survey blames low morale on chief: Officers admit slacking off to stay out of trouble. *The Record*, p. A21.

Sisk, R. (2002, October 25). Finally it's hats off to the chief: Moose defiant, emotional. *Daily News*, p. 28.

Son of city's police chief is arrested on drug charges (1997, September 15). *Seattle Post-Intelligencer*, p. B2.

Sperry, P. (2003, April 9). Police union probes Moose. *World Net Daily*. Retrieved May 16, 2003, from www.worldnetdaily.com/news.article.asp?ARTICLE_ID=31951.

Statement of Montgomery County executive Douglas M. Duncan regarding the resignation of police chief Charles Moose (2003, June 18). Montgomery County Maryland Press Archives. Retrieved July 9, 2004, from http://search.montgomerycountymd.gov.

Sterngold, J. (2002, February 6). Fraying ties with blacks, Los Angeles mayor opposes rehiring police chief. *The New York Times*, p. A14.

Stewart, J. (1997, August 21). News flash: He's an adult. After Willie Williams, Bernard Parks could come off as a genius simply by doing the obvious. *New Times Los Angeles*, Columns.

Stogdill, R.M. (1974). *Handbook of leadership: A survey of theory and research*. New York: Free Press.

Suspect, chief served in guard (2002, October 25). *The Oregonian*, p. A1.

Terzian, P. (2003, March 26). Commentary—Justice for Chief Moose. *Providence Journal-Bulletin*, p. B5.

Top sniper cop in tome-ly deal (2003, January 23). *The New York Post*, p. 12.

Tsao, E. (2003, January 23). Police chief shares lessons of snaring D.C. area snipers. *The Sunday Oregonian*, p. B4.

Van Auken, P. (1992). Leading in four arenas. *Supervision*, 53 (3), 9–12.

Video Monitoring Service (1997, November 5). KPTV-TV. Retrieved May 18, 2003, from Lexis-Nexis.

Villegas, M. (2003, July 2). Ludlow takes oath as 10th district councilman: Four new members, plus Bernard Parks, are sworn in as city council gets new look. *Wave West*, 1–8.

Vital stats: Chief Charles Moose (n.d.). Retrieved May 16, 2003, from www.bet.com/articles/1,clgb4346_5042,00.html.

Washington, W. (2002, October 26). The sniper case arrests: Sniper probe earns praise and criticism. *The Boston Globe*, p. A1.

Whitaker, B. (2000, June 9). Man held in killing of police chief's relative. *The New York Times*, p. A18.

Wilborn, P. (2002, April 9). LA police commission votes against second term for Chief Parks. *The Associated Press*, state and local wire.

Yukl, G. (1994). *Leadership in organizations* (3rd ed.). Englewood Cliffs, NJ: Prentice Hall.

# 8

# Doing Things Right
# or Doing the Right Thing

*Contingency Theory*

## OVERVIEW OF THE THEORY

Contingency theory posits that certain leaders are compatible with certain situations, depending on variables such as leader-member relations, task structure, and position power. In this chapter, the theory is examined through the prism of two chiefs who were faced with extremely high-profile incidents: Chief O'Brien of the Miami Police Department, who had to manage the highly politicized Elian Gonzales case, and Chief Koby of the Boulder Police Department, who oversaw the murder investigation of the child beauty pageant star Jonbenet Ramsey. The question for contingency theory is whether their particular mix of styles was right for managing these situations.

Fiedler's contingency theory is one of the most widely researched leadership theories, yet it is also the most controversial (Saha, 1979). Most studies indicate that the model is of limited or no success in predicting leadership effectiveness (Hill, 1969; Kuehl, 1977; Peters et al., 1985; Saha, 1979; Schriesheim et al., 1994; Utecht & Heier, 1976); however, it has some empirical support

## Fiedler's Contingency Theory

- It is the most widely researched leadership theory.
- It has limited success in predicting leadership effectiveness.
- The theory makes intuitive sense.
- Careful observation indicates that no one style of leadership behavior is always effective; sometimes an authoritarian person is very successful and other times is a failure.

from meta-analytic studies (Strube & Garcia, 1981). A particular strength of this model is that it makes intuitive sense. "Careful observation of leadership behavior indicates that no one style of leadership behavior is always effective; sometime an authoritarian person is very successful, at other times he is a failure" (Hill, 1969, p. 35).

The theory represents an application of Lewin's (1951) postulation that behavior is a function of the interaction between the person and the situation (person x situation) (Strube & Garcia, 1981). The primary concept of the theory is that task-oriented leaders will perform more effectively under very favorable or very unfavorable conditions. Relationship-oriented leaders will be most effective in situations of moderate favorableness (Fiedler, 1967). According to Rice and Kastenbaum (1983), Fiedler defines situational favorableness as "the degree to which the situation enables the leader to exert . . . influence and control over his/her group situation. Treatment of the situation then became a matter of identifying specific variables that affect situational favorableness and formulating appropriate rules for combining such variables into a meaningful metric of situational favorableness" (pp. 377–378). However, as Rice and Kastenbaum explain, the situational variables are not measured directly. Instead, what is measured is that which is assumed to affect situational favorableness: leader-member relations, task structure, and position power. Furthermore, the theory assumes that the interaction between the leader (measured by the Least Preferred Coworker [LPC] scale) and the situation accounts for most of the variance in a group's performance (Kabanoff, 1981).

## Work Groups

- *Coacting groups* work independently on common tasks.
- *Counteracting groups* work together to negotiate and reconcile conflicting opinions and processes.
- *Interacting groups*, the focus of the theory, have situational favorableness based on three variables: leader-member relations, task structure, and position power.

(Fiedler, 1967)

Fiedler assumes that work groups can be classified as coacting, counteracting, or interacting. Coacting groups work independently on a common task. Counteracting groups work together, but to negotiate and reconcile differences in viewpoint and approach (Fiedler, 1967). Interacting groups are the focus of the theory in that these types of groups have situational favorableness based on the three variables of leader-member relations, task structure, and position power (Hill, 1969). To sum up the above, leaders behave in either a task- or relationship-oriented style, which is appropriate or inappropriate given the situational favorableness (based on leader-member relations, task structure, and position power).

Furthermore, in developing the Leader Match program, Fiedler sought to train managers to engineer a situation to match their particular leadership style. The training program assumes that leaders' styles are difficult to change; therefore, situations are what can be altered (Schriesheim et al., 1994). Fiedler (1998)

## Leader Orientation

Behavior is a function of the interaction between the person and the situation.

- *Task-oriented* leaders will perform more effectively under very favorable or very unfavorable conditions.
- *Relationship-oriented* leaders will be most effective in situations of moderate favorableness.

(Lewin, 1951)

provides the following concrete suggestions for engineering a situation:

1. *To increase leader-member relations.* A leader can spend more time with subordinates, organize after-work activities, increase availability, and listen attentively to subordinates' problems, share information, and reward subordinates.

2. *To decrease leader-member relations.* A leader can spend less time with subordinates, see subordinates only by appointment, keep contact business-oriented, avoid becoming involved in subordinates' personal problems, and bring new members into the group.

3. *To increase task structure.* Leaders can outline tasks and break them down into smaller steps and seek formal training.

4. *To decrease task structure.* Leaders can include group members in planning and decision making and can let higher-ups know the challenges and problems their unit faces.

5. *To increase position power.* Leaders can acquire expertise in order to depend less on subordinates, ask for higher-up approval on decisions that affect their unit, exercise power fully, make sure all information passes through them as leaders, and set a good example.

6. *To decrease position power.* Leaders can give more responsibility to group members, share decision-making powers, and deemphasize organizational ranks.

---

### Leader Match Program

- *Increase L-M relations.* Spend more time.
- *Decrease L-M relations.* Spend less time.
- *Increase task structure.* Break down tasks into smaller steps.
- *Decrease task structure.* Include more members in decision-making process and inform the higher-ups about the challenges.
- *Increase position power.* Acquire expertise and depend less on subordinates.
- *Decrease position power.* Give more responsibility to group members, share decision-making powers, and deemphasize organizational ranks.

(Fiedler, 1998)

---

## MILITARY LEADERS AND CONTINGENCY THEORY

Utecht and Heier (1976) studied whether the contingency model could predict successful military leadership. They tested the main component of contingency theory: that task-oriented leaders will perform more effectively under very favorable or very unfavorable conditions, while relationship-oriented leaders will be most effective in situations of moderate favorableness. Military success for the purposes of this study was defined as an officer who has attended or is attending a top military academy. Data were collected by questionnaire from classes of Air Force, Army, and Navy war colleges. Part of the questionnaire consisted of the LPC in order to elicit information about leadership style. Questions about the respondent's last six leadership functions measured task structure information. Rank status inferred position power. Chi-square analysis of the data yielded results indicating that the model was no better than chance in predicting military success. From this, the authors postulate that the model does not work in high structure settings such as the military. They further speculate that this conclusion could be generalizable to "structured non-military organizations" such as the police (Utecht & Heier, 1976, p. 618).

## COGNITIVE RESOURCES THEORY

Related to contingency theory is cognitive resources theory, a theory Fiedler developed in his later work (Fiedler & Garcia, 1987). The main corollary is that intelligent, competent leaders make more effective plans, decisions, and strategies and that leaders communicate these through directive behaviors. In early theoretical discussions, Fiedler had indicated that intelligence was irrelevant to the effectiveness of leadership. However, in his later development of the cognitive resources theory, he added the variables of intellectual ability, competence, and experience to the contingency model (Vecchio, 1990). In fact, in early studies of Fiedler's contingency model, the lack of factoring in intellectual and technical abilities was often cited as a potential weakness of the model (Fiedler, 1967; Hill, 1969; Saha, 1979). However, Fiedler continues to draw a distinction between possessing intellectual capacity and being able to effectively harness it (Fiedler, 1996). Cognitive resources theory is an improvement on pure trait theory (see Chapter 12), which views traits in a vacuum. With cognitive resources theory, situational forces are important because they can have differential effects on the trait-performance association. The theory implies that leaders should be selected based on their valued traits of expertise, experience, and intelligence and that work situations should be engineered to have low stress and group support of the leader (Bryman, 1986).

## LEADER SUBSTITUTES THEORY

The leader substitutes theory is based on the notion that group processes can produce effects similar to interpersonal hierarchical leadership (Tosi & Kiker, 1997). The idea was developed by Kerr and Jermier (1978) from the observation that situational factors can actually negate a leader's ability to be effective. The model makes a distinction between two kinds of situational variables: substitutes (what makes leader behavior unnecessary or redundant) and neutralizers (what nullifies the effects of the leaders) (Yukl, 1994). For example, in a highly structured organization, any attempt on the part of the leader to increase structure is neutralized by the existing structure.

Kerr and Jermier even suggest that leaders may be superfluous in some situations. They seem to mean that formal leadership may be unnecessary in the presence of capable subordinates. "For some substitutes, behavior by the designated leaders is merely replaced by similar leadership behavior carried out by peers or informal leaders" (Yukl, 1994, p. 110).

## VROOM-YETTON CONTINGENCY MODEL

Vroom and Yetton's (1973) contingency model focuses on the autocracy-participation dimension of leadership style. It aims to determine the impact of participative leadership on the quality of decision making in an organization. The model looks at leadership as a problem to be solved. In order to handle the problem, the leader may or may not share his/her decision making with subordinates. The level of participation represents a continuum of five levels of employee participation, from none to democratic participation. The leader decides which of the five levels to adopt based on seven rules, which are designed to either protect the quality of the decision or protect the acceptance of the decision by subordinates. According to the model, a single leader should be flexible enough to vary his/her style across the continuum as needed; therefore, a person has the capacity to be both autocratic and participative (Bryman, 1986). Contrastingly, Fiedler's contingency theory assumes that leadership style is fixed.

## DYADIC APPROACH TO CONTINGENCY THEORY

Vecchio (1979) integrates Fiedler's contingency model with Graen's notion of vertical dyadic linkage (see LMX theory, Chapter 4). The dyadic view counters the notion of studying leader behavior in relation to an entire group. Rather, the focus is on the interaction that occurs between each group member and the leader. Leaders are "discriminating among and dealing with them as individuals, such that certain subordinates receive leader-exchange opportunities while others are merely supervised" (Vecchio, 1979, p. 591). Subordinates fall into one of two categories: the "trusted assistants" (the in-group) and the "ordinary members" (the out-group). Under this theory, low LPC leaders will be more productive relative to high LPC leaders when the environment contains both good and poor leader-member relations. Moreover, leaders are differentially affected by the groups and alter their styles depending on whether they are interacting with an employee in the in- or out-group. Out-group members are best motivated by a leader who emphasizes extrinsic motivators (external pressures on the group which demand performance). In-group members perform better when motivated by intrinsic factors (for example, personal commitment to the leader).

## CRITICISMS OF CONTINGENCY THEORY

There are two important criticisms of contingency theory in general. The first is that the theory assumes that factors that affect situational favorableness are congruent with each other in a given situation. There is no prescription for how a leader should respond when one part of a situation suggests one style but another part of the situation suggests the opposite (Bryman, 1986). The second criticism is the problem of order of the variables. The theory assumes that a leader's style works in one direction to affect performance. There is no reverse causality or any notion of a dialectical relationship implied. Korman (1973) points out that empirical research into contingency theory tends to look at static relationships under the assumption that the variables are ordered in the way that the model assumes.

## CONTINGENCY THEORY OF LEADERSHIP AND THE CASES OF CHIEF WILLIAM O'BRIEN AND CHIEF TOM KOBY

The contingency theory of leadership, in essence, states that not all leaders are good for all situations. The theory attempts to match the best possible leader to a given situation. Situations in police environments can be complex and extreme, for example, because of political pressure (such as that faced by Chief William O'Brien and the Elian Gonzales problem) or sensitivity due to the extremely tragic nature of a case (such as that faced by Chief Tom Koby and the Jonbenet Ramsey situation). In these types of cases, only a specific individual possessing certain qualities and skills can truly be a leader. All those with a different orientation are destined to fail, primarily due to the nature of the situation.

Leadership during a particular situation can be measured in two ways. It can be seen as a failure from an organizational perspective (for example, the police organization within the pyramid of local politics). The same result can also be seen as a success for an individual within this system (for example, on a personal moral level). Whether such a moral victory makes a person a bad leader depends on which perspective is more important—organizational or individual. In this book about police leadership, the focus is on police organizations, not on individual police officers. The examples focus on individuals as they reflect the nature of police work generally rather than the work of one specific police officer. As a result, it is sometimes the case that a police chief whom this author holds in high esteem has nevertheless for those very reasons failed according to the contingency theory and the organizational view of leadership.

As in the situational and style theories, contingency theory researchers focus on the interaction between the leader and the situation, and they delineate between task- and relationship-oriented behaviors. What is different with contingency theory, and particularly with the Vroom-Yetton contingency model (1973), is that the phenomenon of leadership is considered a problem to be solved. Of course this depiction of leadership can be and probably is applicable to every chief described in this book; however, both Chief O'Brien and Chief Koby faced very specific events that presented them with unique problems to be solved. Both had other difficult cases in their careers that they managed differently. These particularly high-profile incidents and the interpretation of them were chosen specifically to illustrate this theory.

Police corruption and misconduct, riots, increases in crime, or even serial killers are the bread-and-butter problems faced by police leaders on a daily basis. However, the purely political and internationally covered case of a child who has to be returned to a parent in another country or the high-profile murder of a child of very wealthy and influential parents who themselves become the major suspects—these cases are indeed the problems that defined the success or failure of those chiefs' leadership. No other problems either chief faced in his career as a police leader were as critical. Chief O'Brien and Chief Koby are prime illustrations of the Vroom-Yetton contingency model's definition of leadership as a function of the success or failure with which a problem is solved.

The only argument one might have with this author is about the distinction between success and failure. Although Chief O'Brien was the man for the Gonzales situation and he handled it properly, he was simply not the right man for the larger existing political configuration. He put the idea of policing before the idea of police organization. Although on an individual and moral level he was a successful leader, based on the contingency model and in the sense of responsibility first to the organization, he failed. Also according to contingency theory, Chief Koby failed in handling the Jonbenet Ramsey case; he was simply not the right man for the situation.

## CAREER HIGHLIGHTS  Contingency Theory

### Chief William O'Brien and the Elian Gonzales Case
*Miami Police Department, Florida*

William O'Brien was born in 1944 and raised in LaGrange, Illinois. He earned his bachelor's degree in political science from the University of Miami (Driscoll, 2000). From 1968 to 1973, he was an Air Force pilot, attaining the rank of captain ("Biography," 2000). He also served in the Vietnam War (Driscoll, 2000). From 1975 to 1998, he was an officer in the Miami Police Department, spending 18 years on the Special Weapons and Tactical (SWAT) team ("Biography," 2000). O'Brien started the first sexual battery unit in the department and also served as commander of Internal Affairs for more than three years (Driscoll, 2000).

O'Brien served as chief of the Miami Police Department from 1998 to 2000. On taking the job in 1998, O'Brien cautioned his officers to "maintain their integrity and stay away from politics" (Driscoll, 2000, p. 1B). Officers told the press that under his leadership the department's morale was high. They also indicated that the equipment improved and that training was more comprehensive. O'Brien was described as "a professional leader" by one sergeant (Driscoll, 2000). However, others criticized O'Brien for being merely a puppet to the city manager, Donald Warshaw, who previously held the post of police chief (Epstein, 1998).

O'Brien appeared open to outside review of the department. O'Brien supported one federal investigation of five police officers accused of planting a gun on an innocent man ("Federal investigation," 1998). He also supported the city's investigation of the records of a crime-prevention group, Do the Right Thing, which was run by Warshaw when he was chief ("City," 1999). In April 2000, O'Brien suspended two officers without pay; one was suspected of causing the death of an inmate, and the other was a sergeant who ordered that the report be falsified to make the death seem accidental ("Police officer," 2000).

The war on drugs preoccupied the Miami Police Department during O'Brien's tenure, and the department often worked with federal agencies. In January 1999, 26 federal indictments were handed down for drug dealing in connection with a gang known as the John Doe Boys. O'Brien was quoted as saying he hoped that such a massive drug bust would act as a general deterrent (Cherfils, 1999).

In January 1999, the chief joined with black religious leaders to plead with a drug gang member to surrender after perpetrating 11 shooting deaths in the previous five months (Kidwell, 1999). Indeed, early in his tenure, O'Brien reached out to the African-Caribbean community in Little Haiti, a particularly crime-prone neighborhood. O'Brien pledged to increase police presence (Casimir, 1998). However, O'Brien also took criticism from the black community, particularly after the shooting of an unarmed black 19-year-old by an officer in September 1999. The officer reportedly shot the victim because he believed the victim was reaching for a gun. Black activists called for a federal investigation, although O'Brien indicated he believed the shooting was justified (Zarella, 1999).

O'Brien's tenure as police chief was overshadowed—and ultimately doomed—by the Elian Gonzales incident that divided Miami in 1999 and 2000. Elian, a six-year-old Cuban child, was a shipwreck survivor rescued off the coast of Florida on November 25, 1999. The ship intended to secretly dock in Florida to facilitate illegal Cuban immigration. Elian's mother perished in the immigration attempt. His Cuban-American relatives in Miami hoped to keep the boy in the United States (as his deceased mother clearly had wished to immigrate), at the home of relative Lazaro

(*continued*)

Gonzales, stating that Elian had a right to live in freedom in the United States. However, his father in Cuba sought his return, and as a Cuban citizen, Elian was potentially deportable. During the federal appeals process, the Cuban community in Miami staged several protests in support of Elian's relatives ("Elian," 2000). The federal government, under the direction of then Attorney General Janet Reno, staged a raid on April 22, 2000, to seize Elian from his Miami relatives (Davis & Black, 2000). Tens of thousands of demonstrators took to the streets in Miami to protest and counterprotest in the weeks after the seizure ("Elian," 2000). More than 300 people were arrested, and tear gas was used for crowd control ("Miami in turmoil," 2000).

According to press reports, Cuban-American citizens initially criticized O'Brien over the police response to a January 6, 2000, exile protest during which the police used tear gas (Jimenez, 2000). The main issue, however, stemmed from the seizure of Elian on April 22, 2000. Federal authorities alerted O'Brien to the raid before it happened. Yet O'Brien informed neither Mayor Joe Carollo nor City Manager Don Warshaw. Furthermore, one of O'Brien's top assistants, who had been the police liaison to the federal government during the investigation, accompanied federal agents on the raid, even though the mayor had pledged that the Miami police would not help in the federal plan to seize Elian (Branch & Bridges, 2000). Reportedly, O'Brien was reluctant to tip off Carollo because Carollo had openly sided with Elian's relatives and O'Brien was worried that telling him would compromise the mission (Bragg, 2000a). After the raid, O'Brien stated, "This was a police issue, not a political issue" ("Mayor sacks manager," 2000). He also said, "If word had gotten out, there would have been a confrontation astronomically greater than there was, putting not only law enforcement personnel at risk but the people in [Elian's] house at risk, the child himself, the demonstrators, and even the media at the scene" (Bragg, 2000a, p. A9). However, Carollo, a Cuban American, was infuriated by O'Brien's failure to disclose information about the raid and told the city manager to fire O'Brien.[1] Warshaw refused to fire O'Brien and so Carollo fired Warshaw. However, Carollo stated the firing had nothing to do with Elian's case but rather with Warshaw's pattern of lying to him ("Mayor sacks manager," 2000).

On April 29, 2000, O'Brien resigned, saying he could no longer work for a divisive mayor. The resignation was emotional, with O'Brien shedding tears ("Miami in turmoil," 2000). Cuban exiles applauded the mayor's desire to fire O'Brien (Cubans make up 60 percent of the city's voters). People from other groups (whites, blacks, and some Hispanics),

[1]According to municipal laws, only the city manager can fire the police chief.

however, expressed criticism, saying Carollo was not observing the rights of anyone but Cuban Americans (Bragg, 2000a). In his resignation speech, O'Brien took responsibility for the events associated with the seizure of Elian (Jimenez, 2000). When O'Brien resigned, officers showed their support for him. The INS officer who led the Elian raid called O'Brien a "hero of the mission" by maintaining operational security.

The new police chief, Raul Martinez, became the first Hispanic to hold the position in Miami. Warshaw, who was appealing his termination by Carollo and who was in the 10-day grace period for terminating the position, hired Martinez despite Carollo's desire to conduct a nationwide search for a chief. Carollo then accused Warshaw of misusing public funds, blackmailing him, and "grabbing at anything he can to keep himself in power" (Richards, 2000). By May 10, 2000, Carollo had replaced City Manager Warshaw with Carlos Gimenez, who was previously the city's fire chief. This added to the Cuban-American majority on the city commission (now three out of five) (Bragg, 2000b).

When Chief O'Brien warned his officers to stay away from politics when he took command of the police department, it was almost a premonition of what was to come in his career. For generations, police chiefs and champions of the idea of policing, both academics and practitioners, have expressed the desire to separate policing from politics and politics from policing. No matter how noble this concept and how much one believes in its importance for creating an effective, efficient, and, above all, truly professional police force, it is absolutely unachievable. Police always were and will forever remain a tool in the hands of the ruling government. Ideally, should the police be separated from government as far as professional decision making is concerned? Yes, they absolutely should be. Unfortunately, these strictly professional decisions will probably remain only in the sphere of the acquisition of new equipment and the choice of color and shape of new uniforms. Everything else will remain political, to either a greater or a lesser degree, maybe, but still political.

A friend recently confronted this author; he said the word "political" has become a disparaging term because anything and everybody can be portrayed as doing something political. This criticism is valid. There can be no doubt that everyone is motivated by some overt or covert agenda, consciously or subconsciously. Therefore, it becomes imperative to clarify what exactly is meant by the word "political" in any given context where it is used. In the context of Chief O'Brien and in the context of policing in general, when the word "political" is used, it means that the police chief or commissioner is asked to engage in action or inaction by the local politician in charge. In Miami, it was the refusal of Chief O'Brien to inform the mayor, who happened to be sympathetic to the community backing one side in the controversy, about the decision to act. O'Brien's decision was based on a

*(continued)*

strictly professional assessment of the situation at hand (the problem) and devoid of any political considerations. His professional assessment made him the right man for the problem, but his lack of political consideration made him the wrong leader for the case. From the individual standpoint, he made the right personal choice; looking at the police as a profession, he made the right professional choice. But from the organizational standpoint—looking at police organization as the tool of the local government and therefore, by default, being accountable to it—he failed.

## CAREER HIGHLIGHTS    Contingency Theory

**Chief Tom Koby and the Jonbenet Ramsey Case**
*Boulder Police Department, Colorado*

Tom Koby was born in 1949 in Cleveland, Texas. He grew up in Houston, joining its police department in 1969. In 1985, he was the commander of the burglary and theft division and earned the Manager of the Year award. By 1987, he was deputy chief and, four months later, assistant chief. Lee P. Brown, the chief who promoted Koby, described him as an "intelligent, bright and energetic police officer. He cared for the police officers under him. He understood that you have to be out in the community" (McPhee, 1997a, p. B4). While working as a police officer, Koby earned his bachelor's degree in business administration in 1973 (McPhee, 1997a).

In May 1991, Koby became chief of the Boulder Police Department, a force with 213 employees (140 officers); he served until 1998. The town of Boulder had 100,000 residents at the time he took over the force. Koby was reportedly hired because of his commitment to community-oriented policing (McPhee, 1997a). One change he implemented was to assign one officer per shift to specifically handle calls and complaints about burglar alarms in order to cope with the 8 percent of calls that were false alarms. This freed up other officers to form additional patrols of downtown and the campus of Colorado University (McCullen, 1996). In addition, because of his concern for order maintenance, Koby opposed the opening of a methadone clinic in downtown Boulder, stating that it would bring drug problems into the city (McCullen, 1997f). He had observed increased crime, such as drug peddling and the selling of stolen goods, near Houston methadone clinics. However, in the first few weeks of the clinic's opening, no problems were reported (Robey, 1998).

Koby tagged underage drinking as one of the larger concerns in Boulder, a college town. He believed that many crime problems in the community could be attributed to alcohol. Rather than giving out more driving under the influence (DUI) tickets, Koby reached out to community leaders (including sorority and fraternity members) at Colorado University to encourage a change in campus attitudes about drinking (McPhee, 1997a). However, on May 2, 1997, a riot erupted on campus. During the riot, students started fires and threw bottles. Police officers responded with tear gas and rubber bullets. Several people were injured and 35 people were arrested (McPhee, 1997b). Approximately 1,500 people had gathered on campus during the unrest ("Hundreds fight," 1997). Reportedly, the melee was fueled by student frustration with the city and school administrations over efforts to control underage drinking. Beer was no longer permitted in the stadium during football games. Fraternity and sorority leaders claimed they were coerced into banning liquor in 1995. But the most commonly cited reason for the unrest was that a fraternity had its charter revoked because of alcohol-related violations (McPhee, 1997b). Some sources reported that the riot also stemmed from a celebration of the end of the semester ("Hundreds fight," 1997). Additional unrest occurred two nights later when a crowd leaving a theater began lighting fires and breaking windows. Police controlled them with tear gas and rubber bullets ("Hundreds fight," 1997).

Regarding the riots, Koby told the press, "Friday night was a mob mentality. Blaming it on students not being able to drink as much as they wanted is crap. This is about drunks. They got drunk and tore the town up to show they have the right to get drunk" (McPhee, 1997b, p. B1). Koby subsequently met with campus leaders to encourage them to help stop the violence by handing out flyers and chalking the sidewalks with messages to remain calm (McPhee, 1997b).

Even as early as 1994, Koby faced police union criticism over his lack of communication with his executive staff, lack of enough staffing in the communications center, and lack of training in the department. In May 1994, Officer Beth Haynes was killed in a shootout. A dispatcher did not relay information that there was an armed man involved in the unfolding incident, and backup was slow to assist her; the police union held Koby responsible (McCullen, 1994).

Koby's tenure as police chief was consumed by the investigation into the death of 6-year-old child beauty pageant star Jonbenet Ramsey, who was strangled in her home on December 26, 1996. That morning, police responded to a call by her mother, Patsy Ramsey, that Jonbenet had been kidnapped; Jonbenet's mother allegedly found a ransom note. Later that day, Jonbenet's father, John Ramsey, and a neighbor found the body of the dead girl in the basement of the Ramsey home (McPhee & Chronis, 1997). In the early stages of the investigation, Koby provided few details to the public, indicating his frustration with the national media attention the case received[1] (Richardson, 1997). For example, by late January 1997, he would only say that there were more than seven suspects, but little else (Brooke, 1997a). Koby also expressed confidence in the ability of his officers to

[1]Since resigning as police chief in 1998, Koby has not made any public statement concerning the murder case (Brennan et al., 1999).

(*continued*)

handle the investigation (Richardson, 1997). His decisions in the case were publicly supported by the city council and city manager. Unlike in most homicide cases, Koby debriefed the city manager regularly on developments (McCullen, 1997b).

Koby was criticized for the police handling of the case in the early stages of the investigation. Specifically, questions arose as to why John Ramsey and a neighbor were permitted to look for Jonbenet when this activity is usually limited to the police. Unsupervised by authorities, John Ramsey picked up his daughter's body when he found her and moved her upstairs, thus disturbing the crime scene (Richardson, 1997). Moreover, the Ramseys and five friends had free rein throughout the home in the seven hours before Jonbenet's body was found, thus threatening the integrity of evidence at the scene. For example, the autopsy results showed that Jonbenet's skull was fractured by a blunt instrument. The first patrol officers at the house noticed a heavy flashlight on the kitchen counter, but it was missing by the end of the day (Brooke, 1997b). Despite this, on January 9, 1997, Koby denied that the moving of the body destroyed evidence at the crime scene (Richardson, 1997). He stated, "I've been in communication with police personnel around the country and most legal experts will tell you we've done it quite right" (McCullen, 1997a, p. A4).

Further criticisms involved the special treatment allegedly given the Ramseys. Detective Linda Arndt, the first detective on the scene, was accused of "bonding" with the parents rather than keeping them under suspicion, as is standard practice when conducting such an investigation (McPhee, 1997a). In addition, the Ramseys were not formally interviewed immediately after the crime, which drew national criticism (McPhee, 1997a). Additionally, Arndt placed a sheet over the body of Jonbenet as it was being taken out of the house, potentially disturbing evidence (Brooke, 1997b). The department was also criticized for the delay of two and a half hours between Patsy Ramsey's 911 call to police and the arrival of a detective (though patrol officers responded immediately) (Brennan & McCullen, 1997). In mid-May 1997, Arndt was taken off the investigation, reportedly because fewer detectives were needed. More likely, it was her inappropriate compassion for the Ramseys that made Koby lose confidence in her. This lack of skepticism about the Ramseys was cited as the reason it took seven hours to find Jonbenet's body (Brennan & McCullen, 1997).[2]

---

[2] Arndt later sued Koby, the subsequent police chief Mark Beckner, and the city for ruining her reputation as an investigator by taking her off the case. She also complained that Koby failed to defend her against criticisms, using her as a scapegoat for a failing investigation (McCullen, 1998a, 1998d; "Trial begins," 2001). By not allowing her to speak to defend herself, Arndt allegedly had her First Amendment rights violated. In 2001, after the case went to trial, the judge ruled that she failed to prove that she was prevented from speaking to defend herself ("Ex-detective's suit," 2001; "Trial begins," 2001).

Koby also refused help from the Denver Police Department, which investigates approximately 100 murders a year, compared to the 1 or 2 that occur annually in Boulder[3] (Brennan et al., 1997). This inexperience led to poor decisions; for example, the police were going to turn the home back over to the Ramseys just hours after the body was discovered—not usual procedure in homicide investigations. Moreover, Koby refused an FBI offer to monitor the Ramseys, their relatives, and their associates for any suspicious activity. In fact, prior to the Ramsey investigation, Koby had never led a murder inquiry (Brennan et al., 1997).

In one of the most controversial investigative decisions, Koby was criticized for using Jonbenet's body as a bargaining chip to secure an interview with her parents. The Boulder Police told the parents they would only get her body back for burial if they gave formal statements. Then the police miscalculated by agreeing to submit written questions to the Ramseys instead of holding a normal police interrogation during which police have the additional tactical edge of using follow-up questions and psychological techniques (Brennan et al., 1997).

Internal and external conflict also characterized the Ramsey investigation. The police and the district attorney's office did not get along; in one instance, the police withheld DNA evidence from the district attorney (Brennan et al., 1997). The reasons were not disclosed to the press but were interpreted as reflecting a conflict (Brooke, 1997b). The evidence was finally handed over six weeks after the police received it (Richardson, 1997). However, on September 15, 1997, Koby and District Attorney Alex Hunter met with private attorneys advising the team on the case in an apparent show of cooperation (Brennan, 1997b). In addition, detectives on the case had conflicting attitudes and strategies (Brennan et al., 1997). For example, there were allegations that leaks to the media were coming from Sergeant Larry Mason;[4] however, this may have been a retaliatory accusation related to the different strategy that Mason advocated. On the first day of the investigation, he was vocally critical of other detectives for not separating the Ramsey parents, not interviewing them in depth, and not ridding the home of milling friends and family in order to conduct a proper search (Brennan et al., 1997).

In May 1997, Boulder Police who were union members delivered a no-confidence vote on Koby over a variety of issues. Subsequently the city manager, who was also criticized for supporting Koby, resigned

---

[3] Of the 16 homicides that occurred between 1990 and 1997, 11 were solved by the Boulder Police Department, a percentage only slightly higher than the national average (McCullen, 1998d).

[4] In September 1997, Koby intended to submit the Ramsey detectives and their superiors to lie detector tests to find out who might have been leaking information to the media; however, the contract with the police union prohibited polygraph tests of officers (Brennan, 1997a).

(*continued*)

(Richardson, 1997). The primary issues were his response to the riots at Colorado University (McCullen, 1997c) and his implementation of community-oriented policing ("Chief," 1998). Regarding community-oriented policing, officers complained about the department moving away from basic police services to an ineffective "feel good" department (McCullen, 1997e). Critics also said Koby mismanaged the media in the Ramsey case ("Chief," 1998), although there was no specific reference to the Ramsey investigation in the documentation of the no-confidence vote (McCullen, 1997c).

More than 10 months after the Ramsey investigation began, in October 1997, Koby admitted that the early stages of the investigation were not handled well, in contradiction to previous comments. "If we had to do it all over again, we would do it differently," Koby told reporters ("Belated acknowledgement," 1997, p. A41). At that time, Koby replaced the commander in charge of the investigation, James Eller, with Mark Beckner (who would later succeed Koby as chief) (McCullen, 1998c). Koby also added three more detectives. Yet the press in a *Rocky Mountain News* editorial believed that the reorganization would do little to save the mishandled case ("Belated acknowledgement," 1997). Beckner did help to promote the investigation team as hardworking (McCullen, 1997g). An editorial in *The Denver Post* similarly opined that the mishandled case could not be salvaged (Green, 1999). Koby also lamented that the case dominated police time and that only one-quarter of the 1,150 criminal cases requiring investigation received any attention in 1997 (Brooke, 1998).

On November 19, 1997, Koby announced his plan to retire in December 1998. The date was set to permit him enough time to wrap up the Ramsey investigation (Robinson, 1997b; "The Jonbenet Ramsey case," 2001). The police union president indicated, however, that within the ranks anti-Koby and pro-Koby factions were developing that were threatening cohesiveness in the department. By setting a resignation date, the union president believed Koby wanted to mitigate these divisions (McCullen, 1997d). On March 31, 1998, however, Koby was asked to continue as police chief and to act as a special project coordinator for the city manager. Mayor Bob Greenlee indicated that Koby's announcement that he would resign in December 1998 resulted in an even further decrease in confidence because the department appeared unstable. "When you set a course, people need to be confident you will keep steering the course," Greenlee said (McCullen, 1998b, p. A5). Koby worked on special projects for the city manager until approximately December 1998, when Koby went into retirement ("Former Boulder cop," 1999). A year later, Koby left retirement to take a position at Tango Partners, a Boulder firm that invests private resources in Internet technology companies and then gives the proceeds to nonprofit charities ("Former Boulder cop," 1999).

Despite the departure of Koby, the Ramsey investigation continued to languish. Hundreds of thousands of dollars were spent during the 16-month investigation, producing 30,000 pages of documents. A grand jury failed to indict anyone for Jonbenet's murder by the end of its term in October 1999 ("Former Boulder cop," 1999). The investigation by the police department finally ended in February 2003 when the case shifted to being solely the domain of the district attorney's office (Weller, 2003).

One of the most frightful situations in police work deals with parents who have lost their child to a violent crime. The only thing that is more frightful is to consider those parents as prime suspects. If the parents also happen to be very powerful socialites from a relatively small local community, nobody can envy the job of the local police chief. Nonetheless, if Chief Koby had engaged in task-oriented behavior instead of relationship-oriented behavior prior to the murder case, his leadership style could have saved him from major criticism. After his appointment as chief of police of the Boulder Police Department, he had introduced many initiatives with the officers' and the community's well-being in mind. However, this relationship orientation took him too far away from the task of the police organization. The task was not just to maintain a good relationship with the community and introduce community-oriented programs but also to deliver professional policing, based inter alia on well-trained and experienced police officers. Koby closed Boulder's police academy and sent his officers to regional academies. This measure alone took away from his ability to have any input into the ways officers are and should be trained. This move was motivated by cost savings for the community, but it was not a task-oriented move and later prevented Koby from being able to handle the Jonbenet Ramsey investigation in a more professional manner.

During the investigation, when his officers did not handle the crime scene in a proper manner, Koby had his relationship orientation put to the test. When he further refused help from the FBI, his task orientation became even more diluted. His lack of effective cooperation with the district attorney's office might have earned him some support from his subordinates but certainly did not contribute to the task at hand. The murder case was never solved, and even if his relationship with the community had not been strained, it may not have saved him from criticism. Both his mismanagement of the murder case and the "feel good" approach to community policing contributed to the demand for his resignation. The biggest problem he faced—the murder case of Jonbenet Ramsey— required a leader whose primary orientation was task rather than relationship. Koby's relationship orientation cost him his career as chief of the Boulder Police Department.

*(continued)*

**Exercise**

The police chiefs detailed in this chapter have been examined through the prism of contingency theory. Using what you have learned from other theories in this book or from the summaries (as indicated in the Introduction) you have read thus far, it is possible to consider their approaches through the lens of different theories. What other theories can you find applicable to these chiefs? Are there lessons to be learned from those applications, or do those theories indicate alternative paths or approaches that might have yielded a more successful outcome?

# REFERENCES

Belated acknowledgement (1997). *Rocky Mountain News*, p. A41.

Biography of Chief William O'Brien (2000, April 28). *The Associated Press*, state and local wire.

Bragg, R. (2000a, April 29). Miami police chief quits in raid fallout. *The New York Times*, p. A9.

——— (2000b, May 10). Legacy of a Cuban boy: Miami city hall is remade. *The New York Times*, p. A20.

Branch, K. & T. Bridges (2000, April 23). Carollo slams chief over role. *The Miami Herald*. Retrieved June 15, 2003, from www.miami.com/mld/miami/news 2059832.htm.

Brennan, C. (1997a, September 20). Koby cancels lie detector tests. *Rocky Mountain News*. Retrieved August 21, 2003, from http://denver.rockymoutainnews.com/extra/ramsey/0920jon/htm.

——— (1997b, September 16). Boulder officials hold talks: DA, police meet over Jonbenet murder. *Rocky Mountain News*, p. A4.

——— & K. McCullen (1997, June 8). Ramsey case a tragedy of errors: Inexperience, sympathy, unwillingness to ask for help combine to trip up investigation. *Rocky Mountain News*, p. A4.

——— K. McCullen & L.G. Everitt. (1999). Koby looks like "someone who has retreated from the world." *Rocky Mountain News*, p. A21.

Brooke, J. (1997a, January 31). After slaying of girl, family and town are in uneasy limbo. *The New York Times*, p. A17.

——— (1997b, July 2). Case of Jonbenet Ramsey stalls on error and rivalry. *The New York Times*, p. A14.

——— (1998, April 22). Grand jury refocuses spotlight on Jonbenet case. *The New York Times*, p. A12.

Bryman, A. (1986). *Leadership and organizations*. London: Routledge & Kegan Paul.

Casimir, L. (1998, December 17). Chief on the beat: Miami's O'Brien reaches out. *The Miami Herald*, p. 8.

Cherfils, M. (1999, January 7). U.S. attorney's office unseals 26 indictments in gang wars. *The Associated Press*, state and local wire.

Chief who led initial investigation into Ramsey murder gone (1998, December 31). *The Associated Press*, state and local wire.

City asked for review of anti-crime group's records (1999, September 19). *The Associated Press*, state and local wire.

Davis, P. & C. Black (2000, April 30). 1,000 march in Miami protest over Elian. *CNN.com*. Retrieved June 15, 2003, from www.cnn.com/2000/US/04/29/cuba.boy.03.

Driscoll, A. (2000, April 29). Bill O'Brien bids farewell. *The Miami Herald*, p. 1B.

Elian protests split Miami (2000, April 29). *BBC News Online*. Retrieved June 12, 2003, from http://news.bbc.co.uk/2/hi/americas/730885.stm.

Epstein, G. (1998, October 22). Miami's new chief: Veteran of streets called "right man for the job." *The Miami Herald*, p. 1B.

Ex-detective's suit dismissed (2001, June 13). *The New York Times*, p. A31.

Federal investigation targets Miami cops (1998, December 14). *The Associated Press*, state and local wire.

Fiedler, F.E. (1967). *A theory of leadership effectiveness*. New York: McGraw-Hill.

——— (1996). Research of leadership selection and training: One view of the future. *Administrative Science Quarterly*, 41 (2), 241–250.

——— (1998). The leadership situation: A missing factor in selecting and training managers. *Human Resources Management Review*, 8 (4), 335–350.

——— & J.E. Garcia (1987). *New approaches to leadership: Cognitive resources and organizational performance*. New York: John Wiley.

Former Boulder cop to work for philanthropic firm (1999, December 29). *The Associated Press*, state and local wire.

Green, C. (1999, October 14). So now a killer walks.*The Denver Post*, p. A1.

Hill, W. (1969). The validation and extension of Fiedler's theory of leadership effectiveness. *Academy of Management Journal*, 12, 33–47.

Hundreds fight police near Colorado campus (1997, May 5). *The New York Times*, p. A12.

Jimenez, J.L. (2000, May 4). Elian made a tough guy cry. *Miami New Times*, News.

Kabanoff, B. (1981). A critique of leader match and its implications for leadership research. *Personnel Psychology*, 34, 749–764.

Kerr, S. & J. Jermier (1978). Substitutes for leadership: Their meaning and measurement. *Organizational Behavior and Human Performance*, 22, 374–403.

Kidwell, D. (1999, January 1). Shooting suspect urged to surrender. *The Miami Herald*, p. B1.

Korman, A.K. (1973). On the development of contingency theories of leadership: Some methodological considerations and a possible alternative. *Journal of Applied Psychology*, 58, 84–87.

Kuehl, C.R. (1977). Leader effectiveness in committee-like groups. *Journal of Business*, 50 (2), 223–230.

Lewin, K. (1951). *Field theory in social science*. New York: Harper.

Mayor sacks manager who wouldn't fire chief (2000, April 28). *The Associated Press*, state and local wire.

McCullen, K. (1994, June 15). Cops' union at odds with chief. *Rocky Mountain News*, p. A20.

———— (1996, December 30). 15 new cops on the block in Boulder, 7 jobs added: More manpower due downtown, on the Hill. *Rocky Mountain News*, p. A22.

———— (1997a, January 10). Chief defends investigation: Boulder police don't think serial killer is loose in city, deny preferential treatment. *Rocky Mountain News*, p. A4.

———— (1997b, March 6). Ramsey investigation called "on track": Boulder city manager confident about inquiry, police chief says probe hasn't busted budget. *Rocky Mountain News*, p. A30.

———— (1997c, May 23). Cops vote on confidence in chief, Boulder police react to management of riot involving CU students. *Rocky Mountain News*, p. A52.

———— (1997d, November 19). Boulder police chief to retire in December 1998: Koby plans to stay until decision is made in Jonbenet slaying. *Rocky Mountain News*, p. A5.

———— (1997e, September 22). Police union watches, waits on Koby: Chief says he's working to solve staffing, morale problems in department. *Rocky Mountain News*, p. A26.

———— (1997f, October 30). Plan for methadone clinic disturbs Boulder officials: Police chief concerned with "bringing people with drug problems into the heart of the city." *Rocky Mountain News*, p. A35.

———— (1997g, December 6). A different style of doing things: New lead investigator in Jonbenet case has a more open attitude in dealing with public. *Rocky Mountain News*, p. A5.

———— (1998a, February 5). Detective taken off Ramsey case to sue: Investigator wants $150,000, claims chief won't defend her in media or let her speak out. *Rocky Mountain News*, p. A5.

———— (1998b, April 1). Boulder police chief loses job: Acting city manager decides to move Koby to another post to work on special projects. *Rocky Mountain News*, p. A5.

———— (1998c, September 21). Ramsey case pulls careers into "vortex": Inquiry's complex swirl has battered many people whose scars have yet to heal. *Rocky Mountain News*, p. A5.

———— (1998d, January 18). Boulder's unsolved murders: Jonbenet's killing one in five in '90s being studied by police. *Rocky Mountain News*, p. A39.

———— (1998e, September 24). Lawsuit against former Boulder police chief out on hold: Ramsey investigation prompts 90-day delay in action on Koby case. *Rocky Mountain News*, p. A38.

McPhee, M. (1997a, February 9). Koby weathers storm over his silence: Boulder chief known as manager, thinker. *The Denver Post*, p. B4.

———— (1997b, May 6). Riot police keep uneasy peace in Boulder. *The Denver Post*, p. B1.

———— & P. Chronis (1997, January 1). Neighbors, police tight-lipped. *The Denver Post*, p. A1.

Miami in turmoil as police chief quits: Resignation came after mayor fires (2000, April 29). *The Florida Times-Union*, p. A6.

Peters, L.H., D.H. Hartke & J.T. Pohlmann (1985). Fiedler's contingency theory of leadership: An application of the meta-analysis procedures of Schmidt and Hunter. *Psychological Bulletin*, 92 (2), 274–285.

Police officer, sergeant investigated in inmate's death (2000, April 20). *The Associated Press*, state and local wire.

Rice, R.W. & D.R. Kastenbaum (1983). The contingency model of leadership: Some current issues. *Basic and Applied Social Psychology*, 4 (4), 373–392.

Richardson, V. (1997, July 14). Jonbenet's killer may never be found: Cops still hopeful, others lose faith. *The Washington Times*, p. A1.

Robey, R. (1998). New clinic no trouble so far. *The Denver Post*, p. B2.

————— (1997b, November 19). Koby reveals retirement goal: Boulder chief sets date at end of '98. *The Denver Post*, p. B1.

Saha, S.K. (1979). Contingency theories of leadership: A study. *Human Relations*, 32 (4), 313–322.

Schriesheim, C.A., B.J. Tepper & L.A. Tetrault (1994). Least preferred co-worker score, situational control, and leader effectiveness: A meta-analysis of contingency model performance prediction. *Journal of Applied Psychology*, 79 (4), 561–573.

Strube, M.J. & J.E. Garcia (1981). A meta-analytic investigation of Fiedler's contingency model of leadership effectiveness. *Psychological Bulletin*, 90, 307–321.

The Jonbenet Ramsey case day-by-day (2001). Retrieved August 21, 2003, from http://us.cnn.com/US/9703/ramsey.case/timeline5.html.

Tosi, H.L. & S. Kiker (1997). Commentary on "substitutes for leadership." *Leadership Quarterly*, 8 (2), 109–113.

Trial begins in Jonbenet Ramsey case (2001, May 30). *The New York Times*, p. A18.

Utecht, R.E. & W.D. Heier (1976). The contingency model and successful military leadership. *Academy of Management Journal*, 19 (4), 606–618.

Vecchio, R.P. (1979). A dyadic interpretation of the contingency model of leadership effectiveness. *Academy of Management Journal*, 22 (3), 590–600.

————— (1990). Theoretical and empirical examination of cognitive resources theory. *Journal of Applied Psychology*, 75 (2), 141–147.

Vroom, V.H. & P.W. Yetton (1973). *Leadership and decision-making*. Pittsburgh, PA: University of Pittsburgh Press.

Weller, R. (2003, February 10). Boulder avoids suit with new probe into case. *The Associated Press*, state and local wire.

Yukl, G. (1994). *Leadership in organizations* (3rd ed.). Englewood Cliffs, NJ: Prentice Hall.

Zarella, J. (1999, September 27). Federal probe demanded after Miami police shooting. *CNN.com*. Retrieved June 16, 2003, from www.cnn.com/US/9909/27/police.shooting.

# CHAPTER

# 9

# Winning Minds and Hearts

*Path-Goal Theory*

## OVERVIEW OF THE THEORY

Path-goal theory matches leadership style with the characteristics of subordinates and the work environment. In this chapter, the theory is examined through the approach and innovations of Commissioner William Bratton, whose career included three major U.S. police forces: Boston, New York, and Los Angeles. It also looks at Chief Richard Pennington of the New Orleans Police Department, who was charged with turning around a highly corrupt force.

Path-goal theory takes into consideration a complex combination of situational variables that combine to moderate the effects of leader behavior (Jermier, 1996). The leader chooses from four styles: directive, supportive, achievement-oriented, and participative (Northouse, 2004).[1] These leader behaviors are moderated by the personal characteristics of

---

[1]However, Wofford and Liska (1993) note that most of the empirical tests of the theory have focused merely on supportive versus directive styles. These styles are measured using the Leadership Behavior and Descriptor Questionnaire (LBDQ) family of scales, which were developed for style theory testing of consideration and structure. Therefore, achievement-oriented and participative styles have been largely ignored by researchers. Furthermore, Schriesheim and Von Glinow (1977) state that the dimensions of the Ohio Leadership Study scales differ greatly from the theory. They contain "punitive, autocratic and production oriented items . . . which are extraneous to the measurement of the theory's leadership constructs" (p. 399).

subordinates (for example, preference for external structure, need for achievement, self-perceived ability) and environmental factors (task structure, work group norms, organizational formalization). These variables determine the best type of leader behavior to use so subordinates can accomplish their goals. Leadership behavior is ineffective if it is redundant when considering environmental factors or if it is incompatible with subordinate characteristics. In essence, path-goal theory seeks to predict how situational variables will affect the impact of leader behavior on subordinates (Indvik, 1986).

Path-goal theory was derived from the expectancy theory of motivation articulated by Vroom (1964) and Georgopoulos et al. (1957). The expectancy theory states that subordinates' motivation is a function of their expectation that their behavior will lead to a specific outcome. Uncertainty and ambiguity, therefore, are considered stressful and counterproductive. Uncertainty makes it hard for subordinates to identify outcomes as they relate to personal utility. It also obscures the likelihood that outcomes can be predicted based on what the subordinates do to accomplish tasks (Dessler, 1972). In addition, another articulation of the theory proposes that subordinates choose levels of effort that they are willing to employ. A high level of effort only results from subordinates' perception that it leads to good performance (Bryman, 1986). In another formulation of the theory, subordinates adjust their level of effort or motivation in light of whether it will lead to personally desirable outcomes (higher pay, recognition of achievement, promotion, enjoyment) versus undesirable ones (layoff, stress, rejection by coworkers, reprimand, accident) (Yukl, 1994).

From the foundation provided by expectancy theory, House (1971) developed the path-goal framework, which combined leader structure, task uncertainty, and subordinate attitudes. In a nutshell, the leader attempts to clarify the goals of subordinates as well as the route subordinates should take to accomplish them.

Yukl (1994) provides a schematic of the causal relationships of directive and supportive leadership on subordinate effort. Causal variances (leader behaviors) plus intervening variables (subordinate expectancies) as well as situational variables (such as the characteristics of the task and environment and the characteristics of subordinates) lead to the end result of subordinate effort and satisfaction (Yukl, 1994). In directive leadership, if the leader reduces role ambiguity and increases expectations of effort and performance, or increases the magnitude of incentives and thus the desire for task success, or strengthens the reward contingencies and thus the performance reward, it will result in increased subordinate effort (Yukl, 1994). In supportive leadership, if the leader reduces boredom, it will increase the intrinsic valence of the work, or if the leader increases the workers' self-confidence and lowers anxiety, it will increase expectations regarding effort and performance and again lead to increased subordinate effort (Yukl, 1994).

Anti-elitism is embedded in the theory (Jermier, 1996). Because the theory focuses on the needs of followers, the assumption is that leaders should modify their behavior accordingly. It focuses on followers' perceptions of whether a particular activity helps or hurts their likelihood of attaining a goal. The perceptions may or may not reflect the true nature of the situation. Yet the theory bases the leader behavior on the perceptions rather than on the reality (Evans, 1970). In essence, subordinates' perceptions drive the leadership style and the resulting effectiveness of the organization.

The theory places a great deal of emphasis on the responsibility of leaders to adapt to subordinate circumstances on a day-to-day basis. "It reduces the emphasis on measurement of leadership styles and replaces it with an emphasis on the leader's breadth of available behaviors and sensitivity to the combination of situational variables" (Wofford and Liska, 1993, p. 875). Unlike in previous theories, in path-goal theory, the leader must be flexible, depending on subordinate demands in a given situation. Much like the situation in Fiedler's contingency theory, the leader must be able to make a situational diagnosis, which in the case of the path-goal theory is based on subordinate needs. The leader must 1) determine key factors that would affect subordinate motivation, 2) identify the degree to which these factors are provided by the organizational environment, and 3) predict the effects of different types of leadership that could be employed. However, the theory fails to provide a framework on which to base this diagnostic analysis (Schriesheim & Neider, 1996).

Path-goal theory can be considered a dyadic rather than a group phenomenon. Leaders affect each subordinate's motivation individually. The theory challenged the "uniformity and consistency of group leadership and opened the field up to considering individualizing approaches to managerial leadership" (Jermier, 1996, p. 312).

The theory also implies that there are situations in which leadership is irrelevant. Although House did not develop this corollary,

Jermier (1996) states: "[A] major feature of the path-goal theory of leadership that made it interesting was that it bordered on denying the importance of leader behaviors in certain situations, thereby raising to awareness the fundamental assumption of the field" (p. 313). The fundamental assumption referred to here is that some form of leader behavior always impacts effectiveness.

Critics of the theory emphasize that the theory is very broad in explanations and encompasses too many possibilities. The reformulated theory developed by House (1996) includes 10 classes of leader behavior, individual differences of subordinates, and task moderator variables. However, the meta-proposition of the theory does reduce to one simple concept. "The essence of the theory is the meta proposition that leaders, to be effective, engage in behaviors that complement subordinates' environments and abilities in a manner that compensates for deficiencies and is instrumental to subordinate satisfaction and individual and work unit performance" (House, 1996, p. 47).

## PATH-GOAL THEORY AND MILITARY LEADERSHIP

Mathieu (1990) studied the moderating influence of subordinates' needs for achievement and affiliation as it relates to the relationship between instrumental and supportive leadership and subordinates' satisfaction. His sample consisted of 298 Army and Navy ROTC cadets (81 percent men and 19 percent women) who completed questionnaires. The questionnaires measured subordinate achievement and affiliation needs using the Manifest Needs Questionnaire (MNQ). Leader behaviors were measured in the questionnaire using a scale developed by House and Dessler (1974). Cadets were asked to rate their leaders. Regarding cadet satisfaction, the Minnesota Satisfaction Questionnaire (MSQ), which assesses attitudes about job security, compensation, and promotion, was used. Results indicated that subordinates with a high need for achievement prefer leaders who clarify the path toward goals "such that their efforts may be best translated into performance" (House & Dessler 1974, p. 185). However, contrary to prediction, individuals with a high need for affiliation were more satisfied with instrumental leadership behaviors (as opposed to supportive leader behaviors). Mathieu (1990) states that this result could indicate that the task-related activities of structured leaders also provide opportunities for social interactions.

## PATH-GOAL THEORY AND THE CASES
## OF COMMISSIONER WILLIAM BRATTON
## AND CHIEF RICHARD PENNINGTON

The path-goal theory aims to understand and predict how situational variables will affect leader behavior toward subordinates and focuses on how leaders can motivate subordinates to accomplish their goals. The leaders who adopt the path-goal approach tend to engage in one of the following styles: directive, supportive, achievement-oriented, or participative. The two police chiefs chosen to illustrate this leadership approach both chose different styles of the path-goal theory. Of course, their careers were far too complex to be generalized and summarized into a single category, but overall, for the purposes of illustrating the path-goal theory, Commissioner William Bratton of the New York Police Department adopted the directive leadership style, while Chief Richard Pennington of the New Orleans Police Department engaged in the achievement-oriented style.

The directive style sets standards of performance and rules for tasks, and it clarifies goals and expectations. According to this approach, the leader tells the subordinates what to do, when to do it, and how to do it. This more difficult part of the directive style can and should be sweetened by guidance and adequate supervision of subordinates. Such guidance and supervision should motivate the employees/police officers and should also transmit knowledge to those in need of such directives. The achievement-oriented style establishes a high standard of excellence whereby the employees are expected to excel based on the situational variables created by the leader.

Both styles require what Richards (2002) calls "the art of winning minds and hearts." Whether choosing the directive or achievement-oriented approach, one has to win both the minds and hearts of the subordinates in order to accomplish the clearly defined tasks (see Table 9–1). To win minds, the objective is to convince people and to make them understand the purpose of what they are asked to do, no matter how detailed and directive the explanation. To make them excel, one has to win their hearts, where the objective is to move people to increase their commitment and motivation. The medium for winning minds is information; the medium for winning hearts is emotion.

Both Bratton and Pennington engaged in the art of winning minds and hearts despite the fact that both chiefs had most, but not all,

**TABLE 9–1** ART OF WINNING MINDS AND HEARTS LEADERSHIP COMPETENCIES NEEDED

| Art of Winning Minds | Art of Winning Hearts |
|---|---|
| *Objective:* Convincing people—make them understand the purpose | *Objective:* Moving people—increase their commitment/motivation |
| *Medium:* Information | *Medium:* Emotion |
| • Relevance<br>• Cogency<br>• Showmanship<br>• Questioning<br>• Dialogue<br>• Promotion of discovery<br>• Atmosphere of intellectual safety | • Authenticity<br>• Empathy<br>• Listening<br>• Rapport<br>• Optimism<br>• Trust in intuition<br>• Atmosphere of emotional safety |

(Richards, 2002)

of the leadership competencies needed to win both minds and hearts. They were not missing innate qualities or skills; the nature of police organization itself stymied some of those competencies. It is hard, if not impossible, to create intellectual and emotional safety in the punitive and semi-military structure of a police department. It is even harder to do in a police environment that is fraught with problems such as corruption, lack of accountability, poor training, and high crime rates. These challenges are topped by a civil service personnel structure in which hiring and firing cannot easily be tailored to the chief's vision. Things can be demanded, created, and implemented, but success will be limited without winning minds and hearts.

**CAREER HIGHLIGHTS**   Path-Goal Theory, Directive Leadership Style

**Commissioner William Bratton**
*New York Police Department, New York*

William Bratton, whose career has included heading police departments in several major American cities, is likely best known for the sweeping changes he introduced while commissioner of the New York Police Department (NYPD) from 1994 to 1996.

Bratton was raised in the Dorchester section of Boston. He earned a bachelor's degree in law enforcement from Boston State College/University of Massachusetts. He is also a graduate of the FBI National Executive Institute ("William J. Bratton," n.d.) and has honorary doctorates from

*(continued)*

John Jay College of Criminal Justice, New York Institute of Technology, and Curry College (Dussault, 1999).

Bratton joined the Boston Police Department (Metropolitan District Commission Police) in 1970, where he rose through the ranks to become superintendent of police, the highest sworn rank, by 1980 ("William J. Bratton," n.d.). As a patrol officer in Boston, he was awarded the Schroeder Brother's Medal of Honor for talking down a bank robber and rescuing a hostage (Dussault, 1999). In 1983, he was chief of the Massachusetts Bay Transportation Authority and was credited with facilitating a 37 percent reduction in crime in the jurisdiction. Bratton returned to the Boston police in 1986, resuming his superintendent role. He emphasized affirmative action initiatives and hired the first female chief of patrol. In 1990, he moved to his first position in New York City as the chief of police/senior vice president of the New York City Transit Authority. During his service there, subway crime was reportedly reduced by 50 percent ("William J. Bratton," n.d.) due to his quality-of-life policing campaign, which involved arrests of young New Yorkers for fare evasion as a method of reducing the occurrence of more serious crimes (Greene, 1999). As the *Economist* reported, as a harbinger of things to come,

> Mr. Bratton reinvigorated New York's transit police by improving equipment, but also through a dose of Druckerish "Management by objectives": the transit cop's task became to cut crime, not merely to respond to it. Morale soared, and subway crime was cut in half. ("NYPD, Inc.," 1995)

The following year, Bratton again returned to the Boston Police Department as superintendent in chief, serving from 1992 to 1993 (Newfield & Jacobson, 2000; "William J. Bratton," n.d.). He brought community-oriented policing to Boston and was supported by community leaders for respecting the concerns of community residents as this style of policing was introduced ("A test," 1993; Lakshmanan, 1993). He also added more police officers and computers to compile crime statistics by neighborhood. Bratton focused on reducing community members' fear of particular crime-prone blocks or neighborhoods in the city. Each officer received 40 hours of professional development in community-oriented policing in the first few months of Bratton's tenure. Recruits were required to attend a weeklong problem-solving training course ("New Boston police chief," 1993).

Boston officers generally supported Bratton, although his career path led to criticism and speculation that he wanted to return to New York City as police commissioner. He was said to be so ambitious that he was "willing to hurt a department, even a friend, to help himself" (McGrory, 1993, p. 15). However, the executive director of the Police Executive Forum in 1993 stated that Bratton recognizes "people's strengths and weaknesses and delegates power and gives them tools. . . . He is a big picture person, who has five or six things going on at the same time. He doesn't micro-manage. He understands policing" (McGrory, 1993, p. 15). Bratton did return to lead the New York City Police Department in 1994.

In New York, Bratton is associated with the zero-tolerance style of policing, which emphasizes quality-of-life issues for the average law-abiding citizen by enforcing laws against petty drug dealers, prostitutes, graffiti artists, and "squeegee men." Bratton directed patrol officers to stop citizens and search them for violating minor laws, to conduct warrant checks, or to question citizens about criminality in their neighborhood. Bratton thus put into practice Wilson and Kelling's "broken windows" theory, which suggests that serious crackdowns on low-level disorderly behavior would reduce serious crime because such order-maintenance problems attract predatory criminals (Greene, 1999). Criticizing a 1995 cost-saving initiative city judges put forward for decriminalization of minor offenses, Bratton explained:

> Go out in Brooklyn any night of the week. All these characters out there on the corner, drinking, urinating. Once they get a few drinks under their belt, out come the knives, out come the guns, out come the loud mouths . . . little things count . . . little things like quality of life. One of the reasons why this city and this country were in [a] mess . . . was nobody paid attention to the small things." (Marzulli, 1995, p. 2)

Under Bratton, the number of misdemeanor arrests jumped from approximately 133,000 annually to 205,000 between 1993 and 1996 (Walker & Katz, 2002).

Commentators criticized Bratton for using military campaign metaphors ("Don't mention," 2003; Greene, 1999). In fact, Bratton described one anti–drug crime initiative, Juggernaut (never implemented), in the following terms:

> We would literally roll through the city, like securing a beachhead. And after we secured the beachhead, unlike the previous initiatives in this city, we wouldn't just let the area sink back; we would move in the occupation forces which would be the community police and the beat cops. (Newfield & Jacobson, 2000, p. 52)

Citizens, often minorities, complained about overzealous policing and brutality. The proportion of "general patrol incidents" made up 29 percent of the complaints in the last year of the Dinkins administration and increased to 58 percent the next year under Mayor Rudolph Giuliani and Bratton (Greene, 1999). Bratton reportedly responded to this increase by pointing out that the board dismisses 75 percent of the complaints as unsubstantiated prior to investigation. The increase in complaints also correlated with the creation of an independent (civilian), rather than internal, complaint board (McQuillan, 1995). However, the number of complaints to this Civilian Complaint Review Board increased more than

(continued)

60 percent between 1992 and 1996. Regardless, relations with minority communities were reportedly particularly strained as a result of the zero-tolerance policing style. At a community meeting in the South Bronx in July 1995, a critical crowd of approximately 500 Hispanic people met Bratton and Giuliani, complaining about police brutality. Bratton told them, "You're acting like a bunch of fools. You're making a fool of your-selves. You're the same group that shows up at every one of these meet-ings and we're not getting anywhere" (Lewis & Siemaszko, 1995, p. 4). Yet in an earlier *New York Times* editorial regarding police brutality, Bratton got good marks for his response to the death in custody of Ernest Sayon. That victim had died after a struggle with the police, who restrained him using a controversial choke hold (banned by the NYPD). Bratton initiated a task force review of the department's policies and training programs on handling violent arrestees ("Mr. Bratton's wise policing," 1994).

Bratton strengthened command and discipline, and he empha-sized officer accountability ("Community policing," 1994), making an analogy that he ran the police department as if managing a private business in which the profit is crime reduction. He devolved power to precinct commanders, whom he then held accountable for the crime statistics in their precincts. Initiating the computerized statistics (COMPSTAT) program, Bratton collected data on arrests, calls for serv-ice, and complaints, and he analyzed and mapped them at the precinct level. At weekly meetings, crime trends were examined and precinct commanders were questioned about their crime-control strategies. Those who could not reduce crime in their precincts were reassigned to less challenging positions (Walker & Katz, 2002). Bratton described these often-intense meetings:

> The reality is that COMPSTAT does produce some tension. If you go to school without doing your homework, you are scared to death the teacher is going to call on you. In COMPSTAT, you are guaranteed to be called on. So if you don't prepare, if you don't participate in the team, you are going to be embarrassed right out of the room. (Dussault, 1999)

As a result, there was high turnover in precinct commander positions. For the year prior to September 1995, three out of five precincts had new commanding officers (George, 1995).

Bratton also attacked corruption (Blood, 1995). Internal Affairs sting operations increased 10-fold, from 50 to 500 investigations, over the year ending August 1995 (Lewis & Siemaszko, 1995). In addition, the depart-ment focused on the problem of cop alcoholism, a problem highlighted after a deputy inspector of a Brooklyn precinct showed up drunk at 7 a.m. for a strategy session with departmental bosses (George, 1995; Lewis & Siemaszko, 1995). That officer lost his command. That same year, 30 NYPD officers at a convention in Washington, D.C., went on a beer-soaked spree, groping women and running around naked. Bratton responded by devoting Internal Affairs resources to combating the cultural factors in policing that encourage both alcoholism and corruption; he also sent a series of self-help videotapes to the home of each officer in the city (Lewis & Siemaszko, 1995).

Late in Bratton's tenure, he publicly feuded with Mayor Giuliani (Wilborn, 2002). Bratton felt that Giuliani was taking all the credit for the much-lauded policing initiatives in order to bolster his own political ambitions (Newfield & Jacobson, 2000). He also said that the rift was caused by a difference in police strategies, which developed over the course of their working together. In a 1997 feature in *The New Yorker*, Giuliani said he had to do the work of the police commissioner because Bratton was too concerned with his media image to police effectively (Wilborn, 2002).

After leaving the police commissioner job in 1996, Bratton founded The Bratton Group, LLC, and was a consultant with Kroll Associates, which oversaw the federal consent decree with the Los Angeles Police Department. Simultaneously, from 1993 to 1996, he was elected president of the Police Executive Research Forum (PERF) ("William J. Bratton," n.d.). In October 2002, Bratton took the helm of the Los Angeles Police Department (LAPD), which was reeling after the breaking of the Rampart scandal.[1] Many have speculated that Bratton was selected to run the LAPD because its image was so tarnished by corruption and he was known as a results-oriented police leader (Wilborn, 2002). Secondly, he had experience with the issues facing the city after serving on the committee overseeing the implementation of the federal consent decree. Finally, commentators have pointed out that Mayor James Hahn wanted to implement community policing as operationalized by Bratton in New York (Laird, 2002).

As expected, Bratton has decentralized authority to geographic bureaus within the department and updated the computer system to replicate New York's COMPSTAT (Stockstill, 2002). Bratton believes that increasing officers in problem areas such as South Central Los Angeles, where violent crime has dramatically increased, is the key to effective policing, but he has been granted only modest increases in force strength due to budget constraints in 2002 and 2003 (Broder, 2003; Nash, 2002).[2]

---

[1] The scandal was named after an immigrant community where 70 LAPD officers were investigated for a pattern of corruption, including planting evidence and fabricating stories to explain unjustified shootings. As a result, in more than 100 cases, convictions were overturned or charges dropped. Despite the internal investigations into the affair, it has engendered citizen mistrust, prompting Bratton to call for an outside review in February 2003 ("Bratton," 2003).

[2] In 2002, the authorized strength was 10,196 officers (Nash, 2002).

(*continued*)

Bratton has made combating gangs foremost on the department's agenda, likening the gangs to the Mafia in New York. There are more than 200 gangs with 100,000 members operating in the LA area. The number of homicides in Los Angeles was the highest in the nation in 2002 (Leovy, 2003).[3] Most commentators attribute the homicide spike to increased gang activity, particularly by the Rolling 60s Crips (Kandel, 2002). Bratton promoted a captain as an antigang "czar" and has been encouraging officers to stop suspected gang members for minor infractions, again using the "broken windows" theory to influence a reduction in serious gang activity. In November 2002, Bratton personally responded to two homicides, saying, "I want to go to homicide scenes so that I can be angry. I want to have intimacy with that," (Nash, 2002, N3).

When Bratton joined the NYPD, he was faced with a number of critical problems. The NYPD was a decentralized bureaucracy with very serious communication and accountability problems. Six months of logs containing reports of arrests, youth violence, and drug and gun activities all pointed to dysfunction and a lack of control, direct outcomes of overall bad management and an overwhelming lack of accountability. At the time, Jack Maple, one of the engineers of COMPSTAT, told this author that the commanding officers of the precincts had reached such a level of comfort in their inertia that when shown a map of their own precinct, they were not even able to identify it.

Bratton's approach to these serious problems was clearly one of a directive leader. He improved communication by dividing the organization into smaller entities to facilitate communication patterns and accountability at a precinct level, he instituted new programs to deal with youth violence and drug and guns activities, he fired many mid-level and senior managers, and he made it clear that promotions would be tied directly and exclusively to merit. The greatest innovation of all, with regard to personal and organizational accountability, was the now-infamous COMPSTAT, the statistical database that made precinct commanders and other ranking officers almost personally accountable for crime rates. However, despite the obvious advantages of COMPSTAT, it did not consider the human factor, the need for creation of both intellectual and emotional safety—minds and hearts—in order for police officers to buy into the concept. Bratton's idea of reengineering a police department was definitely a worthy effort. However, his path-goal approach, exhibited through the directive leadership style, did not factor in the missing component: One must buy the minds and hearts of one's subordinates when introducing highly innovative and extreme approaches. Attrition and elevated levels of cynicism were only some of the negative side effects of Bratton's directive style of leadership.

---

[3]The murder rate in Los Angeles increased by 10 percent in 2002 over the previous year, compared to 2.3 percent nationally.

**CAREER HIGHLIGHTS**  Path-Goal Theory, Achievement-Oriented Leadership Style

Chief Richard Pennington
*New Orleans Police Department, Louisiana*

In the eight years he served as New Orleans Chief of Police, Richard Pennington addressed some of the major problems on the force, most notably with regard to police corruption. He has since transferred some of those strategies to the position he occupies, at the time of writing, in Atlanta.

Pennington was born in Little Rock, Arkansas, and raised in Gary, Indiana. After earning a high school degree, he enlisted in the Air Force and served in the Vietnam War. In 1968, he was discharged and subsequently took a job as a police officer in the Washington, D.C., Police Department (Stirgus, 2002). Pennington climbed the ranks of the Washington, D.C., Police Department from 1968 until 1994 (Suggs, 2002b). From 1992 to 1994, he was an assistant police chief. In the early 1990s, as a district commander, Pennington initiated the first community-policing pilot program in the department, putting more officers on foot patrols and bicycles and increasing community contact. Reportedly, between 1991 and 1992, homicides in Washington, D.C., were reduced from 137 per year to 108 (Alpert, 1994).

Pennington has a bachelor's degree in criminal justice from American University and a master's degree in criminal justice from the University of the District of Columbia. He is also a graduate of the FBI National Academy ("Richard J. Pennington," 2002).

### Chief of the New Orleans Police Department (1994–2002)

When he was appointed chief of police in New Orleans, Pennington inherited a force rife with corruption in a city losing its battle with serious crime. Pennington is credited with cutting the New Orleans murder rate in half (Perlstein, 2003). In 1994, New Orleans had 425 homicides and was considered the murder capital of the nation. By 1999, the murders had declined to 159, the largest crime-reduction rate of the nation's 34 biggest cities (Suggs, 2002b). Murders dropped 64 percent between 1994 and 1999 (St. Bernard, 1999). Policies credited with this success include increasing the visibility of officers in public housing complexes, boosting the number of homicide detectives by 40 percent, and reducing caseloads per investigator from 12 to 8 (Varney, 1995). Pennington also raised officer pay, decentralized the detective bureau, and held commanders responsible for crime reduction (via a COMPSTAT-like focus on statistics) (Perlstein, 1999c).

Pennington is also noted for addressing police corruption in New Orleans (Suggs, 2002e). The problem had been significant. At a party celebrating his inauguration as chief, an FBI agent reportedly pulled him

*(continued)*

aside to let him know that a drug ring was operating within the department. To make a break from past practice, early in his tenure Pennington replaced the Internal Affairs Department with a Public Integrity Division (PID) (Varney, 1995). Two FBI agents were hired for the division in order to provide an outside perspective (Perlstein, 1999a).

Under Pennington's command, more than 350 officers were indicted, fired, or disciplined for misconduct stemming from PID investigations (Suggs, 2002b). In 1994, as aforementioned, Officer Len Davis was convicted of ordering the murder of a woman who filed a police brutality report against him (Alpert, 1998). In 1995, a veteran patrolman was charged with attempted murder for firing shots into a car filled with teenagers, two officers were charged with raping a 14-year-old while responding to a call (Perlstein, 1995), and an officer was a suspect in the killings of 24 women, although that officer was never charged and was later cleared in the killings (Perlstein, 2003). In 1998, an officer was charged with extorting money from a massage parlor (Philbin, 1998), and the second-highest-ranking officer was reprimanded for deceptive bookkeeping practices for the department's purchasing department ("High-ranking police official," 1998). In addition, in 1999, an officer was arrested for rape during a traffic stop ("Officer arrested," 1999), and another officer faced federal extortion charges for demanding money from a business owner in exchange for information about a criminal investigation against her (Perlstein, 1999b).

Another of the ways Pennington fought corruption was by limiting the number of hours that officers could devote to moonlighting jobs, particularly since some off-duty security jobs involved criminal employers. The regulation not only reduced criminal elements in the police association but also eliminated the relevance of "power brokers," cops who controlled such off-duty hiring; it also cut down on the number of police who reported to work dangerously fatigued (Campbell, 2002).

Pennington also kept an open dialogue with police critics, such as local civil rights attorneys and the U.S. Attorney General (Stirgus, 2002). These contacts influenced Pennington to widen his war on police corruption by exploring citizen complaints of racial profiling. In 1998, he urged citizens to come forward with complaints of racial profiling so that he could investigate the alleged problem (Donze, 1998).

Recently Pennington himself was accused of wrongdoing. In January 2003, a state audit of the Southern University at New Orleans uncovered potential salary fraud in the university's compensation to Pennington, and a complaint was filed in the local district attorney's office. He was paid $44,000 over two and a half years to teach two graduate courses for five semesters, a large salary for a part-time instructor. Some signatures on Pennington's time sheets appeared to be forged. However, according to a Pennington spokesperson, he provided services in addition to teaching that included establishing a master's degree program in criminal justice and advising and recruiting students. A director of the school indicated that Pennington had indeed provided the services for which he was paid ("Ex-chief's pay," 2003; Young, 2003).

In other controversies, it was recently revealed that under Pennington's command, New Orleans police wrongly destroyed evidence. The current chief of the city's police department made no accusations of intentional wrongdoing on the part of Pennington but indicated that a massive evidence storage clean-up effort, which took place in 2001, may have destroyed important evidence needed in three ongoing cases (Filosa, 2003).

Upon resigning as chief in 2002, Pennington received standing ovations in New Orleans restaurants, showing the respect he had earned from many citizens (Stirgus, 2002). However, his 2002 bid for election as a Democratic mayor of New Orleans failed (Grace, 2001; Mullener, 2002). During the campaign, rumors surfaced that he abused his wife (Mullener, 2002). Furthermore, the two police unions in the city endorsed his opponent (Stirgus, 2002).

After leaving New Orleans, Pennington brought many of the same approaches to Atlanta, where he has served as chief of police since 2002. Priority issues for him include low officer morale, community policing, dangerous police practices, corruption, and police accountability.

Upon taking the job, Pennington made changes to the command staff and promoted officers in an effort to confront low morale, which he identified as one of the biggest problems with the force he inherited. Of particular note, he promoted an officer who had previously blown the whistle on the department's underreporting of crimes and had spent five years in an exiled position (Suggs, 2002e). Low morale also stemmed from complaints about low pay and a 400-member officer shortage (Niesse, 2002). Pennington announced plans to hire an additional 500 police officers in his first two years (Suggs, 2002a). Pennington also inherited a department that was deficient in necessary equipment (old motorcycle helmets and a shortage of uniforms), which he vowed to correct (Suggs, 2002c).

His inaugural promises included training new officers in community policing ("Pennington sworn in," 2002). Using New York City's quality-of-life campaign as a guide, Pennington initiated a Quality of Life Task Force to confront homelessness and panhandling in March 2003. The group was to crack down on nuisance violations, clean up litter and graffiti, and increase outreach services for homeless people. According to Pennington, panhandling, trash, and graffiti make "going downtown unpleasant, even scary" (Suggs & Ippolito, 2003, p. 1D). He has also spoken of building partnerships with the black community, in particular, on the issue of intraracial crime (Suggs, 2003).

(continued)

Pennington was clear on his expectations from the force itself. On his first day on the job, Pennington called a meeting of his new command staff and stated:

> So don't B.S. me, because I have seen it all and I have done it all. Be straight-forward with me, because I can see through a lot of B.S. I am not coming here under the assumption that this is a bad police department with bad people. I like to surround myself with good people until they prove to not be capable of doing the job. Then I have no trouble replacing you. (Suggs, 2002e, p. 1E)

He also emphasized that he is a uniformed police chief because it sends the message that he is part of the department and because it is a sign of authority (Suggs, 2002e).

In November 2002, Pennington reformed the department's policy on high-speed chases. In the previous six months, there had been five fatalities after high-speed chases, and only one of the chases stemmed from a serious crime. Under the new policy, chases are only permitted for serious offenses against people, such as murder, rape, or robbery. Pennington implemented a similar policy as chief in New Orleans, and the numbers of high-speed chase injuries and fatalities were subsequently reduced (Suggs, 2002f).

In recent controversies, the Atlanta Police Department shot 12 people (5 fatally) between January and August 2002, more than in any of the previous six years. The press reported that community mistrust of officers was on the rise as a result. Some community members accused the department of racial profiling, particularly of blacks driving expensive cars, which described at least one of the shooting victims. Pennington responded by suspending undercover vice operations and ordering a review of department policies on the use of lethal force. One of the shootings involved a cop shooting at a car that was veering toward him at a high speed, which prompted Pennington to order a specific review of the policy regarding shooting at cars (such shootings were prohibited when Pennington headed the New Orleans police). He also stated, however, that the department did not have a history of problems with excessive use of force ("Atlanta suspends undercover vice unit," 2002; Niesse, 2002). Pennington indicated that he was open to a federal investigation into the shootings if that would help resolve the controversy as to what happened and the appropriateness of the police response. He also stated, "I just want my officers to know that we are going to thoroughly investigate shootings. If they have not done anything improper, they have nothing to worry about" (Suggs, 2002d, p. 3D).

Moreover, Pennington has advocated for a rejuvenated civilian review board (although Atlanta has one, it was not active in 2002). This commitment to civilian review was praised by an editorial in *The Atlanta Journal and Constitution* as an important check against a perceived blue wall of silence (Tucker, 2002).

Pennington exhibits the achievement-oriented approach to the path-goal theory. The problems he faced when taking on the position in New Orleans were even more serious in nature than the ones faced by Commissioner Bratton. The level of corruption of the New Orleans Police Department was absolutely unprecedented in the history of modern policing in the United States. The cleaning up of the ranks, changes in the training procedures, pay raises, establishment of new mechanisms of accountability—all were far-reaching steps in a major attempt not only to clean up the department that was often referred to as "the most corrupt police department in the United States" but also to elevate it to a police department that would become a model for others.

Chief Pennington came to New Orleans with an ambitious plan. Its success was dependent on the effective motivation of those officers who remained on the force, so they would be an asset to build on in the creation of a new environment while breaking away from the old image and sub-culture. He, as well as Bratton in New York City, had to buy both the minds and hearts of his officers to achieve this reengineering. Establishing high standards definitely has its merits in environments of highly questionable integrity and scarce resources for change. Chief Pennington was not a man of incremental steps, which would have been more realistic; his changes were extreme and swift and innovative. However, he was not able to create the intellectual and emotional safety needed to successfully "purchase" the minds and hearts of those who needed to maintain the high standard of excellence that the chief demanded. When he ran for mayor, police unions endorsed his opponent.

One of his biggest problems in not being able to create this intellectual and emotional safety was his inability to change the force in the most extreme way by purging the force of those officers who needed to be fired. At a certain point, many officers were charged with criminal misconduct and subsequently fired from the force. Although these officers were charged and found guilty, many more officers witnessed these officers' misconduct yet remained on the force and were never charged or disciplined. With so many officers who had been contaminated by the previous misconduct and wrong practices remaining on the force, it was impossible for Chief Pennington to buy enough minds and hearts to enable the commitment and motivation to sustain the changes he ultimately sought.

## Exercise

The police commissioner and chief detailed in this chapter have been examined through the prism of path-goal theory. Using what you have learned from other theories in this book or from the summaries (as indicated in the Introduction) you have read thus far, it is possible to consider their approaches through the lens of different theories. What other theories can you find applicable to the commissioner and the chief? Are there lessons to be learned from those applications, or do those theories indicate alternative paths or approaches that might have yielded a more successful outcome?

# REFERENCES

A test for Commissioner Bratton (1993, October 2). *The Boston Globe*, p. 10.

Alpert, B. (1994, October 15). Community patrols big with new chief. *The Times-Picayune*, p. A1.

—— (1998, July 8). Rights group praises Pennington's efforts, but brutality problems persist, it claims. *The Times-Picayune*, p. B8.

Atlanta suspends undercover vice unit after fatal shooting (2002, August 6). *The Associated Press*, state and local wire.

Blood, M. (1995, June 10). NYPD vows to improve tarnished reputation. *The Record*, p. A4.

Bratton calls for independent Rampart probe (2003, February 28). Retrieved June 22, 2003, from http://www.kcal9.com/topstories/topstoriesla_story05919851.html.

Broder, J.M. (2003, June 16). Los Angeles city council retaliates against mayor: Fracas over police and rejection of budget. *The New York Times*, p. A12.

Bryman, A. (1986). *Leadership and organizations*. London: Routledge & Kegan Paul.

Campbell, C. (2002, July 23). Police problems need action from new chief. *The Atlanta Journal and Constitution*, p. 2B.

Community policing, Bratton style (1994, January 31). *The New York Times*, p. A16.

Dessler, G. (1972). A test of a path-goal motivational theory of leadership. *Proceedings of Academy of Management*, 178–181.

Don't mention the war: A delicate task for William Bratton in Los Angeles (2003, March 22). *Economist*, 366 (8316).

Donze, F. (1998, November 17). Police behavior overtakes budget: Won't tolerate misconduct, Pennington vows. *The Times-Picayune*, p. B1.

Dussault, R. (1999, August). The taking of New York: Former NYC police commissioner William Bratton talks about how technology helped make the streets safer. *Government Technology*. Retrieved June 22, 2003, from www.govtech.net/magazine/gt/1999/aug/brattonfldr/bratton/phtml.

Evans, M.G. (1970). Leadership and motivation: A core concept. *Academy of Management Journal*, 13 (1), 21–102.

Ex-chief's pay target of investigation (2003, January 15). *The Associated Press*, state and local wire.

Filosa, G. (2003, February 6). Evidence lost, police chief concedes. *The Times-Picayune*, p. 1.

George, T. (1995, September 3). Bratton's new breed of blue. *Daily News*, p. 1.

Georgopoulos, B.S., G.M. Mahoney & N.W. Jones, Jr., (1957). A path-goal approach to productivity. *Journal of Applied Psychology*, 41, 345–353.

Grace, S. (2001, November 21). Pennington launches campaign for mayor. *The Times-Picayune*, p. 1.

Greene, J.A. (1999). Zero tolerance: Police policies and practices in New York City. *Crime and Delinquency*, 45 (2), 171–187.

High-ranking police official gets reprimand, suspension (1998, September 17). *The Associated Press*, state and local wire.

House, R.J. (1996). Path-goal theory of leadership: Lessons, legacy, and a reformulated theory. *Leadership Quarterly*, 7 (3), 323–352.

————— (1971). A path-goal theory of leader effectiveness. *Administrative Science Quarterly*, 16, 321–328.

————— & G. Dessler (1974). Path-goal theory of leadership. *Journal of Contemporary Business*, 3, 81–97.

Indvik, J. (1986). Path-goal theory of leadership: A meta-analysis. *Proceedings of Academy of Management*, 189–192.

Jermier, J. (1996). The path-goal theory of leadership: A subtextual analysis. *Leadership Quarterly*, 7 (3), 311–316.

Kandel, J. (2002, November 21). Dial L.A. for murder: Movie capital leads nation in homicides. *The Daily News of Los Angeles*, p. N1.

Laird, L. (2002, October 4). Bratton pledges to restore LAPD's "tarnished" reputation as police chief. *Metropolitan News Enterprise*, p. 8.

Lakshmanan, I. (1993, June 30). Community leaders say Bratton able, ambitious, and some officers express optimism. *The Boston Globe*, p. 15.

Leovy, J. (2003, January 1). L.A. crime edges up, led by 10% jump in killings. *The Los Angeles Times*, p. B6.

Lewis, D.L. & C. Siemaszko (1995, July 12). Bratton blows top. *Daily News*, p. 4.

Marzulli, J. (1995, November 8). Bratton sez judges killing city's quality of life. *Daily News*, p. 2.

Mathieu, J.E. (1990). A test of subordinates' achievement and affiliation needs as moderators of leader path-goal relationships. *Basic and Applied Psychology*, 11 (2), 179–180.

McGrory, B. (1993, June 30). Bratton seen as a leader in "new school" of policing. *The Boston Globe*, p. 15.

McQuillan, A. (1995, August 24). Gripes vs. cops skyrocket under independent CCRB. *Daily News*, p. 36.

Mr. Bratton's wise policing (1994, May 31). *The New York Times*, p. A30.

Mullener, E. (2002, May 24). Farewell to the chief. *The Times-Picayune*, p. 1.

Nash, J. (2002, November 20). Bratton backs off 12,000 goal: Cash-strapped city to add 270 to LAPD. *The Daily News of Los Angeles*, p. N3.

New Boston police chief outlines his priorities for the department (1993, July 11). *The Boston Globe*, p. 2.

Newfield, J. & M. Jacobson (2000, July/August). An interview with William Bratton. *Tikkun*, 15 (1), 51–54.

Niesse, M. (2002, August 21). Killings by Atlanta police raise racial tensions. *Chattanooga Times Free Press*, p. NG4.

Northouse, P.G. (2004). *Leadership: Theory and practice* (3rd ed.). Thousand Oaks, CA: Sage.

NYPD, Inc. (1995, July 29). *Economist*, 336 (7925), 50.

Officer arrested in sexual assaults (1999, August 26). *The Advocate*, p. B6.

Pennington sworn in as new Atlanta police chief (2002, July 9). *The Associated Press*, state and local wire.

Perlstein, M. (1995, May 23). 2 N.O. cops booked with raping 14-year-old. *The Times-Picayune*, p. B1.

―――― (1999a, July 26). Reformed NOPD is hot topic globally: Its top cop active on lecture circuit. *The Times-Picayune*, p. B1.

―――― (1999b, October 2). N.O. cop booked in extortion scheme: FBI says cop traded information for cash. *The Times-Picayune*, p. B3.

―――― (1999c, October 15). Murder rate nearly half, chief says. *The Times-Picayune*, p. B1.

―――― (2003, May 29). Manhunt thrusts Pennington back into N.O. spotlight. *The Times-Picayune*, p. 1.

Philbin, W. (1998, April 15). Cop held in massage parlor sting. *The Times-Picayune*, p. A1.

Richard J. Pennington, chief of police (2002, July 29). Retrieved June 9, 2003, from www.atlantapd.org/cstaff/chief/html.

Richards, D. (2002). *Convincing minds and winning hearts.* Louisville, KY: Brown Herron Publishing.

Schriesheim, C.A. & M.A. Von Glinow (1977). The path-goal theory of leadership: A theoretical and empirical analysis. *Academy of Management Journal*, 20, 398–405.

―――― & L.L. Neider (1996). Path-goal leadership theory: The long and winding road. *Leadership Quarterly*, 7 (3), 317–321.

St. Bernard, S.C. (1999, August 6). N.O. police chief shares inspiration at breakfast: Pennington gets spiritual on crime. *The Times-Picayune*, p. B1.

Stirgus, E. (2002, April 14). New Orleans chief enters city's folklore. *Cox News Service*, Domestic.

Stockstill, M (2002, October 29). Bratton lays out priorities for LAPD command staff. *City News Service.*

Suggs, E. (2002a, May 31). Pennington names Atlanta's top cop. *The Atlanta Journal and Constitution*, p. 1C.

―――― (2002b, June 6). New chief wants raise for officers. *The Atlanta Journal and Constitution*, p. 1JN.

―――― (2002c, July 13). Inside the mind of the new chief. *The Atlanta Journal and Constitution*, p. 1H.

―――― (2002d, July 26). Atlanta chief welcomes U.S. probe of shooting. *The Atlanta Journal and Constitution*, p. 3D.

―――― (2002e, October 19). Chief shifts police brass. *The Atlanta Journal and Constitution*, p. 1E.

―――― (2002f, November 8). Deadly high-speed chases. *The Atlanta Journal and Constitution*, p. 1C.

―――― (2003, May 23). Area chief joins efforts to fight black crime rate. *The Atlanta Journal and Constitution*, p. 2F.

―――― & M. Ippolito (2003, March 27). Mayor, police chief focus on homeless. *The Atlanta Journal and Constitution*, p. 1D.

Tucker, C. (2002, July 17). Cops needn't fear scrutiny of civilians. *The Atlanta Journal and Constitution*, p. 16A.

Varney, J. (1995, June 30). Department cleaning up act, Pennington tells commission. *The Times-Picayune*, p. B1.

Vroom, V.H. (1964). *Work and motivation.* New York: Wiley.

Walker, S. & C.M. Katz (2002). The police in America (4th ed.). New York: McGraw-Hill.

Wilborn, P. (2002, October 3). With Bratton LA lands a star for its police chief. *The Associated Press*, state and local wire.

William J. Bratton, chief of police (n.d.). Retrieved August 10, 2004, from http://www.lapdonline.org/c_o_s/bratton_w_bio.htm.

Wofford, J.C. & L.Z. Liska (1993). Path-goal theories of leadership: A meta-analysis. *Journal of Management*, 19 (4), 857–876.

Young, T. (2003, January 14). Auditor questions ex-chief's SUNO pay. *The Times-Picayune*, p. 1.

Yukl, G. (1994). *Leadership in organizations* (3rd ed.). Englewood Cliffs, NJ: Prentice Hall.

# 10

# Leadership and Command of the Critical Incident

*Psychodynamic Approach*

## OVERVIEW OF THE APPROACH

The psychodynamic approach to leadership can be traced to Sigmund Freud and primarily focuses on the leader as a charismatic individual (Stech, 2004). Deep-seated emotional factors, including lifetime experiences, affect leadership behavior. This approach is examined through the example of New York Police Department (NYPD) Commissioner Bernard Kerik, who oversaw the department through the September 11, 2001, terrorist attacks on the World Trade Center.

Max Weber's treatment of charismatic leadership set the stage for psychoanalytic theories (Hummel, 1975). For Weber, there are three bases of legitimate authority: traditional, legal, and charismatic. The traditional basis represents the habitual orientation of followers to conform based on ancient patriarchal cultures. Legal authority rests in the acceptance of the rationality of rules made in a particular organization or society. Charismatic authority resides in individuals who have personal confidence and heroism, such as prophets (Weber, 1964).

---

## Three Bases of Legitimate Authority

### Traditional

• Habitual orientation based on ancient patriarchal culture

### Legal

• Acceptance of the rationality of rules

### Charismatic

• Authority of individuals with personal confidence and heroism, such as prophets

(M. Weber, 1964)

---

Weber says that people do not obey leaders based on tradition or statute but rather because people believe in them. This has occurred in all places and in all historical epochs (Weber, 1973). Weber further states that charisma exists when followers experience a moment of distress, which sparks complete devotion to the leader.

In *Group Psychology and the Analysis of the Ego* (1921), Freud describes the needs of a group: continuity, definition, interaction (with other groups), and traditions. These needs counter a primitive state characterized by an intellectual disintegration and a decline of conscience. In *Moses and Monotheism* (1939), Freud describes the beginning of civilization as a struggle with the leader of the primitive clan. He recites a scientific myth that the primal father of the first group was the target of envy and was slain by his son. After the killing, love for the father did not have an object, and the son underwent a melancholic state of object loss. To fill the void, love is projected onto a new leader.

According to Freud, since then, groups require organization and leadership in order to fend off negative unconscious desires and narcissism. Freud develops the concept of libido as the glue that holds subordinates to leaders. Libido is the energy necessary for love. If an individual follows a leader, he/she does it out of love for that leader (Freud, 1921; Winer et al., 1984–1985). For Freud, charisma is a particular type of love. The leader represents a father figure, who is a source of love and fear. Followers believe in the leader, who becomes a surrogate for the father whose image they incorporate into their superego. Furthermore, subordinates behave like family siblings in relation to each other and may experience rivalry (Bass, 1990).

Kohut (1976) discusses the pathology of the self that can be found in both leaders and followers. Under his paradigm, charismatic leaders have experienced a particular trauma, which then propels them to use leadership in order to bolster their own self-esteem. Subordinates, meanwhile, cope with their shame, jealousy, and hate by idolizing leaders (Bass, 1990).

LaBarre (1972) posits that subordinates' fascination with their leaders stems from leaders' narcissistic fascination with themselves. This fascination was derived from the fascination that their mother had for them. Leaders emerge in response to crisis situations in which cultural norms fail. LaBarre's conception of culture is that it is a defense mechanism protecting people from anxiety and stress (Winer et al., 1984–1985). Similarly, Kets de Vries (1980) indicates that leaders have a sense of grandiosity, which emerges in times of crisis. Simultaneously, their subordinates have a sense of helplessness, thus bringing the two together. Leaders apply their paranoid potential to the problem at hand in order to lead effectively.

Winer et al. (1984–1985) interpret the psychoanalytic approach to mean that an individual's personal suffering is an impetus for personal transformation. In repairing the self, the individual gains the capacity to lead others. Charismatic leaders, after suffering through a trauma, unconsciously feel passive, "powerless," and acted upon by the object, despite the fact that they have become the "doer" rather than "the done to" (p. 169). Followers have a matching unconscious sense of self. The leader is attracted to the followers as a paradigmatic reenactment of the original trauma:

> In the unconscious fantasy, [the leader] remains passive and helpless despite success after success. . . . The leader seeks followers in order to immerse himself repeatedly in the traumatic situation and repeatedly reverse it both for himself and others. (Winer et al., 1984–1985, p. 170)

The psychoanalytic study of leadership has focused on the pathology of leadership, labeling leaders schizoid, obsessive, paranoid, and narcissistic (Bass, 1990).

One problem associated with the psychoanalytic approach is the focus on the pathology of leaders and followers. There is a lack of explanation for the charismatic behavior of healthy leaders (Strozier & Offer, 1985). Zaleznik (1974) recognizes that some leaders may have a healthy development of self, related to the psychoanalytic concept of "introjection." When individuals internalize the mother or father figure in childhood (which occurs in stable, emotionally healthy families), they can draw on the strength of the internalization in times of object loss. In essence, they have introjected their objects of needs and are not propelled to crisis. Zaleznik (1977) believes that charismatic leaders have introjected objects, which provides the basis for their ties to followers. An internal audience (mother or father) forms the leaders' inner life and helps them negotiate difficulties on behalf of others.

In addition, the psychodynamic approach has utilized the works of Carl Jung and Joseph Campbell to explore heroic archetypes and myths. In exploring self-actualization in the workplace, David Whyte (1994) writes:

> Once basic necessities are taken care of, there are other more immediate urgencies central to human experience, and it is these urgencies that are continually breaking through our fondest hopes for an ordered work life. The split between what is nourishing at work and what is agonizing is the very chasm from which our personal destiny emerges. Accepting the presence of this chasm we can begin to deal, one step at a time, with the continually hidden, underground force that shape our lives, often against our will. (p. 5)

Using poetry, such as the tale of *Beowulf*, Whyte describes the archetypical descent into the darkness of the soul, drawing on the work of Campbell and his notion of the hero's journey. In the same vein, Jungian psychology focuses on the notion of the shadow self—the part of the psyche that is denied because it is considered unacceptable (Stech, 2004). Whyte encourages workplace leaders to become aware of their shadow selves, described as unresolved forces that affect their behavior. Without awareness, leaders unconsciously play out the same struggles and cannot be personally fulfilled or effective. "The empowered manager [is] one who has some understanding of his or her own dark side and inner struggles" (Whyte, 1994, p. 65).

## BIRTH ORDER

Birth order has also been proposed to be related to leadership. Adler (1928) states that intellectual development and a need for power are more prevalent in firstborn children. They are overrepresented among U.S. presidents, British and Australian prime ministers, members of the U.S. Congress, and U.S. state governors. Most researchers along this line of inquiry believe there is an indirect relation between birth order and leadership. One hypothesis is that firstborns are differentially parented in that they initially receive all their parents'

---

### Birth Order

- Intellectual development and a need for power are more prevalent in firstborn children.
- An indirect relation exists between birth order and leadership.
- Firstborns are differentially parented in that they initially receive all their parents' attention and resources.
- Firstborns have a dual experience: leaders of their younger siblings and followers of their parents.
- Unlike singletons, firstborns experience sibling rivalry, preparing them for the political struggle of being a leader.
- Dethronement—when new siblings are born—causes in firstborns a crisis of deprivation, from which emerges the need to seek power to compensate.

---

attention and resources. Also, they have a dual experience as leaders to their younger siblings and as followers of their parents. This theoretically prepares the individual for leadership roles later in life. In addition, unlike singletons ("only children"), they experience sibling rivalry, preparing them for the political struggle of being a leader (Andeweg & Van Den Berg, 2003).

In a more Freudian version of the above, Adler (1928) refers to the "dethronement" of the first child when subsequent children are born, which sparks a crisis of deprivation (compare this to Freud's notion of object loss). From this crisis emerges the need to seek power in order to compensate. Andeweg and Van Den Berg (2003) conducted a survey of Dutch politicians about birth order. It confirmed earlier notions of the overrepresentation of firstborns in leadership positions. Their study revealed that gender (being female) did not mitigate the effects of birth order, despite their expectations that in a relatively patriarchal society, this would be the case.

## TRANSACTIONAL ANALYSIS

Another psychological model applied to leadership is transactional analysis. According to Berne (1961), there are three ego stages (parent, adult, and child) in every individual. Leaders should attempt to develop into an adult ego state, which is characterized by being able to assess a situation and to fairly and accurately develop solutions.

Recently management consultants at McKinsey & Co. explored training employees in transactional analysis, which they refer to as transpersonal psychology. According to their model, managers and employees alike desire to grow and want a deeper emotional connection to their work. Role-playing and reflection in training workshops enable individuals to "tap into their rational and subconscious hope for the future" (Bellin & Rennie, 2003, p. 37). This growth is similar to Berne's notion of maturing into an adult ego state in order to be able to maximize cognitive abilities considered connected to psychoemotional needs.

## PSYCHOHISTORY

Psychohistorians have attempted to explain political leaders in terms of the psychoanalytic approach. Freud and Bullitt analyzed the strained relationship Woodrow Wilson had with his father. According to their research, Wilson idealized his father to the point of obsession. He resented his father's authority while he admired his father's articulateness. This led to Wilson's political ambition to undertake such grandiose projects as the failed League of Nations (Bass, 1990). George and George (1998) built on the psychohistorical account of Wilson's life in *Presidential Personality and Performance* by identifying the trauma and patterns of Wilson's childhood, which led to the idealization and resentment of his father. Similarly, Eric Erikson (1993) wrote a psychohistory of Martin Luther, proposing that the Protestant Reformation was driven by Luther's psychological need to rebel against his father.

## PERSONALITY AND LEADERSHIP

Psychologists study leadership using personality instruments such as the Myers-Briggs Personality Profile (Stech, 2004). Kroeger and Theusen (1992) propose that being aware of the personality profiles of followers, or "typewatching," can allow the leader to be more effective. This approach does not condone any particular personality type as being more conducive to leadership; it merely proposes that the leader's awareness of his/her type and that of his/her followers can lead to better communication, productivity, time management, stress management, and conflict resolution.

---

### "Typewatching"

- Being aware of the personality profiles of followers can allow the leader to be more effective.

- This approach does not condone any particular personality type as being more conducive to leadership.

- The leader's awareness of his/her type and that of followers may result in better communication, productivity, time management, stress management, and conflict resolution.

(Kroeger and Theusen, 1992)

---

Mann (1959) performed a meta-analysis of 28 studies concerning the relation between personality and evaluations of leadership in small groups. He found that measures of intelligence, adjustment, extroversion, and dominance are positively related to effective leadership. Although this study may be considered related to trait theory, it can also be argued that traits are derived from personality, which may be related to psychological and emotional development. One study found that between 48 percent and 82 percent of the variance in leadership ability was due to the leader's personality (Kenney & Zaccaro, 1983, as cited in Hogan et al., 1994).

More recently, psychologists considered leadership in relation to the big five model of personality. This model states that personality can be described along five dimensions—"surgency" (extraversion), agreeableness, conscientiousness, emotional stability, and intellect. Leaders should decide who their ideal subordinate is, based on these personality dimensions, and build their team accordingly (Hogan et al., 1994).

Zaleznik (1977) contrasts managers and leaders based on their personality characteristics. Managers are viewed as bureaucratic short-term thinkers embedded in routine and inflexibility. Leaders, on the other hand, have characteristics that help them to develop new ideas for long-standing problems. They are an ideal in terms of shaping the bigger picture of an organization. "Leaders are like artists and other gifted people who often struggle with neuroses" (Zaleznik, 1977, p. 75). Zaleznik (1977) emphasizes talent over learned skills; however, individuals with such talent need mentoring in order to actualize their potential. "The only sure way an individual can interrupt reverie-like preoccupation and self-absorption is to form a deep attachment to a great individual or other person who understands

## Effective Leadership

Behaving as and becoming an effective leader is a secondary by-product of an intense commitment to a purpose.

and has the ability to communicate with the gifted individual" (p. 75). The notion of mentorship also relates to Campbell's hero journey. Under his paradigm, there is a guide who assists the individual along his/her journey.

## PSYCHODYNAMIC APPROACH TO LEADERSHIP AND THE CASE OF COMMISSIONER BERNARD KERIK

Out of all the leadership theories this author researched, the psychodynamic approach appears to be one of the most straightforward to explain behaviors of certain leaders, providing of course that one can find enough information on the background of the individual to explain and understand the behaviors described. This type of leadership is very closely associated with the personality of the individuals and the insights they have into themselves. Those insights allow them to have a better understanding of the situation and people involved.

The key question is whether such individuals are capable of using this knowledge and understanding to manipulate subordinates rather than simply working with them. Does awareness that one has a "dark side" translate into control over it, in an attempt to avoid errors of judgment? Or will someone who is aware of his/her inner struggle and inner demons justify the manipulation of subordinates by using the existence of this "dark side" as an excuse?

Whatever the answers to these questions, it is a deeply emotional approach to the concept of leadership. In police environments, emotions should be kept under control to maximize effort. No other situation or event in contemporary history has called for more self-restraint and the need to keep emotions under control than the events of 9/11. Commissioner Bernard Kerik handled the NYPD response to this unforeseeable disaster. Although media accounts and the force itself indicate that the department was prepared for a disaster of that magnitude better than any other police force in the United States, there can be no doubt that without having a competent leader at the helm, the response would have fallen apart. Kerik's competence may have many roots and origins, but this author believes his childhood experiences enabled him to pull the force together and prevent this horrible disaster from becoming even more traumatic. Of course, this is merely one incident, and only one perspective on his leadership during that incident, but it is an excellent illustration of how the psychodynamic approach can apply in a policing context.

CAREER HIGHLIGHTS    Psychodynamic Approach

**Commissioner Bernard Kerik**
*New York Police Department, New York*

Bernard Kerik was born on September 4, 1955, in Newark, New Jersey. His parents separated in 1957, and his mother took him to live with her in Ohio (Kerik, 2001). However, she then abandoned him one year later when he was three years old (Marzulli, 2001b), leaving Kerik in the care of her boyfriend's mother. After abandoning Kerik, his mother worked as a prostitute and was killed in 1964. In 1959, his father regained custody of Kerik and brought him back to Newark, where he grew up under the care of his aunt Clara (Kerik, 2001). Kerik dropped out of high school and never went back to finish (Kerik, 2001). However, he trained in martial arts as a teenager, which helped him to segue into a career in the military. In 1974, Kerik join the U.S. Army (Kerik, 2001). He was stationed in Korea in 1975, where he fathered a daughter whom he lost track of after 1978. After investigating his daughter's whereabouts extensively, Kerik was reunited with her in 2002 after her mother had watched Kerik on the *Oprah Winfrey Show* in 2001 ("Former police commissioner," 2002).

After being discharged from the Army in 1977, Kerik worked for the Interstate Revenue Research Center helping to investigate cigarette smugglers in South Florida. From 1978 to 1981, he worked as a military security officer in Saudi Arabia, protecting American architects, engineers, and construction crews building a military base near the Iraq border. Kerik then became a Passaic County, New Jersey, corrections officer. In 1982, he returned to Saudi Arabia for a second tour, which lasted until 1984. In 1985, Kerik became assistant commander of the Sheriff's Emergency Response Team (SERT) in Passaic County. In 1987, he joined the New York City Police Department and had a career as a narcotics task force officer before rising through the ranks.

From 1998 to 2000, Kerik was New York City's corrections commissioner (Pyle, 2001). Bernard Kerik became the police commissioner of the NYPD in August 2000. During his tenure, serious crime dropped 13 percent, part of a downward trend that began in the mid-1990s. He tried to ease minority tensions, which were high after the 1997 torture of Abner

Louima and the deadly police shootings of Amadou Diallo in 1999 and Patrick Dorismond in 2000. Kerik accomplished this by requiring officers to attend community meetings, which he often also attended; reportedly, he received praise from local civil rights leaders (Hays, 2001).

### September 11, 2001, Terrorist Attacks

The terrorist attacks on September 11, 2001, provided the most formidable challenge in Kerik's career as NYPD Police Commissioner. The World Trade Center towers' collapse formed the infamous Ground Zero, where emergency workers (including police) sifted through the piles of debris for human remains and evidence for what was deemed the most extensive crime scene in history (Kerik, 2001).

As soon as Kerik heard about the attack on the morning of September 11, he drove to the scene. Initially, before the towers fell, he was on Liberty and Barclay Streets as people ran by screaming hysterically, and he witnessed people jumping from the burning towers. In the hours after the attack, Mayor Rudolph Giuliani, Kerik, and their aides narrowly escaped death when they were trapped inside a building at 75 Barclay Street near Ground Zero. At the time, Giuliani was on the phone with the White House. The mayor, Kerik, and their aides dodged debris as it fell from the towers. They were at this particular location because the city command center was located in 7 World Trade Center. The command center was also damaged by the falling debris and other structural impacts from the collapse of the two main towers; it collapsed later that day. The mayor, Kerik, and their aides made their way to Church Street and their cars to regroup. Kerik told the press his initial emotional reaction was anger at the attacks (Marzulli, 2001a). He also said, "If anything happens to any one of us, there's a line of succession. Leaders should lead by example" (Marzulli, 2001a, p. 22).

According to media reports, the NYPD had the most sophisticated antiterrorist strategies of any police force in the nation. They had participated in mock disasters, had set up a high-tech command center, and had advised the mayor on constructing a $7 million emergency bunker. However, the 9/11 attacks proved too overwhelming for the department's antiterrorist preparedness. After the towers fell, phones and e-mail went dead at the command center at Police Plaza. The department was credited with innovating a response. Within a few hours of the disaster, Kerik called all off-duty officers to work. By the end of the day, shifts were elongated from 8 to 12 hours. To add to the 1,000 officers already at Ground Zero, Kerik also deployed an additional 10,000 officers—from narcotics officers to precinct detectives—to help at the scene. Other officers continued to patrol New York City's streets; crime dropped 30 percent during the first few days of the crisis (Rashbaum, 2001). However, according to Kerik, bias attacks against people perceived as Arab increased in the 10 days after the attacks.

*(continued)*

He indicated that there were 56 anti-Arab incidents, ranging from anti-Muslim graffiti to assaults on Muslims, connected to 9/11 between September 11 and 21, 2001 (Messing & Topousis, 2001).

Three days after the attacks, Kerik addressed the NYPD, expressing "the pride and gratitude I feel for what you have done over the past two days" (Marzulli & Standora, 2001, p. 45). At that point, he indicated that 23 police officers were missing (Marzulli & Standora, 2001); they have since been listed among the dead (Kerik, 2001). Kerik delivered an uplifting message, honoring the heroes of Ground Zero and expressing consolation to the families of victims (Marzulli & Standora, 2001).

The National Commission on Terrorist Attacks Upon the United States (also known as the 9–11 Commission) investigated New York's preparedness in their inquiry into the events of September 11. On the whole, the 9–11 Commission found that the response was effective in saving the lives of those below the impact zone, due to the successful efforts on the day:

> Some specific rescues are quantifiable, such as an FDNY company's rescue of civilians trapped on the 22nd floor of the North Tower, or the success of FDNY, PAPD, and NYPD personnel in carrying nonambulatory civilians out of both the North and South Towers. In other instances, intangibles combined to reduce what could have been a much higher death total. It is impossible to measure how many more civilians who descended to the ground floors would have died but for the NYPD and PAPD personnel directing them—via safe exit routes that avoided jumpers and debris—to leave the complex urgently but calmly. It is impossible to measure how many more civilians would have died but for the determination of many members of the FDNY, PAPD, and NYPD to continue assisting civilians after the South Tower collapsed. (National Commission, 2004, p. 316)

The NYPD was not exempt from criticism, however. At hearings in New York, and in a draft report issued before the hearings, the panel criticized New York's emergency responders for failures and gaps in communication and the lack of coordination between the police and fire departments as well as their failure to convey information to 911 operators (a system supervised by the NYPD) (Shenon & Flynn, 2004). For example, police helicopters that were circling the buildings did not transmit information to fire department personnel inside the building (Shenon & Flynn, 2004). The 911 operators and the fire department dispatchers to whom calls were relayed did not have enough information about the impact zone to be able to advise callers trapped in the buildings about what they should do (National Commission, 2004). However, overall the 9–11 Commission praised NYPD's preparedness, efficient internal communication, and control of the scene, particularly in evacuating civilians who had descended from the towers and ensuring emergency vehicles' access to the site; the NYPD was also was praised for having effective communications (radio) technology (National Commission, 2004).

In another example of effective leadership, in the wake of the anthrax attacks in the fall of 2001, Kerik appointed Phil Pulaski, an NYPD investigator who is also a chemical engineer, as the city's bioterrorism czar. Pulaski had handled the initial anthrax threat detected at NBC head-quarters (Weiss, 2001a).

Additionally, after the terrorist attacks, Kerik ordered mandatory mental health counseling for all 55,000 members of the NYPD, the first time this measure was ever required. By making it mandatory, Kerik removed the stigma associated with counseling, stating that voluntary counseling is often not used by officers for fear they would be perceived as weak. The program began on November 18, 2001, and required every member of the department to participate in group counseling. Second, an emergency telephone line and referral system provided additional anony-mous counseling. Third, discussion groups convened and included spouses and family members affected by the attacks ("NYPD," 2001).

The NYPD also assisted the Justice Department in interviewing 86 Middle Eastern immigrants who may have had information regarding the 9/11 attacks. Kerik indicated that he would not ask about their immigra-tion status, leaving that to the discretion of federal authorities ("NYPD to interview," 2001). In December 2001, Kerik testified in front of a Senate panel urging federal agencies to increase their information sharing with local police departments. He advocated a revision of the security clear-ance system, which granted clearance to some cops while denying it to the cops' superiors (Port, 2001). He stated, "Continuing to maintain walls between federal and state authorities . . . represents the worst kind of dys-functional thinking in government" (Port, 2001, p. 6).

Ironically, Kerik had completed his memoirs (for publication) the night before the September 11 attacks; however, he added an epilogue describing his role in the response to the attacks in the weeks that followed. The book, *The Lost Son* (2001), was rushed to the press for release in November 2001 in order to maximize sales. Some, including City Councilman Sheldon Leffler, believed Kerik was trying to profit from the tragedy (Hays, 2001). A *Newsweek* columnist called the book "unconscionable," and another stated it was a "conflict of interest and an abdication of his responsibilities as police commissioner" (Pyle, 2001). However, according to the media, Kerik, along with Mayor Giuliani and Fire Commissioner Thomas Van Essen, had become a national symbol of heroism after the attacks (Hays, 2001). At a news conference about 9/11 on November 8, 2001, Kerik stated:

> I shouldn't get credit for what happened that day. The everyday cops—they're the ones who should get the credit. . . . This department will get along without me. (Hays, 2001)

Kerik defended the publication of his book, pointing out that it is a memoir. He was police commissioner during 9/11, a historical event in the nation's history; therefore, it must be part of his story. On November 10, 2001, he told the press:

(*continued*)

> I could say at least three times, between Mayor Giuliani and myself, we
> came close to not making it out of there. So I think it would be remiss not to
> write it, or say something. (Pyle, 2001)

He also spoke on the *Oprah Winfrey Show:*

> Being the police commissioner after September 11 is painful. It's heart-
> wrenching. But it also has clearly demonstrated to me that this is the best
> job you could ever have. Because the people that work for [me], there are
> none better. ("Horror and heroes," 2001)

However, another scandal was associated with the book. From May
to October 2001, Kerik used three officers to help him discover how his
mother died in Ohio in 1964. The use of that manpower violated an agreement he had made with New York City's conflicts of interest board, which
allowed him to write his book but which forbade him from using city time
or his official position to obtain any private or personal advantage for
himself or the publisher (De la Cruz, 2002). Kerik was fined $2,500 for
using the officers to do research for his book.

Kerik announced that he would step down from his position as
commissioner on January 1, 2002, despite the fact that mayoral candidates
Michael Bloomberg, Alan Hevesi, Herman Badillo, and Peter Vallone
indicated that they wanted to keep him in the position (Colangelo, 2001).[1]
Subsequently, Mayor-Elect Bloomberg publicly indicated that he wanted
Kerik to remain as commissioner (Weiss, 2001b). But Kerik turned down
the offer in order to spend more time with his family (Hays, 2001). In early
December 2001, Kerik promoted 10 captains, 4 deputy inspectors, and
1 full inspector, rewarding leaders associated with drops in crime rates in
their respective precincts (Messing, 2001).

In June 2002, Kerik became the chairman of the New York State
Athletic Commission. His responsibilities included overseeing boxing
and wrestling matches. He issued licenses, enforced rules and regula-
tions, and reviewed medical and safety standards ("Ex-NYC police chief,"
2002). In 2003, Kerik was the interim Minister of the Interior and senior
policy advisor in Iraq after its liberation by U.S. forces. He rebuilt police
and emergency services in that country ("Bernard Kerik," n.d.).

Kerik's ability to respond competently to the 9/11 attacks is clearly
related to experiences of his early childhood. He was no novice to traumatic situations, and his early-childhood family experiences shaped his
leadership qualities and responses. According to Northouse (2004),
childhood family experiences create leaders who always take a paternal
role with subordinates. Based on family experiences, leaders exhibit

---

[1]Two other candidates, Mark Green and Fernando Ferrer, who were often critical
of the NYPD under Kerik's command did not favor his continuing as commissioner (Pyle, 2001).

behaviors along continuums of authoritative to permissive, supportive to critical, and dependent to counterdependent to independent. Kerik's response in the aftermath of the 9/11 attack represents a combination of the continuums.

Kerik was authoritative when he called all off-duty officers to work extended shifts and to deploy 10,000 officers to support the efforts at Ground Zero; he was supportive when he ordered mandatory mental health counseling, anonymous forms of support, and discussion groups for spouses and family members. He also showed independent decision making by taking an unorthodox position on immigration-related issues when suspects were questioned at a time when such behavior might have been perceived as antagonistic.

Another example shows Kerik's leadership: his support for the Police Studies Certificate (co-created and co-coordinated by the author), which gave NYPD police officers access to courses teaching supervisory leadership skills in a multicultural environment and was the best testimony of his relentlessness of commitment to his troops. The program started the week before 9/11. The first two weeks after the 9/11 events, the officers were absent from classes. Yet by week three they were returning, in great numbers, to continue classes and to enhance their skills to serve the public better—a tribute to their colleagues who died. Commissioner Kerik encouraged the continuation of the program despite the other demands pulling at officers during the troubled weeks and months immediately following 9/11. By the end of the semester, most of the officers had completed the courses.

Although it is unlikely that he was consciously aware of it, Kerik used a formula that can be best summarized by Clawson's (2003) six steps to effective leadership.

---

## Six Steps to Effective Leadership

*Step 1: Clarifying your center*
    What is your life's mission?
*Step 2: Clarifying what's possible*
    What can really be achieved?
*Step 3: Clarifying what others can contribute*
    What can others really do?
*Step 4: Supporting others so they can contribute*
    What resources can you really commit?
*Step 5: Being relentless*
    What degree of confidence and commitment do you/others have?
*Step 6: Measuring and celebrating progress*
    How do you praise, and what kind of positive feedback do you provide?

(Clawson, 2003)

---

*(continued)*

His life mission was to become an innovative leader, and his entire career path points to his various attempts to become successful in many fields. After clarifying what was possible in a given environment and what others could contribute to his success, Kerik assigned them the roles in which they could be successful. He was ready to give credit to and to support his subordinates. For example, Kerik continued to support the Police Studies Certificate program and the enrolled officers despite what must have been an overwhelming temptation to cut extracurricular activities for officers who had just experienced the worst disaster of their careers. Finally, prior to his departure, he made sure that the officers who contributed to his success were properly acknowledged and promoted.

According to the psychodynamic approach to leadership, it takes someone who has experienced much hardship in life to deliver the authoritative yet supportive qualities depicted by Kerik. As Clawson (2003, p. 94) posits, "Behaving as and becoming an effective leader is a secondary by-product of an intense commitment to a purpose." It is hard to question the intense commitment Kerik exhibited to making the NYPD the best it could be.

### Exercise

The police commissioner detailed in this chapter has been examined through the prism of the psychodynamic approach. Using what you have learned from other theories in this book or from the summaries (as indicated in the Introduction) you have read thus far, it is possible to consider his approach through the lens of different theories. What other theories can you find applicable to this chief? Are there lessons to be learned from those applications, or do those theories indicate alternative paths or approaches that might have yielded a more successful outcome?

## REFERENCES

Adler, A. (1928). Characteristics of the first, second and third child. *Children*, 3, 14–52.

Andeweg, R.B. & S.B. Van Den Berg (2003). Linking birth order to political leadership: The impact of parents or sibling interaction? *Political Psychology*, 24 (3), 605–623.

Bass, B.M. (1990). *Bass and Stogdill's handbook of leadership: A survey of theory and research*. New York: Free Press.

Bellin, G. & M.W. Rennie (2004). People want to develop. *McKinsey Quarterly*, 2, 37–39.

Bernard Kerik (n.d.). *Washington Speakers Bureau*. Retrieved January 23, 2003, from www.washspkrs.com.

Berne, E. (1961). *Transactional analysis in psychotherapy*. New York: Grove.

Clawson, J.A. (2003). *Level three leadership: Getting below the surface* (2nd ed.). Upper Saddle River, NJ: Prentice Hall.

Colangelo, L. (2001, October 5). It's goodbye to NYPD on Jan. 1. *Daily News*, p. 39.

De la Cruz, D. (2002, February 28). Kerik agrees to pay fine after conflict of interest found. *The Associated Press*, state and local wire.

Erikson, E. (1962; 1993). *Young man Luther: A study in psychoanalysis and history*. New York: W.W. Norton & Co.

Ex-NYC police chief picked to run group (2002, June 21). *The Times Union*, C2.

Former police commissioner finds long-lost daughter (2002, April 11). *The Associated Press*, state and local wire.

Freud, S. (1921; 1955). *Group psychology and the analysis of the ego*. London: Hogarth Press. (1939; 1964). *Moses and monotheism*. London: Hogarth Press.

George, A. & J. George (1998). *Presidential personality and performance*. Boulder, CO: Westview Press.

Hays, T. (2001, November 9). Kerik announces he'll leave NYPD. *The Associated Press*, state and local wire.

Hogan, R., G.J. Curphy & J. Hogan (1994). What we know about leadership: Effectiveness and personality. *American Psychologist*, 49 (6) 493–504.

Horror and heroes: What he saw at Ground Zero (2001). *The Oprah Winfrey Show*. Retrieved January 23, 2004, from www.oprah.com.

Hummel, P.R. (1975). Psychology of charismatic followers. *Psychological Reports*, 37, 759–770.

Kerik, B. (2001). *The lost son: A life in pursuit of justice*. New York: Harper-Collins.

Kets de Vries, M.F.R. (1980). *Organizational paradoxes: Clinical approaches to management*. New York: Tavistock.

Kohut, H. (1976). Creativeness, charisma, group psychology: Reflections on the self-analysis of Freud. In P.H. Ornstein (Ed.), *The search for the self* (pp. 793–843). New York: International Universities Press.

Kroeger, O. & J.M. Theusen (1992). *Type talk at work*. New York: Delacorte.

LaBarre, W. (1972). *The ghost dance: Origins of religion*. New York: Delta.

Mann, R.D. (1959). Review of the relationship between personality and performance in small groups. *Psychological Bulletin*, 56 (4), 241–270.

Marzulli, J. (2001a, September 27). Giuliani & group of top cops barely dodged death as towers fell. *Daily News*, p. 22.

——— (2001b, October 30). Kerik book with WTC story is rushed. *Daily News*, p. 14.

——— & L. Standora (2001, September 15). Kerik tells troops of NYPD's great tragedy: Says the list of officers missing grows to 23. *Daily News*, p. 45.

Messing, P. & T. Topousis (2001, September 21). Anti-Arab assaults surge here. *The New York Post*, p. 22.

National Commission on Terrorist Attacks Upon the United States (2004). *The 9/11 commission report*. Washington, D.C.: U.S. Government Printing Office. Retrieved August 10, 2004, from http://www.9–11commission.gov/report/index.htm.

Northouse, P.G. (2004). *Leadership: Theory and practice* (3rd ed.). Thousand Oaks, CA: Sage.

NYPD orders entire department to undergo mandatory counseling (2001, November 30). *The Associated Press*, state and local wire.

NYPD to interview 86 immigrants on Justice Department's list (2001, December 5). *The Associated Press*, state and local wire.

Port, B. (2001, December 12). Kerik to pols: Let FBI, cops share info. *Daily News*, p. 6.

Pyle, R. (2001, November 11). Police commissioner brushes off critics of book. *The Associated Press*, state and local wire.

Rashbaum, W.K. (2001, September 17). After the attacks: Safety. *The New York Times*, p. A7.

Shenon, P. & K. Flynn (2004, May 18). Panel Has a Question: Why Wasn't the City Prepared? *The New York Times*, B1.

Stech, E.L. (2004). Psychodynamic approach. In P.G. Northouse (Ed.), *Leadership: Theory and Practice* (3rd ed.). Thousand Oaks, CA: Sage.

Strozier, C. & D. Offer (1985). Introduction. In C.B. Strozier & D. Offer (Eds.), *The leader: Psychohistorical essays*. New York: Pergamon.

Weber, M. (1946; 1973). Politics as a vocation. In *From Max Weber: Essays in sociology* (H.H. Gerth & C. Wright Mills, Trans.). Oxford: Oxford University Press.

———— (1947; 1964). *The theory of social and economic organization* (A.M. Henderson & T. Parson, Trans.). New York: Oxford University Press.

Weiss, M. (2001a, October 19). Kerik taps czar for bioterror. *The New York Post*, p. 22.

———— (2001b, November 1). Bloomy wants Kerik in his corner. *The New York Post*, p. 9.

Whyte, D. (1994). *The heart aroused: Poetry and the preservation of the soul in corporate America*. New York: Doubleday.

Winer, J.A., T. Jobe & C. Ferrono (1984–1985). Toward a psychoanalytic theory of the charismatic relationship. *Annual of Psychoanalysis*, 12–13, 15–175.

Zaleznik, A. (1974). Charismatic and consensus leaders: A psychological comparison. *Bulletin of the Menninger Clinic*, 38 (3), 222–238.

———— (1977, May–June). Managers and leaders: Are they different? *Harvard Business Review*, 55 (3), 67–68. (Reprinted in 1992, *Harvard Business Review*, 70 (2), 126–135.

# 11

# Soliciting and Entertaining 100 Ideas

## *Skills Approach*

## OVERVIEW OF THE APPROACH

The skills approach focuses on the individual leader, rather than on followers, and centers on the development of leadership skills. Due to the many innovations he brought to the department during his decade-long tenure, Commissioner Paul F. Evans of the Boston Police Department is chosen as an example to illustrate this approach.

Skills can be learned and developed over the course of a career. Skills not only are the domain of gifted individuals but also are considered a function of both education and experience (Mumford et al., 2000b). They are capacities that are beyond mere intelligence. With the skills approach, crystallized cognitive abilities are more important than intelligence. These abilities include an exceptional capacity at written and oral expression and comprehension as well as the ability to find and manipulate information (Bass, 1990). According to the model, leadership combines knowledge, problem-solving skills, solution construction skills, and social judgment needed to solve problems (Mumford et al., 2000a).

## Learned Leadership Skills

The notion that leadership skills can be learned appears to have been first articulated by Sheriff (1968), who challenges the dominant leadership mythology that emphasized trait theory (see Chapter 12). "On the whole, this effort to transform leaders into supermen is passé. Nevertheless, the search for innate personality and physical traits is not a thing of the past" (Sheriff, 1968, p. 30). He explains that other than the prerequisite that a potential leader possess intelligence, all other necessary qualities can be learned in the process of skill development. Skills are divided into the following three categories: 1) technical skills, 2) human skills, and 3) conceptual skills. The first refers to the specific methods and techniques associated with a profession. Human skills, including getting along with others, reflect a capacity to work effectively in an organization. Conceptual skills imply the ability to generate, consider, and use ideas. More specifically, Sheriff outlines general developable characteristics that are associated with leadership and that include communication abilities, broad and well-rounded interests, problem-solving abilities, mental and emotional maturity, and motivation. Sheriff (1968) states:

> Undoubtedly there are many other characteristics that correlate with leadership. What is significant is that leadership is not simply a matter of innate personality or physical traits. It appears more profitable to view leadership in terms of a constellation of acquired personality traits and developable skills. (p. 35)

Because the skills are developable, it follows that the use of training programs could be helpful in growing leaders rather than having leaders acquire leadership skills haphazardly throughout their career. Pernick (2001) advocates organizational training programs for subordinates who could become leaders. The advantages of this approach are that "the organization gets to groom the next generation in line with its culture and strategic agenda . . . [and that] the organization has a greater control over the supply of leaders with the requisite skills, making strategic implementation faster" (p. 11).

## Leadership in Context

The skills approach places leaders' development in the context of the specific demands of their jobs. Analysis of skills possessed by leaders begins with identifying the demands placed on leaders (Fleishman &

Quaintance, 1984). Leadership problems are not considered routine problems but rather are characterized as novel, complex, and ill defined. Leadership is considered most crucial when the nature of problems differs from the routine. Unlike approaches such as transformational leadership, "unless leaders can identify significant organizational problems and formulate solutions to these problems, all the planning and all the persuasion in the world are to no avail" (Mumford et al., 2000a, p. 157). As such, a leader's capacity to handle information in solving problems is primary:

> There is a plethora of available information in complex organizational systems, only some of which is relevant to the problem. Further, it may be difficult to obtain accurate, timely information and identify key diagnostic information. As a result, leaders must actively seek and carefully evaluate information bearing on potential problems and goal attainment. (Mumford et al., 2000b, p. 14)

Moreover, the skills model places leaders in real-world settings, recognizing that there are seldom ideal conditions for problem solving. Leaders cannot always sort through every option in limited time frames. They also must be aware of the potential negative effects of any decision as well as keep their stakeholders in mind (Mumford et al., 2000b). In essence, they must be conscious of the social context of their problem-solving endeavor. This places social skills at the center of the approach (Zaccaro et al., 1991). Effective leadership, therefore, is dependent on leaders' ability to solve social problems in organizations despite organizational constraints (Yammarino, 2000).

The skills approach also involves the willingness of leaders to place themselves in a situation in which they can learn. Skill development is a function of leaders interacting with their environment. Certain personality characteristics, such as dominance, may be associated with seeking out such leadership-building situations (Lord et al., 1986). Mumford et al. (2000b) identify the following four types of experiences that are most conducive to leadership development: 1) job assignments with novel, challenging problems; 2) mentoring of subordinates; 3) leadership training; and 4) hands-on experience in solving organizational problems.

Because of the centrality of experience, skills are often slow to develop. According to Ericsson and Charness (1994), it takes approximately 7 to 10 years to acquire the skills required at the top levels of a given career. Mumford et al. (2000c) suggest that it may take 20 years to acquire all the necessary skills to solve leadership problems. Additionally, the types of problems encountered by senior management

---

### Leadership and Intelligence

**Intellectual intelligence (IQ)**

- It is genetic.
- It is revealed in curiosity.
- It is honed by discipline.
- It is supported by a range of experiences.

**Emotional intelligence (EQ)**

- Recognize your own emotions.
- Manage your own emotions.
- Control yourself.

**Social intelligence (SQ)**

- Recognize emotions in others.
- Listen.
- Care about others' emotional states.
- Help others gain control and manage their emotions.

**Change intelligence (CQ)**

- Recognize the need for change.
- Understand the change process.
- Master the change process.
- Find comfort in managing the change process.

(Clawson, 2003)

---

tend to be more complex, novel, and ill-defined and are therefore more beneficial in developing leadership skills. At the same time, the skills approach points to the fact that higher levels of problem solving and social judgment associated with leadership are required at top levels (Mumford, 2000b). Therefore, leadership skills are built up through the problem-solving experiences of leadership itself.

## SOCIAL JUDGMENT AS SOCIAL INTELLIGENCE

One of the components of leadership capacity as described above is social judgment, which is akin to notions of social intelligence. Social intelligence was first identified by E. L. Thorndike in 1920 as the ability to act wisely in human relations. Current researchers tend to define social intelligence as (1) the ability to perceive others' needs and problems and (2) the ability to respond and adapt to different environments (Kobe et al., 2001). This is the same construct that Zaccaro et al. propose (1991), indicating that social perceptiveness and behavior flexibility are the attributes of effective leadership. Social intelligence is distinct from general intelligence. Social perceptiveness refers to leaders' sensitivity to the plights of both subordinates and the organization as a whole. Behavior flexibility is defined as a leader's capacity to respond appropriately and flexibly based on the situation (Kobe et al., 2001).

Kobe et al. (2001) studied 192 undergraduates in order to determine whether people with high social intelligence were more likely to engage in leadership activities. They also tested whether emotional intelligence (see below), as a subset of social intelligence, contributed to leadership participation above and beyond that of mere social intelligence. Social intelligence was measured using biographical data scales. Using regression analysis, the researchers found that social intelligence correlated with the bulk of leadership participation, suggesting that it may be a primary component of leadership ability and effectiveness. Further, emotional intelligence added to the variance in leadership participation above and beyond social intelligence.

## EMOTIONAL INTELLIGENCE

Kobe et al. (2001) characterize emotional intelligence as a specific type of social intelligence. Emotional intelligence is typically measured using Bar-On's Emotional Quotient Inventory (EQ-i). Feldman (1999) characterizes emotional intelligence as the ability to apply emotional and social understanding to positively influence subordinates. He identifies core skills and higher-order skills associated with emotional intelligence. The core skills include (1) knowing yourself, (2) maintaining control, (3) being able to read others, (4) possessing accurate perception, and (5) communicating with flexibility. The higher-order skills set involves (1) taking responsibility, (2) generating options and alternatives, (3) formulating a vision, (4) possessing courage, and (5) having resolve.

Emotional intelligence is most often associated with the work of Goleman (1998), who defines it as the capacity to be aware of and to handle emotions in various situations. He indicates that although general intelligence and technical ability relate to leadership, emotional intelligence is a more central contributor to effective leadership. Like the skills approach in general, one's emotional intelligence quotient (EQ) can be raised as a result of a learning process, according to Goleman. The learning process is specific to the context of the particular leader and involves learning about group interaction and information sharing. It also describes the potential for emotions to be contagious within an organization. Increases in EQ are accomplished through behavior change associated with awareness of others in the emotional domain. Goleman believes that positive feedback that results from understanding and controlling emotions in the workplace will positively reinforce the change (Dearborn, 2002).

## U.S. ARMY STUDIES

In a study of approximately 1,800 U.S. Army officers, complex problem-solving skills, social judgment skills, and leader knowledge were found to predict the achievement of leaders in solving complex problems. Similar results were also found using a sample of civilian Defense Department personnel (Connelly et al., 2000). Using the same sample, another study concluded that knowledge, problem-solving skills, and social skills increased as a function of experience. Assignments, training, and career development all contributed to the bettering of leaders' skills over time. Specific experience was more beneficial at particular points of leaders' careers, suggesting that the path to leadership success may be complex (Mumford et al., 2000c).

## SKILLS APPROACH TO LEADERSHIP
## AND THE CASE OF COMMISSIONER PAUL F. EVANS

The notion of skills approach to leadership is directly associated with the concept of human intelligence as a function of learning and development rather than with some innate quality. Most of us grew up socialized to the concept that people were either smart or stupid (or somewhere in the middle); on a more sophisticated level, people who were smart or stupid were referred to as having a high or low level of intelligence. It was very rare that this level of intelligence was explained as a function of the learning experience or the developmental process; instead, intelligence was perceived as similar to physical qualities such as eye color and hair color. As you were to make the best of your physical qualities, it was assumed you were doomed to live with the amount of intelligence with which you were born.

However, human intelligence received a totally new and different orientation and understanding as social scientists began looking at intelligence as a social rather than physical phenomenon. New levels of intelligence were identified, dividing this quality into four separate categories: intellectual intelligence, emotional intelligence, social intelligence, and change intelligence.

Leadership style can be viewed through this new approach to the concept of human intelligence. Intellectual intelligence (IQ), the only one identified as a genetic trait, is revealed in curiosity and is honed by discipline and supported by a range of experiences. Emotional intelligence (EQ) depends on both ability and level: the ability to recognize and handle one's own emotions and the level of control one exercises over those emotions. Social intelligence (SQ) is the ability to recognize emotions in others, the ability to listen and care about others' emotional states, and the ability to help others to gain control and manage their own emotions. Finally, change intelligence (CQ) is the ability to recognize the need for change, the ability to understand the change process, and the level of comfort in managing it (Clawson, 2003). A successful leader (SL) combines these four elements, as shown in the following formula:

$$SL = High\ IQ + High\ EQ + High\ SQ + High\ CQ$$

This is not to say that anyone who does not fit the above formula cannot be a good or successful leader, but the degree to which someone is deficient in one of the variables will significantly affect his/her overall leadership success.

Commissioner Paul F. Evans is certainly not the only police leader who illustrates the above formula. However, choosing Commissioner Evans for this chapter was partially motivated by an objective evaluation of his career and partially motivated by a very minimal yet influential encounter between this author and Commissioner Evans. This author had the opportunity to participate in a closed conference that took place in Italy in 1999 that gathered a number of academics from around the world and influential police chiefs from the United States for several days to discuss innovations in policing. Observing Commissioner Evans for a few days during the proceedings of the conference enabled the author to draw some conclusions about his leadership style. Hopefully the people reading his biography will have similar reactions.

**CAREER HIGHLIGHTS    Skills Approach**

Commissioner Paul F. Evans
*Boston Police Department, Massachusetts*

Paul F. Evans grew up in a South Boston neighborhood (Cullen, 1996; Negri, 1994). From 1967 to 1969, Evans was a corporal in the U.S. Marines, assigned to an artillery unit during the Vietnam War. He attended college after returning from the war and received his bachelor's degree in political science in 1974 from Boston State College. In 1978, he earned his doctor of law degree (cum laude) from Suffolk University Law School ("Paul F. Evans," n.d.).

Evans joined the Boston Police Department in 1970. From 1986 to 1992, he served as the superintendent in chief of field services. Subsequently he served as superintendent in chief of the Bureau of Investigative Services. From July 1993 to February 1994, Evans was second in command under Commissioner William Bratton, serving as superintendent in chief ("Paul F. Evans," n.d.).

In February 1994, Evans was named acting commissioner of police when Bratton left the position; after his appointment, Evans was confirmed and served until November 2003 (Belkin, 2003; DeMarco, 2003; Lakshmanan, 1994). Evans called a multilevel agency meeting early in his tenure in order to coordinate crime-fighting efforts and promote his vision of neighborhood (community-oriented) policing (Lakshmanan, 1994). The meeting was described as the most inclusive such meeting in many years at the department (Lakshmanan, 1994). Evans outlined his belief that neighborhood policing was a restoration of a style of policing prevalent when he was growing up in South Boston in the 1950s and 1960s. This vision included making uniformed officers more visible and building their integrity in order to make them role models for youths ("Evans takes charge," 1994). He also advocated that the same cops work the same neighborhoods, so they can build trust with local residents (Mallia, 1994).

In pursuit of his neighborhood-policing vision, Evans decentralized the citywide drug unit, giving authority to frontline captains instead of deputy superintendents ("A new openness," 1995). He also increased the number of neighborhood police districts from 5 to 10, actively calling on private citizens to help set goals for the department ("A new openness," 1995; Cullen, 1996). Evans also hired 300 additional officers, acting in a neighborhood capacity, during his first two years as commissioner (Cullen, 1996). "I don't know another department that has done so much outreach," opined Francis Hartmann, executive director of the Program in Criminal Justice Policy and Management at Harvard University ("A new openness," 1995, p. 12). In June 1995, Evans released a list of 100 ideas about public safety compiled from 16 teams of community leaders, including clergy, politicians, and police officers. The goals included developing strategies to deal with delinquent youths and redesigning police stations to make them more appealing for area residents seeking help (Valliancourt, 1995).

Initiatives to curb youth violence were a priority from Evans's early days as commissioner. He attended President Clinton's unveiling of the federal initiative to computerize records and track any guns confiscated in juvenile criminal investigations. Evans also encouraged cross-agency cooperation. The federal initiative was modeled after Evans's program, Operation Scrap Iron, in which gun suppliers and dealers, as well as young offenders, were targeted (McGrory, 1996). In 1995, the department teamed up with local YMCAs to identify 300 at-risk youths, who were then sent to summer camps. Between 1993 and 1997, Boston was nationally known for stemming the tide of crime by youths (ages 14 to 24) by 9 percent (Menendez, 1998).

Evans often spoke in press conferences about the disconnect between crime statistics and citizens' perception of their own safety. Although overall crime was dropping in the late 1990s, Evans indicated that the simultaneous spike in juvenile violence may have negated any sense of safety citizens felt. "Perception is reality. If people don't feel safe, it doesn't matter what the stats say," he said (Cullen, 1996, p. 14). In 2002, Evans told reporters that despite high-profile incidents, such as the murder of 10-year-old Trina Persad on June 2 and a series of sexual assaults, violent crime was at a statistical 31-year low. However, he also recognized that high-profile incidents serve to produce citizen fear (Ranalli, 2002; Rosenwald, 2002a). Evans stated:

> You have the statistics and you have the perception. But perception is reality. I'm not going to downplay any of the high-profile cases we've had in this city. . . . But people's perceptions come from what they see on television. What we have to do is reduce fear, and we're committed to doing that, and solving all these cases. (Rosenwald, 2002a, p. A1)

As commissioner, Evans received local praise from the mayor, politicians, and the press for his leadership during two crises. In a March 1994 incident, a botched police drug raid led to the death of a Dorchester neighborhood minister. Officers mistakenly entered his apartment instead of another dwelling, startling him and causing a heart attack. Evans apologized the next day, an unusual move considering the potential legal liability. The apology was praised by members of the black community (Cullen, 1996). Evans subsequently suspended the responsible officer for 15 days for improperly relying on an informant who had given him the wrong address (Canellos, 1995).[1] In May 1994, an officer was arrested for

---

[1]After this incident, a minority of politicians and community leaders criticized the ostensibly light punishment of the officer responsible. One senator, Dianne Wilkerson, told reporters that a civilian review board should be implemented in order to address the "growing divide between the black community and urban police departments" (Canellos, 1995, p. 14).

(continued)

raping a prostitute, which prompted an immediate review of department policies that addressed police misconduct (Estes, 1994). The officer was immediately put on leave (Chacon, 1996).

Evans fared less well in another high-profile incident on January 25, 1995, in which a black undercover cop (on duty), Michael Cox, was beaten by fellow cops who mistook him for a suspect. Cox was in plainclothes chasing a suspect when he was struck from behind by five uniformed cops who thought he was the target. According to court records in Cox's federal case, once the officers realized they had beaten a cop, they fled the scene ("Judge finds," 1998). Cox suffered a concussion, multiple face cuts, and kidney damage and could not work for six months (Noonan, 1999). A federal judge ruled that the incident constituted a civil rights violation. Evans ultimately conceded that Cox's civil rights were indeed violated; however, his (and the city's) lawyer indicated that this did not mean there was a pattern of brutality in the department ("Judge finds," 1998). The city ultimately settled with Cox for $700,000 ("Evans must act," 1999). The incident and subsequent lawsuits led to criticism that there was a pattern of racist conduct in the department, despite Evans's declaration that thereafter such conduct would not be tolerated. In another incident in 1999, two white officers racially harassed a black officer, hanging a noose made of yellow police tape over his motorcycle ("Evans must act," 1999).

The above racial incidents sparked black community leaders to call for a civilian review board. Evans was against the creation of such a board, intimating that complaints should be handled within the department. He also said, "Racism and harassment are totally alien to the oath we swear to and won't be tolerated" ("Black leaders," 1999).

Evans also was confronted with a lawsuit initiated by eight white cops who claimed they were overlooked for promotions in favor of the promotions of three black officers, based on race. Evans argued that race-based promotions were necessary in order to ensure a racially diverse police force that reflected the citizens of Boston (Martinez, 2002).

Despite much praise by people outside the police department, Evans has been considerably criticized from within. He has largely been seen as a commissioner who bows to public opinion (Rosenwald, 2002b). His relationship with Boston police officers first soured in 1995 when Evans invoked a city provision to disregard union contracts in assignment and deployment in order to accomplish the decentralization of the citywide drug unit (Ford, 1995; Heaney, 1997; "Stand with Evans," 1998). In 1997, his relationship with his patrol officers reached its nadir when a bill went before the city to prevent the commissioner from being able to circumvent union contracts in the name of public safety. Evans, along with the Massachusetts Chiefs of Police Association, opposed the bill (Heaney, 1997). Legislators ultimately sided with the patrol officers, stripping Evans of the power to override collective bargaining agreements ("Controlling the police," 2002).

In 2002, the Boston Police Patrolman's Association voted "no confidence" in Commissioner Paul Evans after he banned police officers from shooting at moving cars unless passengers shot at cops first ("Hub patrolmen," 2002). The policy change was prompted by the death of a passenger in a fleeing car who was shot and killed by a police officer on September 8, 2002. By late September 2002, the patrol officers' union was calling for Evans's resignation. They indicated that the ban on shooting at fleeing automobiles would put their lives at risk. However, community leaders, including the Black Ministerial Alliance, supported Evans ("More support," 2002). Additional supporters were the Garrison Trotter Neighborhood Association, the Boston Chamber of Commerce (Szaniszlo, 2002), Suffolk County District Attorney Dan Conley, and two independent candidates for district attorney (Woodlief, 2002).

Evans, when questioned about his relationship with the rank and file, stated that his top allegiance was to the city. As *The Boston Globe* reported:

> In a town of mythic police solidarity, [Evans] has sought to create a department accountable not only to itself, but to the broadest possible constituency. It's a mandate that has earned him uncommon respect outside the department's walls but also hardened dissent among the very ranks he has held, and climbed, over 32 years. . . . Today, many regard Evans as one of the most progressive police managers in the country. But to earn that regard, he has had to shut down the role that long defined being chief: defending and insulating officers, at any cost, from a critical public. (Rosenwald, 2002b, p. B1)

As was the case in many police departments around the country, the economic recession of the early 2000s meant that Evans had to make do with fewer officers due to budget constraints. In December 2002, he was forced to cancel a class of 60 police recruits because of a hiring freeze in anticipation of a $100 million cut in state aid (Marantz, 2002). In November 2003, Evans retired from the police department to take a position advising the United Kingdom on police leadership practices (Belkin, 2003; DeMarco, 2003; Sennott, 2004). A nationwide search was initiated to find his successor, who was appointed in early 2004 (Rosenwald & Estes, 2004).

Paul Evans was the police commissioner of Boston for almost 10 years. It takes a very skillful individual to head a large city with very serious problems for a full decade and leave the position without accusations related to major scandals (see, for example, the case of Los Angeles, described in Chapters 5 and 8). Nothing illustrates his skills approach to leadership better than the following account, which distills the essence of all four variables from the successful leader (SL) formula. A year after his appointment, he released a list of 100 ideas about public safety in Boston, compiled from 16 different teams of community leaders. Such an initiative not only

*(continued)*

is unprecedented in the history of police leadership but also exemplifies the combination of Evans's ability to recognize the need for change and to recognize that the change can be achieved only by factoring in how others feel about it. Such recognition in turn requires the ability to control one's own emotions, feelings, and vision for a department. All these skills were definitely honed by Evans's military discipline and experience. How much of it was genetic? One can only guess. However, the right combination of all the variables was definitely present, making Commissioner Evans an example of the skills approach to leadership.

### Exercise

The police commissioner detailed in this chapter has been examined through the prism of the skills approach. Using what you have learned from other theories in this book or from the summaries (as indicated in the Introduction) you have read thus far, it is possible to consider his approach through the lens of different theories. What other theories can you find applicable to this commissioner? Are there lessons to be learned from those applications, or do those theories indicate alternative paths or approaches that might have yielded a more successful outcome?

## REFERENCES

A new openness at the BPD (1995, March 22). *The Boston Globe*, p. 12.

Bass, B.M. (1990). *Bass & Stogdill's handbook of leadership: Theory research and managerial application* (3rd ed.). New York: Free Press.

Belkin, D. (2003, November 13). Evans won't name choice for successor. *The Boston Globe*, B4.

Black leaders urge Boston Police Department review board (1999, June 12). *The Associated Press*, state and local wire.

Canellos, P.S. (1995, October). Evans defends action against officer in raid, minister's lawyers criticize suspension. *The Boston Globe*, p. 14.

Chacon, R. (1996, February 11). Commissioner takes a new tack this time. *The Boston Globe*, p. 44.

Clawson, J.A. (2003). *Level three leadership: Getting below the surface* (2nd ed.). Upper Saddle River, NJ: Prentice Hall.

Connelly, M.S., J.A. Gilbert, S.J. Zaccaro, V.K. Threlfall, M.A. Marks & M.D. Mumford (2000). Exploring the relationship of leadership skills and knowledge to leader performance. *Leadership Quarterly*, 11 (1), 65–86.

Controlling the police (2002, September 14). *The Boston Globe*, p. A12.

Cullen, K. (1996, January 7). The neighborhood cop. *The Boston Globe*, p. 14.

Dearborn, K. (2002). Studies in emotional intelligence redefine our approach to leadership development. *Public Personnel Management*, 31 (4), 523–530.

DeMarco, P. (2003, October 26). A look back at the Evans years. *The Boston Globe, City Weekly*, p. 9.

Ericsson, K.A. & W. Charness (1994). Expert performance: Its structure and acquisition. *American Psychologist*, 49, 725–747.

Estes, A. (1994, May 2). Menino stands by police chief, department. *The Boston Herald*, p. 7.

Evans must act quickly (1999, April 27). *The Boston Herald*, p. 26.

Evans takes charge (1994, February 14). *The Boston Globe*, p. 22.

Feldman, D.A. (1999). *The handbook of emotionally intelligent leadership: Inspiring others to achieve results*. Falls Church, VA: Leadership Performance Solutions Press.

Fleishman, E.A. & M.K. Quaintance (1984). *Taxonomies of human performance: The description of human tasks*. Potomac, MD: Management Research Institute.

Ford, B. (1995, February 14). Highs & lows mark top cop's first year. *The Boston Herald*, p. 6.

Goleman, D. (1998, November–December). What makes a leader? *Harvard Business Review*, 93–102.

Heaney, J. (1997, November 12). Evans blasts police bill as union "power play." *The Boston Herald*, p. 18.

Hub patrolmen don't back Evans (2002, October 17). *The Boston Herald*, p. 22.

Judge finds for officers beaten by fellow cops (1998, November 25). *The Associated Press*, state and local wire.

Kobe, L.M., R. Reiter-Palmon & J.D. Rickers (2001). Self-reported leadership experiences in relation to inventoried social and emotional intelligence. *Current Psychology*, 20 (2), 154–163.

Lakshmanan, A.R. (1994, January 15). Evans acting quickly as acting police head. *The Boston Globe*, p. 13.

Lord, R.G., C.L. Devader & G.M. Alliger (1986). A meta-analysis of the relationship between personality traits and leadership perceptions: An application of validity generalization procedures. *Journal of Applied Psychology*, 71, 402–410.

Mallia, J. (1994, April 23). Evans' crime bill is cops key: Neighborhood policing nearing reality. *The Boston Herald*, p. A1.

Marantz, S. (2002, December 25). City nixes new cops in freeze on hiring. *The Boston Herald*, p. 1.

Martinez, J. (2002, March 27). Fed judge rules he'll review race-based cop promotions. *The Boston Herald*, p. 16.

McGrory, B. (1996, July 9). Local officials join Clinton in outlining youth crime bill. *The Boston Globe*, p. 3.

Menendez, J. (1998, August 13). Evans: Keeping city kids busy is key. *The Boston Herald*, p. 27.

More support for embattled police commissioner (2002, September 20). *The Associated Press*, state and local wire.

Mumford, M.D., S.J. Zaccaro, M.S. Connelly & M.A. Marks (2000a). Leadership skills: Conclusions and future directions. *Leadership Quarterly*, 11 (1), 155–170.

———, S.J. Zaccaro, S.J. Harding, D. Francis, T.A. Jacobs & E.A. Fleishman (2000b). Leadership skills for a changing world: Solving complex social problems. *Leadership Quarterly*, 11 (1), 11–35.

————, M.A. Marks, M.S. Connelly, S.J. Zaccaro & R. Reiter-Palmon (2000c). Development of leadership skills: Experience and timing. *Leadership Quarterly,* 11 (1), 87–114.

Negri, G. (1994, February 14). Evans' leadership skills were honed by demands of his bereaved family. *The Boston Globe*, p. 18.

Noonan, E. (1999, October 28). Officer accused in Cox beating terminated from force. *The Associated Press*, state and local wire.

Paul F. Evans (n.d.). Retrieved July 10, 2003, from http://policetraining.rio.maricopa. edu/staff/paul_evans.shtml.

Pernick, R. (2001). Creating a leadership development program: Nine essential tasks. *Public Personnel Management*, 30 (4), 10–17.

Ranalli, R. (2002, July 1). Girl's shooting spurs bad memories: Many fearing a rise in crime. *The Boston Globe*, p. B6.

Rosenwald, M.S. (2002a, August 22). Violent crime at 31-year low in Boston; commissioner acknowledges residents' fears. *The Boston Globe*, p. A1.

———— (2002b, September 29). Evans struggles with responsibility to two worlds: New plans show dilemma in protecting police, public. *The Boston Globe*, p. B1.

———— & A. Estes (2004, February 20). Historic moment for police. *The Boston Globe*, A1.

Sennott, C.M. (2004, May 20). An American police chief in London. *The Boston Globe*, D1.

Sheriff, D.R. (1968). Leadership skills and executive development: Leadership mythology vs. six learnable skills. *Training and Development Journal*, 22 (4), 29–34.

Stand with Evans, a leader (1998, January 8). *The Boston Herald*, p. 24.

Szaniszlo, M. (2002, September 21). Black leaders back police commissioner; union sticks to demand for resignation. *The Boston Globe*, p. 4.

Valliancourt, M. (1995, June 25). Police hear 100 ideas on public safety. *The Boston Globe*, p. 19.

Woodlief, W. (2002, September 24). Evans finds the right thing tough to do. *The Boston Herald*, p. 27.

Yammarino, F.J. (2000). Leadership skills: Introduction and overview. *Leadership Quarterly*, 11 (1), 5–9.

Zaccaro, S.J., J. Gilbert, K.K. Thor & M.D. Mumford (1991). Leadership and social intelligence: Linking social perceptiveness and behavioral flexibility to leader effectiveness. *Leadership Quarterly*, 2, 317–331.

# 12

# Career of Leadership

## *Trait Theory*

## OVERVIEW OF THE THEORY

Trait theory holds that an individual's personal traits, such as intelligence, persistence, self-confidence, initiative, and task knowledge, determine his/her success as a leader. This theory is examined through the example of Chief George Edwards, who led the Detroit Police Department for a short period during the troubled 1960s, as an individual whose entire personality contributed to his leadership of the department.

Trait theory focuses on the characteristics of great leaders throughout history Northouse (2004). Theorists attempted to identify specific traits that distinguished leaders from nonleaders. The earliest trait theorist may have been Plutarch (c. A.D. 100), who compared the characteristics and behaviors of Greek and Roman leaders in *The Parallel Lives* (Bass, 1990).[1]

Early trait theory, also known as the "Great Man" theory, held that leadership characteristics were innate, fixed, and relevant to all situations (Hollander & Offermann, 1993). In the 19th century, the leadership traits included physical characteristics such as height (Bryman, 1992).

---

[1]Plutarch can also be interpreted as a situational theorist, as each leader he describes from Greece had a counterpart in Rome in a similar political context (Bass, 1990).

### Trait Theory

1. According to trait theory, characteristics of great leaders throughout history determine their success.
2. Early trait theory ("Great Man" theory) posited innate characteristics, fixed and relevant in all situations.
3. Leadership traits in 19th-century trait theory included physical characteristics such as height.
4. Modern applications of trait theory note that personal characteristics are important, as are situations.
5. Psychoanalytical spin on trait theory states that leaders are like artists (Zaleznik, 1977).

Pure trait theory is characterized by viewing personality traits as determining leadership in isolation. Particular situations, or the context of the individual possessing the traits, are not emphasized (Bass, 1990; Stogdill, 1974). From approximately 1900 to 1940, leadership researchers attempted to establish intrinsic traits that differentiated leaders from nonleaders by profiling such leaders as Napoleon, Hitler, Gandhi, and Kennedy (Jago, 1982). Sarachek (1968) uses characters in Homer's *Iliad* to build archetypal leadership qualities: Agamemnon represented justice and judgment, Nestor embodied wisdom and counsel, Odysseus possessed shrewdness and cunning, and Achilles represented valor and action (Stogdill, 1974).

## MODERN APPLICATIONS OF TRAIT THEORY

More modern applications of trait theory emphasize that a combination of personal characteristics contributes to successful leadership but that situations may also be important (Stogdill, 1974). Many leadership scholars have declared trait theory dead because it failed the test of social science (discussed below) (Baruch & Lessem, 1997; Jago, 1982; Owens, 1973), but it continues to appear in modern leadership materials. "Trait theory is important, because it seeks a framework based on the qualities of exceptional leaders in terms of personal characteristics. This framework can be used to identify potential leaders" (Rowley, 1997, pp. 80–81).

*Leaders are like artists.* Zaleznik (1977) revitalizes trait theory by giving it a psychoanalytic spin. He contrasts managers and

## Managers vs. Leaders

### Managers

- Are bureaucratic short-term thinkers, embedded in routine and inflexibility (Zaleznik, 1977).
- Join forces to sell goods and services (Bennis & Nanus, 1985).

### Leaders

- Develop new ideas for long-standing problems, shape the bigger picture of the organization, seek out risk and danger, and are often emotionally intense (Zaleznik, 1977).
- Work to create a real change (Bennis & Nanus, 1985).

leaders based on their personality characteristics. Managers are viewed as bureaucratic short-term thinkers embedded in routine and inflexibility. Leaders, on the other hand, have characteristics that help them to develop new ideas for long-standing problems. They are an ideal in terms of shaping the bigger picture of an organization. They are "temperamentally disposed to seek out risk and danger" (Zaleznik, 1977, p. 72). They relate to others in an intuitive and empathetic manner. They are often emotionally intense. "Leaders are like artists and other gifted people who often struggle with neuroses" (Zaleznik, 1977, p. 75). Zaleznik emphasizes talent over learned skills; individuals with such talent need mentorship in order to actualize their potential. "The only sure way an individual can interrupt reverie-like preoccupation and self-absorption is to form a deep attachment to a great individual or other person who understands and has the ability to communicate with the gifted individual" (Zaleznik, 1977, p. 75).

*Leadership traits can be acquired and learned by example.* Bennis and Nanus (1985) interviewed and observed 90 leaders from the public and private sectors in search of the aggregate qualities these leaders possessed.[2] Four major skills emerged after qualitative review of the data. The authors believe these skills "can be learned by anyone,

---

[2]Bennis and Nanus (1985) describe their own work as "transformative" leadership and not trait theory. Northouse (2004), however, states that their work is evidence of recent interest in the trait theory. Yet Northouse also discusses their book in his chapter called "Transformational Leadership."

taught to everyone, denied to no one" (Bennis & Nanus, 1985, p. 27). These are the four skills:

1. *Attention through vision.* Leaders have an agenda and are results-oriented. They are visionaries.
2. *Meaning through communication.* Leaders have the capacity to project meaning to the members of an organization. They articulate what has previously been unsaid, and they construct images and metaphors to mobilize attention to a new outlook or perspective.
3. *Trust through positioning.* Leaders operate with integrity and buy into their own ideals, thereby fostering trust with their subordinates.
4. *Deployment of self through positive self-regard.* Leaders accept people as they are, approach relationships in terms of the present instead of the past, treat those closest to them with the same respect as casual acquaintances, trust others, and do not need constant approval and recognition from others.

Bennis and Nanus also identify myths of leadership that may counter other trait theorists. These myths are that leadership is a rare skill, leaders are born that way, leaders are charismatic, and leadership exists only at the top of the organization. Taken as a whole, the Bennis and Nanus approach seems to democratize trait theory and encourages people to cultivate their own leadership characteristics.

*Certain traits are preconditions to leadership.* Kirkpatrick and Locke (1991) modernize trait theory by stating that certain leadership traits are merely preconditions and do not guarantee success.

---

### Leadership Traits Can Be Learned

1. *Attention through vision.* Leaders have an agenda and are results-oriented.
2. *Meaning through communication.* Leaders have the capacity to project/articulate meaning.
3. *Trust through positioning.* Leaders operate with integrity and buy into their own ideals.
4. *Deployment of self through positive self-regard.* Leaders project acceptance, respect, and trust.

(Bennis and Nanus, 1985)

---

## Certain Traits Are Preconditions

1. Drive
2. Desire to lead
3. Honesty and integrity
4. Self-confidence
5. Cognitive ability
6. Knowledge of the business

If you have these, all you need is skills, vision, and implementation.

(Kirkpatrick and Locke, 1991)

"Leaders who possess the requisite traits must take certain actions to be successful. . . . Possessing the appropriate traits only makes it more likely that such actions will be taken and be successful" (p. 49). Kirkpatrick and Locke identify six core traits that are preconditions to effective leadership: drive, desire to lead, honesty and integrity, self-confidence, cognitive ability, and knowledge of the business. If these traits are possessed, a potential leader must then actualize them by implementing the following actions: skills (as in specific capacities, not the general capacity associated with a trait), vision creation, and implementation of the vision.

According to Kirkpatrick and Locke, trait theory has management implications. Managers should choose employees with the aforementioned traits because these employees are endowed with the characteristics from which leaders can be built. Trait assessment tests should be used to help determine the appropriate staff members. They should then be offered training and experience to facilitate actualization of the leadership traits. "Leaders do not have to be great men or women by being intellectual geniuses or omniscient prophets to succeed, but they do need to have the 'right stuff' and this stuff is not equally present in all people" (Kirkpatrick & Locke, 1991, p. 58).

*Leadership traits are in the eyes of the beholder.* Calder (1977) puts forth that leadership is built on traits but that the traits need to exist only in the perceptions of others for the leader to be successful. People define others as either possessing or not possessing leadership traits. From this approach, called the attribution theory of leadership, the followers' perceptions of leadership qualities determine whether the leader will be effective (Jago, 1982).

---

**Leadership Traits Are in Eyes of Beholder**

The followers' perceptions of leadership qualities determine whether the leader will be effective or not. This is also known as the attribution theory of leadership.

(Calder, 1977)

---

## SOCIAL SCIENTIFIC EVALUATION
## OF LEADERSHIP TRAITS

In research by Stogdill (1974), 124 trait studies were evaluated. Subjects for the studies were obtained by observing behaviors of potential subjects in group situations, doing peer reviews, nominating subjects using researchers, selecting people occupying positions of leadership, and analyzing case history data. The findings of this study are summarized in Northouse (2004). However, a more complete list of traits associated with leadership according to Stogdill's 1948 study is as follows:

1. Capacity (intelligence, alertness, verbal facility, originality, judgment)
2. Achievement (scholarship, knowledge, athletic accomplishments)
3. Responsibility (dependability, initiative, persistence, aggressiveness, self-confidence, desire to excel)
4. Participation (activity, sociability, cooperation, adaptability, humor)
5. Status (socioeconomic position, popularity)
6. Situation (mental level, status skills, needs and interests of followers, objectives to be achieved)

As evidenced above, although traits are important, Stogdill also factors in situational variables. He states, "[T]he pattern of personal characteristics of the leader must bear some relevant relationship to the characters, activities and goals of the followers" (pp. 63–64).

In meta-analytic research by Mann (1959) of 1,400 studies on personality and leadership, the best predictor of leadership success is intelligence. Additional positively correlated traits are masculinity and dominance. These traits also are found to be significant in a subsequent analytic study of Mann's data using updated statistical

## Social Scientific Evaluation of Leadership Traits

1. Capacity
2. Achievement
3. Responsibility
4. Participation
5. Status
6. Situation

(Stogdill, 1974)

---

methods (Lord et al., 1986). However, the two studies disagree as to the correlation of extroversion on leadership. Mann found it to be significant while the later study indicates it was nonsignificant. Mann reviewed studies that measured the concept in four ways: observation of individuals' leadership traits by researchers, peer review of leaders' traits, use of status in an organization as the criterion for leadership, and leaders' self-ratings of their traits. Differing populations and sample sizes complicated the analysis. The median correlations are low; thus the findings are relatively weak even when statistically significant. However, the methodology in the Lord et al. study shows more statistical significance for the traits of intelligence, masculinity, and dominance using the same data.

Jenkins (1947; cited in Stogdill, 1974) reviewed 74 military studies and found that although leaders exhibit a variety of abilities and characteristics that are superior to followers, a pattern of specific traits could not be discerned. From this, he deduces that a trait theory of leadership could not be supported. Rather, he postulates that leadership is situation-specific (Stogdill, 1974).

Bass (1990) states, in his meta-analytic review of leadership studies, that the following traits are strongly correlated with leadership: drive for responsibility, completion of tasks, vigor and persistence, originality in problem solving, social initiative, self-confidence, sense of personal identity, acceptance of consequences, tolerance of frustration and delay, ability to influence others' behavior, and capacity to structure social interaction. However, Bass also argues that there is an interaction effect between the situation and the traits possessed by the leaders. "There is no overall comprehensive theory of the personality of leaders. Nonetheless, evidence abounds that particular patterns of traits are of consequence to leadership, such as determination, persistence, self-confidence and ego strength" (Bass, 1990, p. 87).

## Social Scientific Evaluation of Leadership Traits

1.  Drive for responsibility
2.  Completion of tasks
3.  Vigor and persistence
4.  Originality in problem solving
5.  Social initiative
6.  Self-confidence
7.  Sense of personal identity
8.  Acceptance of consequences
9.  Tolerance of frustration and delay
10. Ability to influence others' behavior
11. Capacity to structure social interaction

(Bass, 1990)

Krimmel and Lindenmuth (2001) researched the desirable and undesirable performance indicators of police chiefs by examining the attitudes of 250 municipal managers regarding police chiefs under their control. The managers answered questions about 45 different leadership indicators of their police chiefs; the questions primarily focused on a list of traits such as "responsible," "shares information," "focused," and "sophisticated" (Krimmel & Lindenmuth, 2001). The list of traits is broken down into six subsets (Krimmel & Lindenmuth, 2001):

1.  *Sad.* This refers to a nexus of responses that demonstrate that the police chief is defensive, dissatisfied, lonely, vulnerable, and unable to delegate authority.
2.  *Upset.* This refers to responses indicating that the chief is insensitive, is arrogant, betrays trust, is inappropriately ambitious, rules with an iron fist, has boot camp values, and denies responsibility. (This style of chief can also be classified as means-end or Machiavellian.)
3.  *Calm.* This subset refers to chiefs who are rated as fair-minded, sincere, reasonable, comfortable with uncertainty, competitive, conscientious, and able to focus on the whole problem and who recognize the value of disequilibrium.
4.  *Sharing.* This subset reflects chiefs who are people persons, collaborators, information sharers, providers of clear visions, developers of new patterns of relationships, motivators of employees, and outgoing people.

5. *Scout*. This refers to the subset of variables reflecting that the chief takes responsibility, is responsible, selects good subordinates, is appropriately ambitious, is well organized, selects and maintains goals, and properly maintains activities.
6. *Bond* (short for James Bond). This subset reflects chiefs who are self-controlled, cautious, reserved, capable, secure, and intelligent.

Krimmel and Lindenmuth found that police chiefs promoted from within the department tended to fit into the calm, sharing, or scout subset. Chiefs hired from the outside were more likely to be categorized in the upset subset. Graduates of the FBI National Academy were more likely to be rated in the calm, sharing, scout, or Bond subset. Chiefs possessing (at best) high school diplomas were more likely to be rated as having leadership problems. Police chiefs with better education were more likely to be evaluated as belonging to the sharing or scout subset. The type of community policed had no effect on leadership indicators. However, police departments that were unionized were significantly more likely to evaluate police chiefs as belonging to the calm, sharing, or scout subset. In summary, police chiefs who have some college credits, have graduated from the FBI National Academy, and have been promoted from within were the least likely to be assessed as having leadership problems (Krimmel & Lindenmuth, 2001).

## TRAIT THEORY AND THE CASE OF CHIEF GEORGE EDWARDS

The trait theory posits that an individual's characteristics determine his/her success as a leader. This theory is thus based on the assumption that leaders are born rather than made. Traits identified as leadership qualities include motivation, drive, and persistence. Although others have been identified, including certain physical characteristics, these three qualities are the best indicators of the leadership skills chosen in this example. One could compose quite a long list of police chiefs and commissioners who, throughout their careers, exhibited these leadership traits, and Chief George Edwards represents just one of many other police leaders who could illustrate this theory.

However important personal characteristics are to trait theory, they are also dependent on the situations the leaders encounter. In other words, one might have the leadership traits or characteristics but never encounter the right situations to be able to make the best decision or judgment and apply those traits. Thus, an interesting spin on trait theory offers the possibility that traits are acquired, not ascribed, as a result of the variety of situations that individuals encounter on their paths to becoming leaders.

---

**CAREER HIGHLIGHTS**    Trait Theory

**Chief George Edwards**
*Detroit Police Department, Michigan*

George C. Edwards, Jr., was born in Dallas, Texas, in 1914. His father was an attorney and socialist activist in the antisegregation movement[1] ("George C. Edwards, Jr., collection," n.d.). Edwards received his bachelor's degree from Southern Methodist University in 1933. He then attended Harvard, where he earned a master's degree in literature in 1934 ("George C. Edwards, Jr., collection," n.d.).

From 1934 to 1935, he worked as the secretary of the League of Industrial Democracy, traveling around the country as a labor activist. He relocated to Detroit in 1936, working in an automobile plant while writing a book (never published). He participated in a sit-down strike in 1937 at the plant and was sentenced to 30 days in jail for defying a court order to disperse ("George C. Edwards, Jr., banned," 1995).

In 1937, he worked as the secretary-director of the Detroit Housing Commission. He was elected to the Detroit Common Council in 1941, subsequently serving four terms. From 1943 to 1946, Edwards was a lieutenant in the U.S. Army ("George C. Edwards, Jr., 80," 1995). In 1945, he investigated Japanese war crimes in the Philippines for the Army (Stolberg, 1998). He then became the national director of the United Auto Workers welfare department ("George C. Edwards, Jr., 80," 1995).

Edwards earned his law degree in 1944 from the Detroit College of Law and subsequently entered private practice. In 1949, he unsuccessfully ran for mayor of Detroit ("George C. Edwards, Jr., collection," n.d.). Edwards was appointed as a judge for Wayne County's Probate Court and revised procedures for handling juveniles. He implemented preliminary hearings within 24 hours of the apprehension of a child and sped up the process in subsequent stages. These reforms came in response to a system in which previously children had been held in limbo for months (Stolberg, 1998). In 1954, Edwards was elected to the Wayne County Circuit Court in Michigan, followed by his 1956 appointment to the Michigan Supreme Court. He left this post in 1962 to serve

---

[1] Edwards wrote a book about his father's life: Edwards, G. (1974). *Pioneer-at-law: A legacy in the pursuit of justice.* New York: W.W. Norton & Co., Inc.

as police commissioner in Detroit ("George C. Edwards, Jr., banned," 1995; "Judge G. C. Edwards," 1995).

After serving as commissioner (discussed below), Edwards served on the 6th Circuit U.S. Court of Appeals from 1963 until 1985, when he semiretired and took a reduced caseload. He was chief judge of the circuit from 1979 to 1983. He is most often remembered for writing the opinion in a 1971 case that established that wiretapping without a warrant was unconstitutional. The opinion was upheld by the U.S. Supreme Court and was later applied to the Watergate proceedings ("Deaths elsewhere," 1995). The case stemmed from the conviction of Lawrence Robert Plamondon, a White Panther party member, on charges that he bombed a CIA office in Ann Arbor, Michigan, in 1969 ("George C. Edwards, Jr., banned," 1995).

Edwards served as commissioner of the Detroit Police Department from 1962 to 1963. Mayor Jerome P. Cavanaugh chose Edwards as police commissioner because of Edwards's record of working for racial integration and harmony (Stolberg, 1998). On the bench, he had been particularly sensitive to constitutional issues associated with racially discriminatory enforcement of the law. Edwards's record was especially suitable given the controversy surrounding a crackdown in Detroit by the previous police chief, William D. Hart. In 1960, in response to the murders of two white women at the hands of a black man, Hart declared a state of emergency and ordered a roundup of street criminals. The black community largely believed the crackdown to be an excuse for police officers to intimidate and harass blacks. Community leaders were becoming increasingly outspoken about the racial divide in the city and viewed the police force as a hostile white enemy (Stolberg, 1998). Furthermore, in 1943, after years of increasing racial tensions, the city erupted into a race riot.

Edwards reportedly deliberated about whether to take the job as commissioner. As a Michigan Supreme Court judge, he already had a high-profile job. However, being commissioner would allow him to explore the practicalities of what already intrigued him: how to balance constitutional safeguards with law enforcement (Stolberg, 1998). In a letter to his son about his decision, he wrote, "I guess I couldn't resist trying to figure out whether it is possible to make the Constitution a living document in one of our great cities" (Stolberg, 1998, p. 36). In response to Edwards's appointment, numerous black civic leaders praised Mayor Cavanaugh. Reaction among Detroit's white residents was reportedly divided. Upon taking the job in 1962, Edwards laid out his main goals for his tenure as commissioner: improve racial equality in the enforcement of the law, target the Mafia, increase minority recruiting in the police department, and develop community-oriented policing (Stolberg, 1998).

(*continued*)

*Improve racial equality in law enforcement.* In 1962, the city of Detroit was one-third black. Edwards's first reform move for racial equality was to overhaul the department's traffic division, which had a bad reputation in the black community for harassment. In an effort to reach out to the black community, he put pressure on the deputy commissioner who headed the division to treat black motorists with respect (Stolberg, 1998). Despite skepticism about whether his overtures to the deputy commissioner would make a difference, within a few weeks, Edwards began receiving letters from black citizens and civic leaders thanking him for the change in police attitudes (Stolberg, 1998).

Edwards's first race-related crisis occurred on January 28, 1962, when Willie Daniels, a black man accused of threatening a woman with a gun, was beaten by police officers when he was apprehended in his home (Stolberg, 1998). Daniels sued the city for his injuries (bruising and swelling on his wrists and stomach), which were verified by a doctor. Meanwhile, Edwards initiated an internal investigation, including a trial board consisting of Edwards and top brass. Despite ongoing complaints of brutality, an investigation had not been initiated since 1957. After conducting the internal trial, the board found the accused officers not guilty, though Edwards made it clear the decision was not unanimous because he believed otherwise. Edwards stated that from the trial he realized that "police morale was a code name for a police officer's obligation to support another police officer, regardless of regulation or law unless he was so far out of bounds that saving him was impossible" (Stolberg, 1998, p. 159 [quoting from Edwards's unpublished manuscript about his commissionership]). Edwards subsequently changed departmental policy, requiring a supervisor to go to every location at which a gun was reported in hopes of decreasing brutality and increasing accountability.

Another brutality issue cropped up near the end of Edwards's tenure. Cynthia Scott, a known prostitute and robber, threatened an officer with a knife while being escorted to a squad car (Stolberg, 1998). After she cut the officer, she ran off. The officer's partner gave chase, and she turned on him with the knife as well. He told her to stop, but she stepped away; the officer subsequently shot her in the back, killing her (Stolberg, 1998). The case was a public relations disaster because the black community felt it was an example of brutality. The incident sparked picketers at the City-County Building. Edwards conducted his own internal inquiry, ultimately agreeing with the attorney general and district attorney, who declined to take action against the officer who shot Scott. Edwards believed the officer was justified because there was little doubt that he was afraid for his life at the time of the shooting (Stolberg, 1998). The case did damage to the black community's perception of the police in spite of the efforts of reform that Edwards had previously been praised for (Stolberg, 1998).

Despite Edwards's commitment to reform and his sensitivity to the black community, he stood against civilian review boards (Stolberg, 1998). He believed that if he made it clear that excessive use of force would not be tolerated, civilian oversight would be unnecessary. On this point, many black leaders disagreed, saying that true reform required civilian review boards (Stolberg, 1998). However, in 1962, Edwards gave the Community Relations Bureau within the department the responsibility for investigating brutality complaints, setting up a specific team that he felt would be unbiased (Stolberg, 1998).

Edwards's handling of security at potentially racially charged events in Detroit also received praise for decreasing tensions and protecting the public safety (Stolberg, 1998). On June 10, 1962, Nation of Islam leader Malcolm X spoke before 3,500 people in the city. Edwards attended the event, although he did not explicitly support the group. Instead, he told the press that the group had a right to meet in the city and be treated with respect as long as they did not pose any threat to lives or property. Edwards had 900 officers on standby in the event of a disturbance, but they were ultimately unneeded. He took a similar approach to the Freedom March staged by Martin Luther King, Jr., on June 23, 1963. Final crowd estimates were between 125,000 and 250,000 people, including Edwards who marched with them. The only trouble reported to the police that day was a broken window and a disoriented man in the middle of a street; there were no violent incidents (Stolberg, 1998).

*Target the Mafia.* While commissioner, Edwards fought against the influence of the Mafia in the city, particularly seeking to disrupt gambling operations (Stolberg, 1998). He was a proponent of the alien conspiracy theory, which holds that mob bosses are connected under a national umbrella (Stolberg, 1998). This was a common conspiracy theory at the time, as 58 mob bosses across the nation were found meeting in Apalachin, New York, in 1957. That same year, the McClellan Commission was set up by the Senate to explore the activities of organized criminals infiltrating labor unions (Stolberg, 1998).

Edwards began his antimob crusade by forcing the shutdown of the Lesod gambling club on the Lower East Side of the city (Stolberg, 1998). He built a case against the establishment via police surveillance and interviews of customers; the mob eventually conceded. He also implemented a policy to discourage other clubs from operating in Detroit by passing an ordinance (with the city council) prohibiting clubs to be open between 2 a.m. and 8 a.m. unless they agreed to a police investigation of their activities (Stolberg, 1998). Edwards's biggest antimob action was the raid on the Gotham Hotel, orchestrated in conjunction with the IRS: 41 people were arrested, $60,000 in cash was seized, and 120,000 betting slips were found. In addition, Edwards

*(continued)*

led a successful investigation against mob boss Giacamo Giacalone
using wiretaps (Stolberg, 1998).

*Increase minority recruitment.* Edwards believed that diffusing racial
tensions required minority recruitment of police officers. At the time of
his appointment, there were only 136 black police officers in a force of
4,300 (which equaled 3 percent black) (Stolberg, 1998). This occurred
despite the fact that blacks made up 28 percent of the applicant pool, similar to their representation in the general population. Furthermore, no
black officer had achieved the rank of inspector. A report by
Commissioner Director Richard Marks found that discrimination in hiring practices was routine (Stolberg, 1998). Higher standards on physical,
mental, and medical tests were applied to black applicants. During his
tenure, Edwards promoted blacks, including a black officer as inspector,
and began a media campaign to recruit minorities. However, he was able
to make only modest gains. By 1967 (four years after Edwards left the
department), there were only 191 officers in contrast to 4,049 white officers (Stolberg, 1998).

*Develop community-oriented policing.* Edwards is credited with envi-
sioning community-oriented policing as an answer to police-community
relations, including race relations (Stolberg, 1998). He hired more officers
and strategically placed them in high-crime areas at peak times. He also
fostered relationships with neighborhood block clubs designed to ward
off crime (Stolberg, 1998).

Edwards also continued police-community meetings that had
begun under the previous commissioner (Stolberg, 1998). In particular,
on June 22, 1962, Edwards organized a conference among civilians and
civic and religious leaders on juvenile delinquency in order to encourage
citizen cooperation in combating the problem. The highlight of the meeting was an appearance by Raymond Burr (an actor who played Perry
Mason on television) (Stolberg, 1998). On November 1, a follow-up conference with public and private school officials was held to discuss local
juvenile delinquency concerns (Stolberg, 1998). Edwards also received
federal funding for a program called Community Action for Detroit
Youth, which researched and developed initiatives to combat juvenile
delinquency at the community level (Stolberg, 1998).

Despite the above reforms that garnered community support,
Edwards did not enjoy popularity among the rank and file (Stolberg, 1998).
At the announcement of his appointment as commissioner, officers largely
disapproved because of his judicial record of liberalism (Stolberg, 1998).
In his first few weeks on the job, Edwards made an effort to visit various
station houses and talk to as many officers as possible in order to reach out
and gain support (Stolberg, 1998). Yet, despite this attempt, officers often
subtly sabotaged his policies. For example, as part of a community-policing
initiative, Edwards asked precinct commanders to meet with school

officials after responding to gang fights. When this did not happen two weeks later, he ordered them to do so and to provide him with written reports (Stolberg, 1998). In another incident, department leaders misreported crime statistics in order to discredit Edwards's approach to crime fighting (Stolberg, 1998).

Despite Edwards's negotiation of a pay increase for officers, on April 16, 1962, department leaders called a meeting to discuss their dissatisfaction with him (Stolberg, 1998). Most of the complaints involved low morale and a sense that their ability to do their job was hindered by various reform policies (Stolberg, 1998). Edwards never commanded the respect of most of the rank and file; however, his primary aim was not to win their support but to win that of the public (Stolberg, 1998). As Edwards stated:

> The issue of whether there will be civilian control of the police . . . is one of the most critical issues of our time. . . . The person who functions as the executive head of the police department should have his eye on the civilian need for his department, not whether he is popular with his rank and file. (Blonston, 1968, cited in Stolberg, 1998, p. 292)

Chief Edwards's experience shows motivation, drive, and persistence. Edwards was also an individual who was exposed to a myriad of situations and experiences throughout his career, especially during the times when he toured the country as a labor activist. There is an old adage: Nothing gives you a better education than travel. There is much to be said about this wisdom with regard to exposure to situations and learning of leadership traits. Changing work environments and even serving time in prison for doing the right thing certainly contributed volumes to Edwards's learning experience.

When one looks at Edwards's life, it is hard to ignore his drive to be successful whatever the endeavor. No matter how unrelated his fields of interest, they share a common thread: Edwards's motivation to complete his task well. It was precisely this motivation, drive, and persistence, paired with the experiences offered by his eclectic career, that made Edwards a suitable candidate to be chosen as the chief of the Detroit Police Department. Edwards did not need the position to advance his political career, as he already had a high public profile. He did not need another challenge, since he already had quite a full plate of challenges. However, it appears that, above all, his motivation to take on the position was a factor of a pronounced leadership trait—the desire to do the right thing.

It is natural to try to consider deeper motivations when trying to understand situations in which we (or others) have become involved that at least superficially seem to bear little, if any, benefit. Frequently we are even asked why we do the things we do or why we involve ourselves in a predicament that might destroy our past accomplishments and bring

*(continued)*

little if any glory to our future. Sometimes actions that appear to make no sense whatsoever are motivated by leadership qualities and traits more than by some irrational drive. Occasionally it is a desire and drive for honesty and integrity, vigor and persistence, and a sense of personal identity as well as an overall burning desire to restore some balance of injustice and to do the right thing.

Chief Edwards's tenure as police commissioner, paired with his life experience in other areas, illustrates a true example of the trait theory of leadership. The way he handled sensitive situations, race-related problems, and the introduction of innovative community-oriented policing (two decades prior to the formal introduction of such concepts by social scientists)—these are just a few examples of a leader who needed to have the right characteristics that enabled him to do the right thing in the politically and socially volatile world of policing in the 1960s.

### Exercise

The police chief detailed in this chapter has been examined through the prism of trait theory. Using what you have learned from other theories in this book or from the summaries (as indicated in the Introduction) you have read thus far, it is possible to consider his approach through the lens of different theories. What other theories can you find applicable to this chief? Are there lessons to be learned from those applications, or do those theories indicate alternative paths or approaches that might have yielded a more successful outcome?

## REFERENCES

Baruch, Y. & R. Lessem (1997). The spectral management inventory—A validation study. *Journal of Managerial Psychology*, 12, 365–382.

Bass, B.M. (1990). *Bass and Stogdill's handbook of leadership: A survey of theory and research*. New York: Free Press.

Bennis, G. & B. Nanus (1985). *Leaders: The strategies for taking charge*. New York: Harper & Row.

Bryman, A. (1992). *Charisma and leadership in organizations*. London: Sage.

Calder, B.J. (1977). An attribution theory of leadership. In B.M. Staw & G.R. Salancik (Eds.), *New directions in organization behavior* (pp. 179–204). Chicago: St. Claire Press/London: MacMillan. (Paperback edition by Meridian Books, New York, 1962.)

Deaths elsewhere (1995, April 10). *Chicago Daily Law Bulletin*, p. 3.

George C. Edwards, Jr.: Banned secret wiretaps (1995, April 9). *Chicago Sun-Times*, p. 61.

George C. Edwards, Jr., collection (n.d.). Retrieved August 26, 2003, from www.reuther.wayne.edu/collections/hefa_10.htm.

George C. Edwards, Jr., 80, was chief appeals court judge (1995, April 9). *The Record*, p. N7.

Hollander, E.P. & L.R. Offermann (1993). Power and leadership in organizations. In W.E. Rosenbach & R.L. Taylor (Eds.), *Contemporary issues in leadership* (pp. 62–86). Boulder, CO: Westview Press.

Jago, A.G. (1982). Leadership: Perspectives in theory and research. *Management Science*, 28 (3), 315–336.

Judge G.C. Edwards dies at 80; rules against secret wiretaps (1995, April 10). *The New York Times*, p. B14.

Kirkpatrick, S.A. & E.A. Locke (1991). Leadership: Do traits matter? *The Executive*, 5, 48–60.

Krimmel, J.T. & P. Lindenmuth (2001). Police chief performance and leadership styles. *Police Quarterly*, 4 (4), 469–483.

Lord, R.G., C.L. DeVader & G.M. Alliger (1986). A meta-analysis of the relation between personality traits and leadership perceptions: An application of validity generalization procedures. *Journal of Applied Psychology*, 71, 402–410.

Mann, R.D. (1959). A review of the relationship between personality and performance in small groups. *Psychological Bulletin*, 56, 241–270.

Northouse, P.G. (2004). *Leadership: Theory and practice* (3rd ed.). Thousand Oaks, CA: Sage.

Owens, J. (1973). What kind of leader do they follow? *Management Review*, 62, 54–57.

Rowley, J. (1997). Academic leaders: Made or born? *Industrial and Commercial Training*, 29, 78–84.

Sarachek, B. (1968). Greek concepts of leadership. *Academic Management Journal*, 11, 39–48.

Stogdill, R.M. (1948). Personal factors associated with leadership: A survey of literature. *Journal of Psychology*, 25, 35–71.

——— (1974). *Handbook of leadership: A survey of theory and research.* New York: Free Press.

Stolberg, M.M. (1998). *Bridging the river of hatred: The pioneering efforts of Detroit police commissioner George Edwards.* Detroit: Wayne State University Press.

Zaleznik, A. (1977, May–June). Managers and leaders: Are they different? *Harvard Business Review*, 55 (3) 67–68. (Reprinted in 1992, *Harvard Business Review*, 70 (2), 126–135.)

# 13

# Into the Future

*The Big Hairy Audacious Goal
and Catalytic Mechanisms*

Nearly 200 years ago, leading police reformers advocated removing the police from politics and politics from the police, in other words, to treat this occupation as a true profession. This task, however difficult to achieve, remains weighty and important. The question resembles the proverbial chicken and the egg: Do we as a society owe it to democracy to maintain a strong and professional police force, or is society democratic because of professional policing?

A good overview of leadership theories must end with Jim Collins's leadership theory, the most relevant approach to socially complex and politically impaired police organizations. Although Collins, similar to other researchers who contributed to the development of leadership theories, did not look specifically at police environments to identify the patterns of behaviors and structures, his approach to leadership is particularly relevant for police organizations. It offers insight into how to turn entities fraught with problems and unachievable goals into progressive and fully operational organizations. Despite the fact that his approach has more of a management than purely leadership slant, it speaks to leadership practice and is easily translated into the realities of police life.

Jim Collins's leadership theory is part of his general management theory outlined in his two books, *Built to Last* (1994 [with

J. Porras]) and *Good to Great* (2001). In general, Collins advocates that companies set ambitious goals. Leaders should act out their organization's core values and goals rather than honing in on their own self-interest. Maximizing profit is not as effective a goal as maintaining core values. Patience is also a major asset, as turnarounds in an organization can take up to seven years (Lenzner, 2003). Collins's leadership theories are often described as "reality-based" (Bryant, 2003, p. 50). These theories are described and illustrated with examples of some of the police chiefs depicted in this book as well as generally applicable reality-based situations from everyday policing.

## ANTICHARISMATIC LEADERSHIP

In *Good to Great* (2001), Collins and his team of 21 researchers sampled 11 large companies that were particularly successful on certain economic indicators, including high cumulative stock returns over a 15-year period and average returns of over three times the market rate. As a comparison, Collins then selected 6 companies that performed poorly on the same indicators. One of the major findings was that charismatic leadership was negatively correlated with successful businesses.

Collins believes that charismatic and transformational leadership is a dead end for businesses. Businesses must overcome the "culture and affliction" of relying on particularly dominant and self-absorbed leaders:

> In the US, we revere the great, egocentric leaders. We have had a generation of leaders that were ambitious first and foremost for themselves and we are now paying the price. (Collins as quoted by Pickard, 2003, p. 8)

The main problem with transformational leadership is that the leader's dominant personality overtakes the reality of the organizational context. Collins explains:

> The moment a leader allows himself to become the primary reality people worry about, rather than reality being the primary reality, you have a recipe for mediocrity, or worse. This is one of the key reasons why less charismatic leaders often produce better long-term results than their more charismatic counterparts. (Collins, 2001, p. 72)

Furthermore, celebrities who take over an organization from the outside are also negatively correlated with business success (Bryant, 2003; Collins, 2001).

When one looks at the police leaders of national prominence who were brought in to transform police organizations fraught with problems of corruption and/or general mismanagement, it appears that there is a striking resemblance between Collins's research findings and their level of success. It is true that in times of extreme distress, a charismatic leader will produce extreme results; however, the question remains how long-lasting those extreme results are going to be. It is true that one can reform an organization in the most extreme manner by introducing innovations. Examples include the use of COMPSTAT, as in New York City, or numerous changes in structure and operational deployment, as in New Orleans. Looking at long-term results, the police forces of New York City or New Orleans or Charlotte-Mecklenburg are not very different than what they used to be prior to experiencing and experimenting with the appointment of their charismatic leaders.

When this point was made in classroom discussions at John Jay College of Criminal Justice, where many students are NYPD officers, it inevitably met with objections. Some NYPD students abruptly disagreed with the notion that the NYPD in the year 2004 was the same as in the year 1994, or 1984 for that matter. However, the sad truth is, it is. It is correct to say that the manner of deployment has changed dramatically, the clearance rate is much higher, the overall level of education and training is better, line officers up to ranking police supervisors are more accountable and effective than their counterparts from years ago, equipment is better, and response time is faster. Nevertheless, this superficially attractive force still suffers from an inability to recruit the best and the brightest, the attrition rate is high, the pay is low, the morale is low, tensions between supervisors and troops run high, and the sense of pride in wearing this particular uniform is nowhere near what it should be. Although these findings were not empirically researched, they are based on the testimonial evidence and close weekly interactions with hundreds and hundreds of NYPD officers from 2001 to 2004.

A fully functional and transformed organization cannot exhibit dysfunctional qualities. One cannot claim both success and change for the better if employees are dissatisfied or potential quality candidates do not fight for a job offer within the organization. When employees wake up in the morning having to go to work rather than wanting to go to work, one can posit that the organization is as dysfunctional as it was years ago, even factoring in major innovations and directional changes. Charismatic leaders who come and go can change only so much. Police organizations, especially the larger ones, struggle with lack of leadership from the very foundation on up. Producing leaders at the very bottom, working on leadership skills and qualities from the first day at the police academy, will produce true insiders who will eventually deliver what is needed at the top of the police organization.

As Collins acknowledges, leadership effectiveness is more likely when leaders rise from within the ranks:

> Ten out of the eleven good-to-great CEOs came from *inside* the company, three of them by family inheritance. The comparison companies turned to outsiders with *six* times greater frequency—yet they failed to produce sustained great results. (Collins, 2001, p. 32)

Insiders are better able to measure progress and stay committed to company goals due to their understanding of and experience within the organizational culture (discussed below) (Bryant, 2003). There is one disclaimer or clarification to be made about insider leaders: Being an insider does not immediately qualify one to be an effective leader of any organization, especially not a police one. That is why we need to develop many potential leaders from whom we will be able to pick *the one,* as defined by Collins in his Level 5 leadership approach.

## LEVEL 5 LEADERSHIP

Instead of charismatic leadership, Collins advocates what he terms "Level 5 leadership," which is a model of executive capabilities (Collins, 2001). The Level 5 leader is the best possible leader and exhibits the following characteristics:

- Is ambitious but puts the needs of the organization first
- Is modest, self-effacing, and understated
- Is driven by the need to produce sustainable results
- Sets up successors for effectiveness

Additional adjectives used to characterize Level 5 leaders are quiet, reserved, shy, gracious, mild-mannered, and understanding (Collins, 2001).

Level 5 leaders also employ the concept of "the window and the mirror" (Collins, 2001, p. 33). They attribute their successes to luck or factors outside their control while taking responsibility for their failures. In other words, they take stock of their problems by looking within the organization while maintaining humility in times of success.

One criticism of "the window and the mirror" is a question posed by Macht (2001): "[H]ow does one get an accurate assessment of a company's success if its leaders are too modest to talk about it frankly?" (p. 122). For Macht, this approach of focusing on leaders' attributions of luck and outside forces actually represents a missed opportunity to delve deeper into what leaders actually did to achieve their goals. According to Collins, however, "the window and the mirror" approach helps leaders to focus realistically on their organizational problems while not suffering from a lack of humility when times are good:

> There is nothing wrong with pursuing a vision for greatness. After all, the good-to-great companies also set out to create greatness. But unlike the comparison companies, the good-to-great companies continually refined the *path* to greatness. (Collins, 2001, p. 71)

Realism is important to Collins's leadership vision. This means fostering a culture of truth in which nothing gets in the way of dialogue with subordinates and a realistic approach to organizational problems. The capacity to actualize a culture of truth rests on having humility and being able to "understand enough to have the answers and then to ask the questions that will lead to the best possible insights" (Collins, 2001, p. 75). It also rests on a paradoxical notion that while confronting the brutal reality, a Level 5 leader also retains faith that the organization will prevail in the end despite difficult circumstances (Collins, 2001).

The game of truth is a dangerous one in today's police organizations, primarily because of the lack of leadership training that needs to be and must be offered at the basic academy level. Too often, police organizations have an overreliance on rank structure and attach ultimate authority to the position one holds. They underdevelop referent power, which stresses and emphasizes authority as a derivative of respect for a supervisor. To develop an environment of truth, one needs to be skilled in many leadership approaches and methods. This skill does not arise from intuition; it comes from years of learning and experimenting. However, this experimentation needs to be part of a structured process of learning and not a function of uncontrolled errors of judgment.

In addition, Collins found no link between executive compensation and company performance, also suggesting the role that humility plays in leadership. Furthermore, flashy technology does not correlate with good business (Macht, 2001). In general, money and hype are considered smoke screens by Collins, who favors leaders with a sense of values and vision. In police environments, in which money and hype are certainly not what the job is all about, this approach to leadership appears to be more relevant than in any other company where Collins might have conducted his research. Although many would say that what attracts them to policing is the prospect of steady employment and salary, it does not take much time on the job to realize that being a police officer is not about money and hype; it is about the war between good and evil and the difference between right and wrong. No matter how romanticized this notion might appear to an outsider reader, this is what police work is all about.

It is unclear whether Level 5 leaders can be trained and developed or whether the traits are innate. Collins has indicated that people can evolve into Level 5 leadership by focusing on the needs of their organization rather than on their self-interests. Pickard (2003) is right when he claims that this core focus is not necessarily fostered by sending people to leadership courses. People need to be introduced to leadership concepts from day one of their learning experience. Just as one will not understand the work of Shakespeare with a kindergartner's comprehension of the English language, it will only be possible to create and develop leadership attitudes through indoctrination of leadership concepts from the onset of one's career.

The Level 5 hierarchical model includes four sublevels, which represent lesser leadership capabilities:

> Level 4—*Effective leader*. "Catalyzes commitment to and vigorous pursuit of a clear and compelling vision, stimulating higher performance standards" (Collins, 2001, p. 20).
>
> Level 3—*Competent manager*. Organizes subordinates and other resources around the effective and efficient pursuit of goals.
>
> Level 2—*Contributing team member*. Provides individual skills and talents for the achievement of goals and works cooperatively with others in groups.
>
> Level 1—*Highly capable individual*. "Makes productive contributions through talent, knowledge, skills, and good work habits".

It is highly possible that finding an effective leader will be fraught with difficulties, especially in the smaller police departments that do not have the luxury of sifting through hundreds or thousands of employee applications to find *the one*. However, it is strongly recommended to strive for Levels 1 through 3 capabilities to achieve the ultimate formula for an effectively run and fully functional organization.

234                                                              CHAPTER 13

## Choice of the Right People

Collins also believes that leaders succeed by attracting and keeping the right employees. Rather than trying to overhaul and train employees for their positions, organizations should pick suitable, adaptable people from the start. Collins believes these are self-disciplined people willing to go to great lengths to fulfill their responsibilities in the workplace. In fact, the question of who should be in the organization should precede the question of what the organization should be doing. The following three practical rules are suggested:

1. When in doubt, do not hire—keep looking.
2. Act on the need to make a change in personnel.
3. Put your best people to work on the biggest opportunities, not on the biggest problems.

The first and third rules are of critical importance for police environments. When force numbers need to be increased, whether the source of that need is political, social, economic, or something else, police organizations tend to lower their standards and hire the needed numbers. It often appears that there is a total and complete sacrifice of quality for quantity. The greatest misconception of police work states that more police officers equal better police work, which is a true disservice to this noble profession. Better policing will always and under all circumstances be delivered with fewer but better cops rather than with more but lower-quality cops. Hiring for the sake of hiring is a formula for disaster and organizational dysfunction; this leadership rule needs to be hammered into the heads of current (and future) police leaders. The third factor involves a paradox: Managing problems can make an employee good, but to achieve greatness, the best employees should be working on the cutting edge of what the organization is doing (Collins, 2001).

According to Collins, companies tend to view personnel structure as "a genius with a thousand helpers" (Collins, 2001, p. 61). This is commensurate with the charismatic leadership that Collins despises—the notion that there is a genius leader who sets the entire vision, with underlings to carry it out. Instead, by picking the right people, the leader can institute a more democratic workplace that encourages freedom and innovation. This culture, however, should be implemented within a framework. Subordinates should be encouraged to take "disciplined action" (Collins, 2001, p. 124). These actions should reflect the values and culture of the organization:

> The good-to-great companies built a consistent system with clear constraints, but also gave people freedom and responsibility within the framework of that system. They hired self-disciplined people who didn't need to be managed, and then managed the system, not the people (Collins, 2001, p. 125).

Furthermore, Collins suggests that the core values an organization adopts are not as important as the process of soul-searching that occurs in outlining core values. Core values are the glue that holds an organization together and that helps to provide direction (Collins, 2001).

## HEDGEHOG RULE OF MANAGEMENT

Leadership requires an understanding of what the organization can *actually* be the best at doing or producing, known as the hedgehog concept. The hedgehog metaphor comes from a Greek proverb: The fox knows many things, but the hedgehog knows one big thing (Lenzner, 2003). Collins has altered the formula, and his "hedgehog" knows three things. According to Collins, 2001, leaders must help organizations reflect on:

1. What the organization can be passionate about
2. What the organization can be the best in the world at
3. What drives the organization's economic engine

The first factor involves fulfilling a sense of mission or passion. Subordinates can get excited about the business at hand when it is something employees are personally passionate about:

> The good-to-great companies did not say, "Okay, folks, let's get passionate about what we do." Sensibly, they went the other way entirely: We should only do those things we can get passionate about. Kimberly-Clark executives made the shift to paper-based consumer products because they could get more passionate about them. As one executive put it, the traditional paper products are okay "but they don't have the charisma of a diaper." (Collins, 2001, p. 109)

The potential problem for police organizations in fulfilling passion is that the mission of the police is largely dictated by its function within a democratic society. In other words, enforcing laws, making arrests, and protecting public safety must be on the agenda regardless of whether the agency is passionate about such work. However, the employees can get passionate about the style or type of law enforcement employed by the agency and about special programs that the police can offer the community. Does the agency feel passionate about community policing, team policing, or undercover work? Running a child fingerprinting program? Providing faster 911 response?

The second factor in police work is also dictated by the constraints and definition of policing. Obviously, each police agency needs to be the best at protecting public safety, if they are the best at anything. However, this success can be measured in many ways. Agencies can decide to be the best in crime-clearance rates or victim support functions, for example.

The third factor involves organizations isolating their fundamental moneymaker. According to Collins, less than 10 percent of organizations understand their true economic indicators (Lenzner, 2003). For public organizations such as police agencies, it may or may not be truly a matter of finances. It could mean having a political sense and the ability to influence local budgetary decision making. It could involve an emphasis on public relations and a sensitivity to the public perceptions of local policing. It could also suggest that leaders should be attempting to obtain grants from outside sources or from the federal or state government for special programs.

## BIG HAIRY AUDACIOUS GOALS (BHAGs) AND THE FORMAL AND INFORMAL GOALS OF POLICING

Collins's most famous theoretical formulation is the notion of the "big hairy audacious goal" (BHAG), developed in *Built to Last* (1994 [with J. Porras]). The first step is to start with role models for the organization and explore how these models accomplished the seemingly impossible (Hall, 2003). This exercise is not about writing empty vision and mission statements; the emphasis is on turning goals into results. Care should be taken to understand what the catalytic mechanisms are that can make a goal reality, providing the link between objectives and performance (Collins, 1999).

In *Built to Last*, Collins and Porras (1994) describe BHAGs as having three key characteristics. First, BHAGs are long-term. Leaders should think in terms of becoming the most powerful, most

## Big Hairy Audacious Goals and Five Catalytic Mechanisms

### First Mechanism

- The mechanism can produce desired results in unpredictable ways.

### Second Mechanism

- The mechanism distributes power for the benefit of the organization and does not concentrate power at the top.

### Third Mechanism

- The mechanism has a "sharp set of teeth" (Collins, 1999, p. 75).
- It creates a system that forces the right things to happen even when those in power have an interest in a divergent outcome.

### Fourth Mechanism

- The mechanism attracts the right people and ejects viruses (problems).

### Fifth Mechanism

- The mechanism produces an ongoing effect.

(Collins and Porras, 1994)

far-reaching, and most successful at what it is their organizations do. They should not sacrifice big long-term goals by focusing on short time frames. Second, BHAGs should be clear and simple. Anything too complicated or nuanced is probably not a large and broad enough goal. Third, BHAGs should connect to the core values of the organization. For example, the BHAG for Granite Rock, a company that sells crushed gravel, is to achieve "total customer satisfaction and a reputation for service" (Collins, 1999, p. 72).

Catalytic mechanisms are the devices to achieve BHAGs. According to Collins and Porras (1994), five characteristics are key to developing such mechanisms, as shown in the box. In essence, BHAGs are an organization's wildest dreams, and catalytic mechanisms are the realistic programs, policies, and initiatives that will allow the organization to achieve those dreams (Collins, 1999). Thinking in terms of leadership, the notion of BHAGs and catalytic mechanisms echoes Level 5 leadership principles—leaders should be able to think big but should remain realistic, focused, and sensitive to input from subordinates. The BHAGs are what police work is all about. The goal of effective policing—policing in a manner that will satisfy both the politicians who deploy police forces and the public who (erroneously) perceive the police as serving them—is a truly big hairy audacious goal.

Police organizations have competing *formal* and *informal goals*. The formal goal of policing is one borne by its outer shield—to serve and protect the public. But simultaneously there is always an informal policing goal—to serve and protect the politician and the political agenda espoused by his/her political reign (for a further discussion of the formal versus informal goals of policing, see M. R. Haberfeld, *Critical Issues in Police Training*, 2002). Police organizations must constantly juggle the burden of these competing goals of policing, and they risk making the goal of an effective and functional police organization a pie in the sky.

Bringing this pie in the sky down to earth will be possible only through tiny and incremental steps. It requires using catalytic mechanisms, tools that are effective only when placed in the hands of effective workers. Those workers can be created only through an intensive exposure to leadership training that should and must start on the first day of the basic academy.

Juggling the impossible can actually prove to be impossible, so delivering an illusion is sometimes as good as we can hope for. Police organizations will never be freed from political influences; experiences like the one lived by Chief O'Brien in managing the Elian Gonzales case will always haunt these environments. However, the true challenge is to be mentally and emotionally prepared. Such preparation relies on maintaining a view of integrity that goes beyond one's personal viewpoints to what effective policing should mean to the politician, the public, the chief, and finally the police officers on the street. The notion of compromise of core values and beliefs is not always necessarily negative in nature. Most beliefs about what is right or wrong merely reflect personal perceptions and are not ultimately correct in each and every situation, particularly if one is prepared to look at problems and decision-making processes from the leadership perspective rather than from a self-centered orientation.

Finally, what is the ultimate goal of this book? The ultimate goal is to achieve what Csikszentmihalyi (1990) defines as "flow" or what Clawson (2003) refers to as the "universal sense of resonance" (p. 127). Both authors describe this phenomenon as akin to the emotional sensation felt when things go well. Most people have experienced it (for example, being "in the zone" while doing sports); individuals can commonly describe a variety of times when they have felt this sense of harmony with their task (for example, when giving birth to a child or while writing computer code)

| Flow | Resonance |
|---|---|
| Characteristics<br>1. Time warps, either speeding up or slowing down.<br>2. One loses self-consciousness.<br>3. One focuses intently on the task.<br>4. One performs at the peak of one's abilities.<br>5. It seems effortless, as if it were flowing.<br>6. The experience is intensely internally satisfying.<br>7. Afterward, one regains a sense of a stronger, more capable self.<br><br>(Mihalyi Csikszentmihalyi, 1990) | Resonance is "the sense of seamless harmony with one's surroundings so that internal experience and external experience are one, the fulfillment of performing at your best without strain."<br><br>(J. Clawson, 2003, p. 137) |

(Clawson, 2003). The goal in the context of leadership is that each one is able to function in a work environment that not only produces the highest level of satisfaction but also enables one to perform at the height of one's ability and, by doing so, to realize the dreams of one's life.

The first requirement in order to get to a point where one can truly achieve this point of flow or resonance is to have a dream—a dream not only of what one wants to be (for example, a professional basketball player or a chief of police) but of how one feels while one is performing at that pinnacle. Clawson refers to this experiential dream as an internal dream (2003). To make it come true, however, involves work. This may involve training, practice, study, travel, reading, changing one's lifestyle, or any number of other activities; it also requires maintaining the necessary energy (by removing negative factors and influences) in order to devote all that is necessary to realize the dream (Clawson, 2003). Furthermore, the cyclical process of achieving resonance is inevitably hindered by setbacks, obstacles, and successes, during which time it will be necessary to reinject energy and revisit the dream in order to maintain the vision (Clawson, 2003). The good news is that because the goal is to achieve a state of mind rather than a concrete job or position, it will be possible to catch glimpses of resonance during the preparation process as one comes closer to making that resonance more of a constant reality.

### Five Key Questions for Resonance Focus

1. How do I want to feel today?
2. What does it take to get that feeling?
3. What keeps me from that feeling?
4. How can I get it back?
5. What am I willing to work for?

(Clawson, 2003)

If there is a work environment that can enable somebody to actually fulfill the dreams of his/her life and at the same time elicit ultimate performance as well as optimum satisfaction and harmony, this environment can and should be found in the field of policing. After all, what more can one hope for in life if not the ultimate sacrifice, devoid of any selfish feelings? Running toward danger instead of away from it—done out of a mission to save others—this is the epitome of the flow and resonance concepts—and the epitome of what police work is all about.

## REFERENCES

Bryant, A. (2003, June 23). Breakout best seller. *Newsweek*, 141 (25), 50.1.

Clawson, J. (2003). *Level three leadership: Getting below the surface.* Upper Saddle River, NJ: Pearson Education, Inc.

Collins, J. (1999, July–August). Turning goals into results: The power of catalytic mechanisms. *Harvard Business Review*, 71–82.

———— (2001). *Good to great.* New York: Harper-Collins.

———— & J. Porras (1994). *Built to last.* New York: Harper-Collins.

Csikszentmihalyi, M. (1990). *Flow: The psychology of optimal experience.* New York: Harper & Row.

DeJarnett, L.R. (1993, summer). The vision thing. *Information Strategy: The Executive's Journal*, 9 (4), 3–4.

Hall, B. (2003, November). BHAGs for 2004. *Training*, 40 (10), 16.

Lenzner, R. (2003, April 28). Room at the top. *Forbes*, 171 (9), 68–71.

Macht, J. (2001, October). Jim Collins to CEOs: Lose the charisma. *Business 2.0*, 2 (8), 121–122.

Pickard, J. (2003, November 6). Collins challenges charm culture. *People Management*, 8.

# Index

## A

Accomplishing stage, in leader-management model, 35
Achievement-oriented style, 28, 160, 164, 175
Adaptation, 22
Adler, A., 183, 184
Affect, teams and, 34–35
Ahear, L., 108, 109
Almeida, C., 132
Alpert, B., 171, 172
Ancona, D.G., 32
Andeweg, R.B., 184
Anticharismatic leadership, 229–231
Asimov, N., 106
Assumptions, self-exploration of, 20
Atwater, L.E., 17
Avolio, B.J., 72, 73, 76, 77

## B

Babwin, D., 88
Baker, T.E., 1
Barnett, J., 127
Baruch, Y., 212
Bass, B.M., 10, 18, 20, 21, 32–34, 72, 73, 76, 77, 99, 101, 115, 120, 181, 182, 185, 197, 211, 212, 217
Bauer, T., 80, 81, 83
Beliefs, self-exploration of, 20
Belkin, D., 204, 207
Belkin, L., 55, 56
Bellin, G., 185
Bennis, W.G., 10, 72, 73n, 213, 214
Berbeo, D., 129, 130
Bergner, L.L., 1, 2
Berne, E., 12, 184, 185
Bernstein, M., 123–126
Bias, leader-member exchange theory and, 52–53
Big five model of personality, 186

Big hairy audacious goals (BHAGs), 236–240
Birth order, 183–184
Black, C., 148
Blackmon, D.A., 80
Blake, R.R., 10, 97–99, 101, 106
Blanchard, K.H., 10, 114–117, 119–122, 128
Bono, J.E., 74
Bostic, H., Jr., 107, 108
Bragg, R., 148, 149
Branch, K., 148
Bratton, William, 160, 164, 165–170
Brennan, C., 153
Brewer, N., 37
Bridges, T., 148
Broder, J.M., 169
Brooke, J., 152–154
Brown, Lee P., 46, 53–66
Brown, Willie, 105
Brubaker, P., 39
Bryant, A., 229, 231
Bryman, A., 11, 74, 116, 143, 144, 161, 211
Bullitt, 185
Burns, J.M., 10, 16, 20, 21, 71, 72
Burritt, C., 109
Bush, George H. W., 85
Bush, George W., 126

## C

Calder, B.J., 215, 216
Caldero, M., 21, 22
Caldwell, C., 19–21
Caldwell, D.F., 32
Campbell, C., 172
Campbell, Joseph, 183, 187
Canellos, P.S., 205
Cannon, L., 86, 87
Cannon-Bowers, J.A., 33

Cartwright, D., 95
Casey, J., 107
Cashman, J.F., 47, 52
Casimir, L., 147
CEASE (Combined Enforcement
　　and Supervision Effort)
　　program, 108
Chacon, R., 206
Chadbourne, J., 116
Change intelligence (CQ), 200, 203
Charisma (charismatic leaders), 73–76
　　need for, 75–76
　　psychodynamic approach
　　　and, 180–183
Charlotte-Mecklenburg Police
　　Department, 107–110
Charness, W., 199
Cherfils, M., 147
Christner, 99
Christopher Commission, 87
Chronis, P., 151
Cincinnati, team policing in, 37
Ciulla, J.B., 16
Clawson, J., 238–240
Clawson, J.A., 193, 194, 203
Clines, F.X., 126
Coacting groups, 140
Cognitive processes, team theory
　　and, 33–34
Cognitive resources theory, 142–143
Cohesion, team performance and, 34
Colangelo, L., 192
Collins, Jim, 228–237
Combined Enforcement and Supervision
　　Effort (CEASE) program, 108
Common goals, committment to,
　　transformational leadership
　　and, 21
Community Mobilization Project
　　(CMP), 85
Community Policing Consortium, 121
COMPSTAT (Command Accountability
　　Strategies), 129, 168–171, 230
Conceiving phase, in leader-
　　management model, 35
Conceptual skills, 2, 12, 198
Conger, J., 72, 75
Connelly, M.S., 202
Contingency contracting, 116–117

Contingency theory, 11, 138–156. *See also*
　　Vroom-Yetton contingency
　　model
　　case studies, 145–156
　　criticisms of, 144–145
　　dyadic approach to, 144
　　military leaders and, 142
　　overview of, 138–141
Contingent reward, 72
Coordination, team leaders and, 35
Corruption, 26
　　definition of, 21
　　economic, 22
Counteracting groups, 140
Craft ethics, 17
Crank, J.P., 21, 22
*Critical Issues in Police Training*
　　(Haberfeld), 4, 238
Crothers, L., 3
Csikszentmihalyi, M., 238, 239
Cullen, K., 204, 205
Curry, T., 87, 88

**D**

Dainty, P., 99, 116
DARE (Drug Abuse Resistance
　　Education), 85
Davis, P., 148
Dearborn, K., 202
Defining Issues Test (DIT), 17
De la Cruz, D., 192
DeMarco, P., 204, 207
Dessler, G., 161, 163
DeVanna, M.A., 75
De Vries, R.E., 74–76
Dinesh, R.M., 52
Directive style, 128, 164, 170
Dobbins, G.H., 34
Doherty, M.L., 48
Dole, Elizabeth, 83
Domanick, J., 86
Donze, F., 172
Dotson, David, 87, 88
Driscoll, A., 146, 147
Drug Abuse Resistance Education
　　(DARE), 85
Duchon, D., 52, 53
Duin, S., 125, 126
Dumaine, B., 31

Dunegan, K.J., 49, 50
Dussault, R., 166, 168
Dvir, T., 78
Dyads (dyadic relationships)
 antecedents to high-quality
  dyadic relationships, 51–52
 effectiveness and, 49–51
 in leader-member exchange
  (LMX) theory, 47–53

**E**

Early career leadership training, 1–3
Eckhart, D.E., 16, 21
Economic corruption, 22
Edwards, George, 211, 219–226
Effective leadership, six steps to, 193
Effectiveness, dyadic relationships
 and, 49–51
Emergent leadership, 36
Emotional affect, teams and, 34–35
Emotional intelligence (EQ), 201–203
Emotional Quotient Inventory
 (EQ-i), 201
Epstein, G., 147
Erdogan, B., 48
Erez, A., 9, 36
Ericsson, K.A., 199
Erikson, Eric, 185
Estes, A., 207
Ethics (ethical leaders), 72
 characteristics of ethical
  leaders, 20–21
 craft, 17
 transactional leadership and, 73
 transformational leadership
  and, 16–18
 underemphasis on, 16
 use of the word, 15
Evans, M.G., 162
Evans, Paul F., 197, 202–208
Expectancy theory of motivation, 161

**F**

Fairness, of transformational
 leaders, 20–21
Feldman, D.A., 201
Fennell, E.C., 82
Fermino, J., 123, 124

Fernandez, C.F., 115, 116
Fiedler, F.E., 11, 138–142, 144, 162
Filosa, G., 173
First-line supervisors, 2, 16.
  *See also* Line officers
Fleischman, 100
Fleishman, E.A., 198–199
Flynn, K., 190
Follower motivation, 71–72
Foote, D., 87
Ford, B., 206
Formal goals, 238
Freud, S., 12, 180, 181, 184, 185
Friedman, D., 88
Fuller, J.B., 76
Functional team leadership, 32–35

**G**

Garcia, J.E., 139, 142
Gates, Daryl, 71, 79, 84–89
George, A., 185
George, J., 185
George, T., 168
Georgopoulos, B.S., 161
Giampetro-Meyer, A., 17, 19, 73
Glionna, J.M., 102–106
Gobdel, B., 48
Goldstein, A., 85
Goleman, D., 201, 202
Gonzales, Elian, 145–149
Grace, S., 173
Graeff, C.L., 116
Graen, G., 9, 47–49, 52, 54, 144
Grant, J.D., 37
"Great Man" theory, 211
Greenberg, Reuben, 71, 79–89
Greene, J.A., 166, 167
Greenleaf, R., 19, 20
Greimel, 124
*Group Psychology and the Analysis
  of the Ego* (Freud), 181
Guy, Robert, 108

**H**

Haberfeld, M.R., 238
Hahn, James K., 131–132, 169
Hall, B., 236
Hallinan, Terence, 104, 105
Halpin, 100

Hardin, J., 81
Harman, David, 31, 38–43
Harrell, J., 39, 40
Hartmann, Francis, 204
Harvard University, leadership-style
        studies, 97
Hays, T., 189, 191, 192
Heaney, J., 206
Hedgehog rule of management,
        235–236
Heier, W.D., 138, 142
Heifetz, R.A., 19
Hemphill, 99
Hersey, P., 10, 114–116, 119–121, 128
Hicks, B., 81
Hill, W., 138–140, 142
Hoegel, M., 35
Hogan, R., 186
Hollander, E.P., 211
Holly, D., 126
Holyoke (Massachusetts), team
        policing in, 36
Honesty. *See also* Integrity
        of transformational
        leaders, 20–21
House, R.J., 10, 12, 73–75, 77, 161–163
Hummel, P.R., 180
Hutchinson, E.O., 130

**I**

Idealized influence, 73
Individualized consideration, 73
Indvik, J., 161
Informal goals, 238
In-groups, leader-member exchange
        (LMX) theory and, 46–48,
        54, 60, 65, 66
Inspirational leadership, 73
Integration of behavior and
        values, 18–19
Integrity, 15–29
        definition of, 15
        five-step approach to manage-
        ment of, 29
        overview of, 31–32
        recruitment and, 21–23
        selection and, 23–24
        training and, 24–26
        triangle of, 21–26

Intellectual intelligence (IQ), 200, 203
Intellectual stimulation, 73
Intelligence
        change (CQ), 203
        emotional, 201–202
        emotional (EQ), 201–203
        intellectual (IQ), 200, 203
        skills approach and, 197,
        198, 200
        social, 200–201
        social (SQ), 203
Interacting groups, 140
Introjection, 182
Ippolito, M., 173
Isenberg, D.J., 35
Israeli Defense Forces, 78

**J**

Jacobs, D., 81, 82
Jacobson, M., 166, 167, 169
Jago, A.G., 212, 215
Janis, I.L., 33
Jenkins, 217
Jermier, J., 11, 143, 160, 162, 163
Jessup, H.R., 36
Jimenez, J.L., 148, 149
Judge, T.A., 74
Jung, C., 12, 183

**K**

Kandel, J., 170
Kanungo, R.N., 18, 20, 75, 84
Kastenbaum, D.R., 139
Katz, C.M., 85, 86, 168
Kennedy, H., 127
Kenney, 186
Kerik, Bernard, 180, 187–194
Kerr, N.L., 36
Kerr, S., 11, 143
Kets de Vries, M.F.R., 182
Kidwell, D., 147
Kiker, S., 11, 143
King, Rodney, 86–89
Kirkpatrick, S.A., 12, 214, 215
Kirmeyer, 101
Klockars, C.B., 15, 21, 28, 29
Kobe, L.M., 12, 201
Koby, Tom, 150–155

Kohut, H., 181
Komacki, J.L., 37
Korman, A.K., 144–145
Korten, D.C., 118
Kozlowski, S.W.J., 33, 35, 48
Kramer, M., 86
Kranes, M., 123, 124
Krimmel, J.T., 218, 219
Kroeger, O., 12, 185, 186
Kropf, S., 83
Kuehl, C.R., 138
Kuhnert, K.W., 10, 17, 20, 76, 79
Kuykendall, J., 120, 121

**L**

LaBarre, W., 182
Laird, L., 169
Laissez-faire management, 72
Lakshmanan, A.R., 204
Lakshmanan, I., 166
Larson, J.R., Jr., 33
Leader Behavior Description
    Questionnaire (LBDQ),
    99, 100, 160*n*
Leader-management model, 35
Leader Match program, 140–141
Leader Member Exchange (LMX)
    instrument, 48–50
Leader-Member Exchange (LMX)
    theory, 9, 46–66
    antecedents to high-quality
        dyadic relationships, 51–52
    bias and, 52–53
    effectiveness and the dyadic
        relationship, 49–51
Leadership (leadership skills). *See also*
    *specific theories and approaches*
    anticharismatic, 229–231
    choice of the right people
        and, 234–235
    definition of, 3
    emergent, 36
    hedgehog rule of management
        and, 235–236
    Level 5, 231–233
    pentagon of, 7–9, 26–29
    of public service workers, 3
    team. *See* Teams
    theories of, 4

Leadership Effectiveness and
    Adaptability Description
    (LEAD) instrument, 116, 120
Leadership styles, 10–11. *See also*
    Style theory
Leadership theories, 8–12
Leadership training
    advanced, 8
    early, 1–3
    gap in, 3–7
Leader substitutes theory, 11, 143
LEAD (Leadership Effectiveness and
    Adaptability Description)
    instrument, 116, 120
Learned leadership skills, 198
LeBlanc, P.M., 48, 49
Legitimate authority, bases of, 180, 181
Lelchuk, I., 102, 103, 113
Lenzner, R., 229, 235, 236
Leovy, J., 170
Lessem, R., 212
Level 5 leadership, 231–233
Lewin, K., 139
Lewis, D.L., 168, 169
Lewis, P., 17, 20, 76, 79
Liden, R.C., 9, 47, 49, 52
Lin, 101
Lindenmuth, P., 218, 219
Line officers, 2–3, 5–6
Liska, L.Z., 160*n*, 162
LMX (leader-member exchange)
    theory, 9, 46–66
    antecedents to high-quality
        dyadic relationships, 51–52
    bias and, 52–53
    effectiveness and the dyadic
        relationship, 49–51
Locke, E.A., 12, 214, 215
Lord, R.G., 12, 199, 217
Los Angeles Police Department
    (LAPD), 79, 84–89,
    129–133, 169
    Rampart scandal, 114, 131–133
    team policing in, 36–37
Los Angeles Police Protective League
    (LAPPL), 130
Lowe, 76
Lundy, S., 81
Lying, 21

## M

McCanse, A.A., 97, 98
McCauley, L., 80
McCormack, F., 81
McCoy, M.C., 34
McCullen, K., 150–152, 154
McGreevy, P., 129, 130
McGrory, B., 166, 167, 205
Macht, J., 232
MacKenzie, A., 35
McPhee, M., 150–152
McQuillan, A., 167
Malkin, M., 127
Mallia, J., 204
Management-by-exception, 72
Management Leadership
    Questionnaire (MLQ
    instrument), 77
Managerial grid, 97–98
Manifest Needs Questionnaire
    (MNQ), 163
Mann, R.D., 12, 186, 216, 217
Manning, 126, 127
Maple, Jack, 170
Marantz, S., 207
Martinez, J., 206
Martinez-Carbonell, K., 16
Marzulli, J., 167, 188–190
Masi, R.J., 77
Mathieu, J.E., 33, 163
Matier, P., 106
Maurer, T.J., 50, 51
Menchaca, R., 81
Menendez, J., 205
Messing, P., 190, 192
Michigan University leadership
    studies, 95–97
Middle management, 2–3
Military leaders
    contingency theory and, 142
    path-goal theory and, 163
    style theory and, 99–100
Minnesota Satisfaction Questionnaire
    (MSQ), 163
Misumi, J., 35, 95, 99
Montclair Police Department
    (New Jersey), 38–43
Moose, Charles A., 114, 122–128
Moral development, 72

Moral reasoning, 17, 19
    transformational theory and, 76
Morgan, S., 129
Morse, R., 106
*Moses and Monotheism* (Freud), 181
Moulton, J.S., 10, 99, 101, 106
Mullener, E., 173
Mumford, M.D., 197, 199, 200, 202
Munday, D., 80
Myers-Briggs Personality Profile, 185

## N

Nahavandi, A., 37, 38
Nanus, B., 10, 72, 73n, 213n, 214
Nash, J., 169, 170
National Commission on Terrorist
    Attacks Upon the United
    States (9-11 Commission), 190
Negri, 204
Neider, L.L., 162
Newfield, J., 166, 167, 169
New Orleans Police Department,
    171–175
New York Police Department
    (NYPD), 189–194, 230
Niehouse, O.I., 117
Niesse, M., 173, 174
9-11 Commission, 190
Nkrumah, W., 124
Noble cause corruption, 21, 22, 26
Noonan, E., 206
Northouse, P.G., 4, 10–12, 48, 95–97,
    115, 160, 192, 211, 213n, 216
Nowicki, Dennis, 94, 101, 102, 107–110
Nurturing, ethical leaders as, 20

## O

Objective needs for leadership, 75
O'Brien, William, 145–150
Offer, D., 182
Offermann, L.R., 211
Ohio State University, leadership
    studies at, 94–95
Operation Scrap Iron, 205
Organizing phase, in leader-
    management model, 35
Orlov, R., 87, 132
Oshiro, G.R., 125
Owens, J., 212

**P**

Parker, William H., 84
Parks, Bernard, 114, 129–133
Participative leadership, 96–97
Participatory leadership, 33
Path-goal theory, 12, 28, 160–175
 case studies, 164–175
 military leadership and, 163
 overview of, 160–163
Pennington, Richard, 160, 164, 171–175
Pentagon of police leadership, 7–9
Perlstein, M., 171, 172
Pernick, R., 198
Peters, L.H., 138
Piacente, S., 82
Pickard, J., 229, 233
Plutarch, 211
Police integrity. *See* Integrity
Police leadership. *See* Leadership
Porras, J., 236, 237
Port, B., 191
Porter, A., 83
Price, T., 17, 18
Proactive training, 5
Psychodynamic approach, 12, 180–194
 birth order and, 183–184
 case study, 187–194
 to Commissioner Bernard Kerik,
  188–194
 overview of, 180–183
 personality and, 185–186
 psychohistory and, 185
 transactional analysis and,
  184–185
Psychohistory, 185
Punch, M., 21
Pyle, R., 191, 192

**Q**

Quaintance, M.K., 199

**R**

Rampart scandal, 114, 131–133
Ramsey, Jonbenet, 150–155
Ranalli, R., 205
Rashbaum, W.K., 189
Reactive training, 5
Recruitment, 8
 integrity and, 21–23

Reddin, W.J., 97, 114
Reiterman, T., 102–106
Relationship-oriented leaders, 95, 97,
  99, 101, 102, 120, 139, 140,
  142, 145, 155
Rennie, M.W., 185
Rewards, situational leadership theory
  and, 117
Rice, R.W., 139
Richards, D., 164, 165
Richards, V., 149, 151–154
Robey, R., 150
Rogers, J., 131
Rosenfeld, S., 106
Rosenwald, M.S., 205–207
Rotated leadership, 36
Rowley, J., 212
Rucker, A., 82

**S**

Saha, S.K., 138, 142
St. Bernard, S.C., 171
Salas, E., 31
Sanders, Earl, 94, 101–107
Sarachek, B., 212
Scandura, T., 51, 52
Schodolski, V.J., 131
Schriesheim, C.A., 47, 138, 140,
  160*n*, 162
Selection of personnel, 8, 234–236
 integrity and, 23–24
Self-exploration of beliefs, values, and
  assumptions, stewardship
  and, 20
Self-managed teams, 36
Self-management, 33
Sennott, C.M., 207
September 11, 2001, terrorist
  attacks, 189–194
Servant leadership, 19
Service-oriented ethical
  leaders, 20
Shah, D.K., 84
Shamir, B., 74, 77, 78
Shapiro, J.S., 84, 87, 88
Shenon, P., 190
Sheriff, D.R., 12, 198
Siemaszko, C., 168, 169
Sisk, R., 124, 126

Situational leadership theory, 10, 114–133
  case studies, 122–133
  employee burnout and, 117
  overview of, 114–117, 122
  policing and, 119–122
  politics and, 118–119
  simplified version of, 118
Skills approach, 12, 197–208
  case study, 202–208
  leadership in context and,
    198–200
  learned leadership skills, 198
  overview of, 197
  U.S. Army studies, 202
Social intelligence (SQ), 200–201, 203
Sperry, P., 127
Standora, L., 190
Stech, E.L., 180, 183, 185
Steidlmeier, P., 18, 20, 21
Steiner, D.D., 52, 53
Stephens, Darrel, 46, 53–66
Sterngold, J., 132
Stevens, K., 80
Stewardship model, 19–20
Stewart, J., 129
Stirgus, E., 171–173
Stogdill, R.M., 10, 12, 99, 100, 114,
    212, 216, 217
Stolberg, M.M., 220–225
Stone, K., 85, 86
Stress, teams and, 34
Strozier, C., 182
Strube, M.J., 139
Style theory, 94–110
  case studies, 101–110
  Harvard University studies, 97
  managerial grid and, 97–98
  Michigan University leadership
    studies, 95–97
  military leadership and, 99–100
  Ohio State University leadership
    studies, 94–95
  overview of, 94
  police leadership and, 101
  as a universal theory, 99
Subjective needs for leadership, 75
Suggs, E., 171–174
Sugiman, T., 35
Supervisory planes, 1–2

Survey of Work Values (SWV)
    instrument, 52
Swanson, C.R., 1, 2, 14
Sward, S., 103–105
Szaniszlo, M., 207

**T**

Tannenbaum, S.I., 33
Task-oriented leaders, 95, 97, 99, 102,
    107, 139, 140, 142, 155
Team policing, 36–43
Teams
  effective team leaders, 32–33
  functional team leadership, 32
Teams (team theory; team leadership),
    9, 31–43
  affect and, 34–35
  cohesion and, 34
  definition of, 31
  functional team leadership,
    32–35
  leader-management model, 35
  self-managed teams, 36
Terzian, P., 126, 127
Tesluk, P.E., 33
Tharp, M., 88
Theories of leadership, 4, 8, 9–12
Theusen, J.M., 12, 185, 186
Thorbourne, K., 40
Thorndike, E.L., 200
Tichy, N.M., 75
Toche, H., 37
Top management, 2
Topousis, T., 190
Tosi, H.L., 11, 143
Training
  early, 1–3
  gap in, 3–7
  integrity and, 24–26
  proactive, 5
  reactive, 5
Traits, 12
Trait theory, 211–226
  case study, 219–226
  modern applications of, 212–216
  overview of, 211–212
  social scientific evaluation of
    leadership traits, 216–219
Transactional analysis, 184–185

Transactional leaders, 10
Transactional leadership, trans-
    formational leadership
    and, 16–18, 72
Transformational theory (transforma-
    tional leadership), 10, 71–89
    charisma and, 73–76
    ethics and, 16–18
    factors in, 73
    meta-analytic studies on, 76
    in military contexts, 77–79
    moral reasoning and, 76
    transactional leadership
        and, 16–18, 72
Tsao, E., 126, 127
Tucker, C., 174
Turner, N., 17, 73, 89
Turque, B., 87
Typewatching, 185, 186

**U**

Uhl-Bien, M., 9, 47, 54
Unsinger, P.C., 120, 121
Utecht, R.E., 138, 142

**V**

Values
    integration of behavior
        and, 18–19
    self-exploration of, 20
Van Auken, P., 118
Van Den Berg, S.B., 184
Van Derbeken, J., 103–106
Varney, J., 171, 172
Vecchio, R.P., 48, 49, 115, 116, 142, 144
Villegas, M., 132
Vinzant, J.C., 3
Viturello, Frank, 31, 38–43
Von Glinow, M.A., 160

Vroom, V.H., 11, 143–144, 161
Vroom-Yetton contingency model,
    11, 144–146

**W**

Walker, S., 83, 85, 86, 168
Weber, J., 18–19
Weber, Max, 73, 180, 181
Webster, William, 88
Weinkauf, K., 35
Weiss, M., 191, 192
Weller, R., 155
Werner, E., 88, 89
Whyte, David, 183
Wilborn, P., 131, 169
Williams, Willie, 88
Wilson, Woodrow, 185
Winer, J.A., 181, 182
Wisby, G., 107
Wofford, J.C., 160n, 162
Woodall, B., 108, 109
Woodlief, W., 207

**Y**

Yammarino, F.J., 48, 77, 199
Yang, J.E., 88
Yetton, P.W., 11, 143, 145, 146
Young, T., 173
Yrle, A.C., 50, 52, 53
Yukl, G., 11, 94–96, 99, 115–117,
    143, 161, 162

**Z**

Zaccaro, S.J., 9, 31–35, 186, 199, 201
Zadrozny, A., 39
Zaleznik, A., 182, 186, 212–213
Zamora, J.H., 102, 103
Zander, A., 95
Zarella, J., 147
Zelditch, M., 97